HOW BLACK COLLEGES EMPOWER BLACK STUDENTS

HOW BLACK COLLEGES EMPOWER BLACK STUDENTS

Lessons for Higher Education

Frank W. Hale, Jr.

FOREWORD BY *Karen A. Holbrook*

STERLING, VIRGINIA

Published by Stylus Publishing, LLC
22883 Quicksilver Drive
Sterling, Virginia 20166-2102

Library of Congress Cataloging-in-Publication-Data

How black colleges empower black students : lessons for
higher education / [edited by] Frank Hale, Jr.—1st ed.
    p.   cm.
ISBN 1-57922-144-0 (cloth : alk. paper)
ISBN 1-57922-145-9 (pbk. : alk. paper)
1. African Americans—Education (Higher)   2. African
American universities and colleges.   I. Hale, Frank W.

LC2781.H677   2006
378.1'982996073—dc22

                                                            2005036251

ISBN: 1-57922-144-0 (cloth) /13-digit 978-1-57922-144-7
ISBN: 1-57922-145-9 (paper) /13-digit 978-1-57922-145-4

Printed in Canada

All first editions printed on acid free paper
that meets the American National Standards Institute
Z39-48 Standard.

Bulk Purchases

Quantity discounts are available for use in workshops
and for staff development.
Call 1-800-232-0223

First Edition, 2006

10   9   8   7   6   5   4   3   2   1

Dedicated to the memory of Novella and Frank W. Hale, Sr.,
without whom I could not have been.

To the memory of Luvada Lockhart,
without whom I could not have become.

To Mignon,
without whom, at this moment in time, I could not be.

CONTENTS

ACKNOWLEDGMENTS

The American people as a whole know little about the successes of historically Black colleges and universities. To some degree, they consider them a tortured and inferior fragment of higher education. There has always been a profound conflict between the value that the African American community has placed on education and the moral ambivalence of a society that slams the doors on equal educational opportunity.

Available eye-opening statistics reveal that many African American women and men have refused to be written off as a liability to this nation and the world. They overcame potent negative forces and followed their own dreams of educational pursuits and human dignity.

They have followed the usual routes to success: purpose, preparation, persistence, and human worth. The atmosphere at institutions of Black higher education has been conducive to their intellectual ascent.

The Black college's role as a molder of youth is highly revered as a part of African American culture. The community has been fascinated by the exalted status that women and men have attained as a result of the rich culture they gained in Black academia.

Black colleges and universities have been more than traditional institutions of higher education. They have been open about their mission to accept students that other institutions would not admit. Their story is a fascinating narrative of dealing with delicate and difficult issues that affect the daily lives of African American youth, their images of themselves, and their willingness and ability to tackle those complicated issues that reflect America in all of its ambiguity.

Yes, I would like to thank those heroic institutions who have courageously endured for so long without the appreciation that is their due. The essayists in this book have served on the front lines of Black higher education. They have been generous with their time and memories. We owe them, like the colleges and universities of which they write, a great debt, for their message is enduring, captivating, heartening, and reassuring.

Additionally, I owe a great deal to Trina Phillips, my secretarial associate, who spent countless hours in the preparation of the manuscript. Peg

Levine's critical eye and perspective provided valuable feedback on matters of substance and style. Finally, I would like to thank John von Knorring, publisher of Stylus Publishing, LLC, who continuously and insistently supports and listens to those whose voices and realities are sometimes shunned.

Karen A. Holbrook

Karen A. Holbrook, who became the thirteenth president of The Ohio State University on October 1, 2002, came to Columbus from The University of Georgia, where she served as senior vice president for academic affairs and provost as well as professor of cell biology and adjunct professor of anatomy and cell biology and medicine at the Medical College of Georgia. At Georgia, she helped create the Biomedical and Health Sciences Institute, two new colleges, and the New Media Institute, and she played a key role in developing the university's Strategic Plan.

Dr. Holbrook was previously an instructor and, later, assistant professor, associate professor, associate chairman, and professor of biological structure and medicine at the University of Washington School of Medicine, where she gained a national reputation for her expertise in dermatology.

In 1993, Dr. Holbrook moved to the University of Florida at Gainesville, where she served as vice president for research and dean of the Graduate School and as professor of anatomy and cell biology and medicine (dermatology). While there, she organized and chaired a meeting cosponsored by the Governor's Office, the University System, private enterprise, and the American Association for the Advancement of Science (AAAS), called "The Future of Science and Technology in Florida: High Tech Florida Means Business."

Throughout her career, Dr. Holbrook has held leadership roles and participated extensively in the activities of professional and honorary societies, including the AAAS, where she is a Fellow and has served as a member of the board of directors; the American Association of Universities; the National Association of State Universities and Land-Grant Colleges; and the Association of American Medical Colleges. She is also on the Board of Directors of ACT, the Institute for International Education, and the American Council on Education.

In Ohio, Dr. Holbrook was appointed by Governor Taft as a member of the Commission on Higher Education and the Economy and the steering committee for the Third Frontier Bond Initiative Campaign. She has also received numerous honors and has published extensively.

Born in Des Moines, Iowa, Karen Holbrook earned her B.S. and M.S. degrees in zoology at the University of Wisconsin in Madison in 1963 and 1966, respectively. After teaching biology at Ripon College for three years, she earned a Ph.D. in biological structure from the University of Washington School of Medicine in 1972 and pursued postdoctoral training in the Department of Dermatology.

There should no doubt in the mind of any intelligent scholar and observer that Black colleges and universities have helped to reverse the spiral of exclusion that was the modus operandi in White southern institutions of higher education prior to the civil rights initiatives of the 1960s. Nowhere has the silence of academics been more damaging than in their failure to acknowledge the rich contributions of Black institutions of higher education. Preoccupied with an obsession to exaggerate the accomplishments of the majority institutions, they have ignored or failed to pay attention to the successes that have had a significant impact on the growth and development of African American college youth.

We in the well-funded educational institutions have not gone far enough toward promoting equity in which all parts of the educational system are able to run smoothly, blessed by an appropriate economic slice of a caring system. Yet these Black colleges and universities have been able to make positive changes in the lives of their youth without the benefit of enormous and unimaginable resources at their disposal. These institutions have endorsed the principle that everyone who desires and needs higher education should be able to obtain it, and that it is a wasteful mockery within the system when they cannot. Thus, Black colleges and universities generally have adopted open door policies to make it possible for youngsters with limited resources and unimpressive credentials to be enrolled. As a result, these institutions have accepted students who have come with an extremely wide range of abilities. The record is unquestionably clear. They have routinely produced a significant level of highly courageous and capable students who through imaginative and artistic insights not only graduated from college but also became highly competent professionals in a variety of fields.

The formula for the success of these young people is not some obscure whisper in the night. I have engaged some of my academic peers who are faculty at Black colleges in conversation. Their approach is not purely cerebral. They have learned to respect students who have learned to plough themselves up through difficult circumstances. Their approach focused on hands-on individual instruction, all the while giving students the encouragement and freedom to discover ways of developing themselves and their potential. They inevitably acquire necessary confidence through which they develop the kind of intellectual and psychological nourishment that ultimately contributes to their success.

The underlying philosophy of these institutions is to make a strong commitment to adjust to the needs of the student, not simply expecting that the student has the total responsibility of adjusting to the traditions, policies, and practices of the institution. They typically try to centralize services in such a way that the student is not held captive by cumbersome requirements that limit his or her effectiveness in the round of activities. There is no single program or discipline that can guarantee a student success. "Availability" is a key word in the lexicon of student needs. It represents a variety of relatively small programs and services that aid in supplementing the student's progress at these institutions. But one cannot underestimate the value of personal connections with faculty, administrators, staff, and student peers. This is particularly vital on Black college campuses. Their day-to-day networks of new contacts, a problem that is particularly acute among racial minorities on White campuses, are wholesome and can significantly add to their comfort level. The less stress, the better is a student able to perform.

This volume provides strong testimonies by Black college administrators about what these institutions do to strengthen the development of their students. It is the evidence they offer that provides a balanced perspective of the value of Black colleges and universities that should challenge the nation to sit up and listen.

Dr. Karen Holbrook, President
The Ohio State University

FOREWORD

Frank W. Hale, Jr.

The history of Black colleges and universities within the American higher education community has all too frequently been ignored and excluded from the forums of educational considerations. As African Americans we have been unduly silent and at times avoided those opportunities to "toot our own horns" concerning our magnificent and glorious experiences at Black institutions of higher education. These institutions have played an increasingly important role in our nation's educational life. For a century and a half these institutions stood tall, even in an environment of neglect, when society was unwilling to recognize their contributions and their worth.

Black institutions of higher education have assumed the burden of responsibility for those students who have hungered for knowledge and the opportunity to gain it. Their collective efforts have reaped rich dividends. It has been a partnership of *one* on *one*.

This volume is an effort to confront the rhetoric of those who would challenge the need for the existence of Black colleges and universities. We have a stake and obligation in keeping the memory of their contributions alive. Among Black professionals they enjoy a sterling reputation, because they were the first to open their doors and to make it possible for their sons and daughters to gain a higher education. Here we listen to the voices of experience—those whose memories are pregnant with life experiences on Black college campuses. Such memories have enabled them to tell their own stories about the essential factors that shaped the lives of those young people who have benefited from these institutions. We have explored ways in which college presidents, active and inactive; senior administrators; and faculty have reflected on the positive effects that Black institutions of higher education have had on their students. These institutions have recognized that they need to give special caring to students who often, as first generation college students, have not been privy to the perspectives, experiences, and lifestyle opportunities available to some of their peers.

It is not too early to tell how Black institutions of higher education have made a permanent impact on public and private higher education. While I acknowledge the skepticism of some critics concerning their value, the magnitude of their contributions is immeasurable and incontrovertible. I stand by my long-run concerns about funding levels that will allow them to maintain viable and effective programs.

I know that the histories and achievements of Black institutions of higher education are integral to the neglected learning that goes on in some colleges. One of the purposes of this book is to facilitate a change in those discussions that undermine the need for these institutions. It is designed as another vehicle to remove the cloud of disbelief and cynicism that would rob these institutions of their credibility.

If we are serious about raising the level of educational aspirations among Black youth; if we want to solve the problems of poverty, unemployment and crime in our cities; and if we want to make it possible for all our youth to become competitive in an increasingly technological society, then we all must shoulder the responsibility to provide those opportunities that will enable Black youth to meet our expectations. Well-run and effective Black colleges and universities and other institutions of higher education depend, in large measure, on partnerships, alliances with parents, alumni, and community support. Such collaboration makes our efforts possible.

Frank W. Hale, Jr.

Dr. Frank W. Hale, Jr., is often referred to as the "Dean of Diversity" in higher education. He is in constant demand as a lecturer and consultant, and his most recent book, *What Makes Racial Diversity Work in Higher Education*, is used in colleges and universities throughout the country.

Dr. Hale is vice provost and professor emeritus at The Ohio State University, where he served from 1971–1988. Before coming to Ohio State University, he served as president of Oakwood College in Huntsville, Alabama. He is a graduate of the University of Nebraska, where he earned bachelor's and master's degrees in communication, political science, and English (1950–1951). He received his doctorate in communication and political science from the Ohio State University (1955) and was awarded a postdoctoral fellowship from the University of London in 1960.

Dr. Hale, who has been in the field of higher education for fifty-four years, has held full professorships at Central State University (Ohio), Oakwood College (Alabama), and the Ohio State University. At Ohio State, he served as associate dean and chairman of the fellowship committee of the graduate school, vice provost for minority affairs, and assistant to the president. Following his retirement in 1988, he served as executive assistant to the president at Kenyon College in Gambier, Ohio, and he returned to Ohio State as distinguished university representative and consultant in the president's office (1999–2005).

Dr. Hale has received hundreds of awards and citations, including the Frederick Douglass Patterson Award, the United Negro College Fund's highest award, and the Distinguished Service Award for Human Rights and Social Change from the National Association of State Universities and Land Grant Colleges (NASULGC).

As a scholar, researcher, author, teacher, administrator, consultant, and civil rights crusader, Dr. Hale engineered many new initiatives at Ohio State, including the Graduate and Professional Schools Visitation Days Program, which he established in 1971, and its undergraduate counterpart, the Minority Scholars Program, instituted in 1982. Through his efforts, approximately twelve hundred minority students received nearly $15 million in graduate fellowship awards. Eighty percent of these recipients earned master's and/or doctoral degrees. During Dr. Hale's tenure, Ohio State was cited as the number one producer of Black Ph.D.s in the 1970s and 1980s. To cap his illustrious career, the Ohio State Board of Trustees voted him vice provost and professor emeritus, naming the Frank W. Hale, Jr., Black Cultural Center in his honor and designating the building in which it is housed as Hale Hall. An endowed scholarship has also been established in his name.

INTRODUCTION
A Tribute to Black Colleges

A Negro university, from its high ground of unfaltering facing of the truth, from its unblinking stare at hard facts does not advocate segregation by race; it simply accepts the bald fact that we are segregated, apart, hammered into a separate unity by spiritual intolerance and legal sanction backed by mob law, and that this separation is growing in strength and fixation; that it is worse today than a half century ago and that no character, address, culture, or desert is going to change it in our day or for centuries to come. Recognizing this brute fact, groups of cultured, trained and devoted men gathering in great institutions of learning proceed to ask, What are we going to do about it? It is silly to ignore the gloss of truth; it is idiotic to proceed as though we were white or yellow, English or Russian. Here we stand. We are American Negroes. It is beside the point to ask whether we form a real race. Biologically we are mingled of all conceivable elements, but race is psychology, not biology; and psychologically we are a unified race with one history, one red memory, and one revolt. It is not ours to argue whether we will be segregated or whether we ought to be a caste. We are segregated; we are a caste. This is our given and at present unalterable fact. Our problem is how far and in what way can we consciously and scientifically guide our future so as to ensure our physical survival, our spiritual freedom and our social growth? Either we do this or we die. There is no alternative. If America proposed the murder of this group, its moral descent into imbecility and crime and its utter loss of manhood, self-assertion, and courage, the sooner we realize this, the better.

W.E.B. DuBois: A Reader
David Levering Lewis

In January of 1944, at age sixteen, I first stepped onto the hallowed grounds of Oakwood College in Huntsville, Alabama. Almost immediately, I became aware that there was nothing in the weather-beaten, whitewashed structures on campus that even faintly resembled the beauty and architectural extravagance of the high school from which I had graduated in Topeka, Kansas. I was making the transition from a materialistic mainstream culture into a Southern subculture that left me crestfallen, wondering if I would do well in such a setting. I was soon to learn that young people from whom teachers expect greater intellectual progress, do, in fact, show significant gains, whatever the appearance of the college buildings.

Over the past six decades, guided by both spiritual and academic principles, Oakwood College has reached unprecedented heights in its quest for excellence. From the time I was first admitted as a student, it has evolved into one of the most magnificent, manicured campus settings among the sisterhood of Black higher education institutions. The circle of committed alumni has remained unbroken during the 110-year history of the college. The Oakwood story can't be limited to giant and stately oak trees, marvelous magnolias, and heady hillside views. Its real story encompasses the dramatic impact that its superior academic and spiritual programming has had on thousands of students who have been beneficiaries of the most passionate, scholarly, and accessible voices of dedicated faculty to be found. The campus embraces more than one thousand acres, and it easily seduces one with its lovely buildings of variegated patterns of modern architectural splendor that reflect radiance and resplendency in multiple colors of light on a sunny day. I have been singularly blessed to have come full circle in my academic experiences there as a student, as a faculty member, as the college president, and ultimately as a member of the College Board of Trustees.

During my generation, there was a tendency to believe that educational superiority resided and remained in the hands of the majority. The proponents of this idea were part of a system that perpetuates unmitigated nonsense and White racism.

The widely accepted myth was that Blacks are incapable of the attitudes and practices that promote creative and enlightened thinking and that the ultimate education of Blacks should be attuned to the competitive and creative strategies of White institutions with long traditions and elite images.

Too often the contributions of Black colleges are overlooked. Many alumni of these institutions have gained prominence in their respective fields and have used their credentials and their gifts to enrich the nation as a whole and to teach young people the importance of acquiring attitudes of mind, knowledge, and qualifications that will enable them to take their place in a competitive society.

It was my good fortune to have been able to play a part as a faculty member in two historically Black institutions: Oakwood College in Huntsville, Alabama, and Central State University in Wilberforce, Ohio. I hasten to add that those two experiences prepared me for the realities of the world. The mission of service is deeply ingrained in the philosophy of Black colleges. Service is the driving force that gives authority to the institution's identity. Black colleges are committed to the spiritual, intellectual, cultural, and economic development of their students. The concept of service goes beyond the rhetoric of the classroom; students are encouraged to become academic activists and to lead the way in responding to the problems that African Americans face on a daily basis.

One of the most essential contributions of Black colleges has been an open admissions process that accepts students who many other institutions with selective admissions would reject. Those Black institutions are citadels of optimism. They expect their youth to succeed. They ever remind them that they were born qualified and that they go to school to certify that fact. They rigorously motivate them to believe that they are capable of learning and that they will be successful if they persevere. In today's world, to what extent do pessimistic teachers train their students to be criminals? Don't these pessimists contribute to student failure when they suggest, directly or indirectly, that some young people are incapable of learning and have no ambition and no future, and that thus they are destined to fail? Such humiliation inflicted upon young students prepares them to become unfortunate examples of the coincidence of crime, illiteracy, and cultural deprivation as meaningless and marginal members of society.

Historical Perspective

It takes no superior intellect to know and understand that institutions of Black higher education provide a sustained climate of welcoming and acceptance for Black students seldom experienced by them in White institutions. The very fact that the issue of affirmative action is front and center in many White institutions speaks to the troubling problems of racial tensions and hostilities. It is no wonder then that students of color find it convenient and comfortable to form their own separate organizations so that minority students can come together and develop a positive climate for themselves, where they can feel fully accepted.

Black students at Black colleges and universities do not face such challenges. Already a homogenous group, they don't face the tensions common in a climate where they are not fully accepted. There should be no confusion around the question of whether Black students at Black colleges enjoy an advantage of acceptance not generally realized on non-Black college campuses. Though Black students were recruited in large numbers at White institutions following the assassination of Dr. Martin Luther King, Jr., they soon discovered how troublesome life would be with the stigma of some thinking that they were less qualified for admission because affirmative action programs played an important role in admissions decisions. The insults of derogatory name calling, mockeries, race-baiting graffiti, and the distribution of neo-Nazi and Ku Klux Klan literature all combined to deepen the divide between Black and White students. Consequently, institutions of higher education saw the need to develop racial harassment policies, to expand their mission statements, to be more inclusive, to infuse their curricula with information that recognized the contributions of people of color; universities needed to conduct retreats on race relations, to establish affirmative action committees and annual affirmative action awards for those departments, colleges, and units that had brought about positive changes in committing themselves to building communities where people learn to value and respect one another for their differences. Historically Black Colleges and Universities have long been models of inclusion for White students and White faculty over the years. Equivocation on this issue has never been a matter of great concern.

Jacqueline Fleming is right when she insists that "proponents of total integration minimize the nature of adjustment problems that Black students must undergo" at predominantly White schools. She continues, "The stress of racial tension and inadequate social lives borne by Black students in White schools generates feelings of alienation that often lead to serious adjustment problems; . . . the factors that provide a positive climate at predominantly Black colleges are largely absent or unavailable to Black students in White schools. Consequently, Black students perform below their ability levels."[1] It stands to reason then that Black institutions are singularly unique in what they contribute to the education of Black students.

Historically, Blacks were almost entirely excluded from traditionally Southern White institutions before the 1960s. Black students who sought to pursue higher education of necessity enrolled at Black institutions of higher education. The current viability of Historically Black Colleges and Universities (HBCUs) should never be in question. These institutions have special relevance because of the success of their graduates in obtaining graduate and professional degrees from Northern White institutions; this cannot be too strongly emphasized. The brilliantly successful career profiles of Martin Lu-

---

[1] Jacqueline Fleming, *Blacks in College* (San Francisco: Jossey-Bass Publishers, 1984), p. 3.

ther King, Jr., Julian Bond, Maynard Jackson, Willie Gary, Spike Lee, Leontyne Price, W.E.B. DuBois, Thurgood Marshall, and Zora Neale Hurston testify to the genius and enhancement that Black institutions of higher education have given to the entire educational enterprise. The depth, strength, and integrity of these institutions have been validated by the incontrovertible achievements and contributions of their graduates. These institutions have admitted students who have come from economically deprived homes where few parents had the privilege of attending college. The Black students whose preparation may not have qualified them to enter predominantly White institutions were, nevertheless, accepted and respected at Black institutions. As a consequence, their experiences were enabling and empowering them rather than crippling them. Without being patronizing, these institutions recognize the importance of galvanizing the students' quests for self-identity by making changes and modifications to meet the needs of students, rather than by assuming that it was the total responsibility of the student to have the sophistication to adjust, without clearly defined goals, to the character of the institution.

Black colleges were established at a time when educational opportunities were not available to Black Americans. It has been over 175 years since Cheney, the first Black college, was founded in 1830. Freed slaves were able to choose to attend only the institutions of higher education open to them. Because of limited financial resources, these institutions lacked liberal arts curricula; thus they could only operate at the level of elementary and secondary schools. The Morrill Act of 1890 established Black public colleges. The Act ruled that states must either provide separate educational facilities for Blacks or admit them to existing colleges. Consequently, Southern and border states hastily chose to establish schools for Blacks. By 1896 the doctrine of separate but equal, highlighted by the *Plessy v. Ferguson* doctrine, placed a heavy emphasis on industrial training for Blacks. It was a doctrine that was underscored by Booker T. Washington's Atlanta Exposition speech of 1895, which also supported the idea that Blacks should focus their training and preparation on the industrial arts rather than the liberal arts. His position was diametrically opposed to that of W.E.B. DuBois, who maintained that a liberal arts curriculum best fits the needs of Black Americans.

I recall the earlier agitation that brought the *Brown v. Board of Education* (1954) issue front and center. As early as 1941, Black parents in Topeka, Kansas, began to agitate for the school system to provide more durable and respectable resources for their children. The textbooks were often hand-me-down backless textbooks that the White schools could no longer use. The desks were scarred and carved upon to the extent that they had little functional or aesthetic appeal. Parents would often meet at St. John's A.M.E. Church on the first Sunday of every month to present their complaints and concerns to Rev. Burrell and to attorney Elijah Scott and representatives of the NAACP. Monroe School and Buchanan School were examples of schools reflecting the sham and hypocrisy of the separate but equal doctrine of education. Determined parents provided the advance guard for what proved to be a reawakening of America to the meaning of equal opportunity in the field of education. Black Americans began to understand that issues had to percolate in society before the status quo could be changed; that ideas relative to the program of Black Americans had to bubble up before they could expect the evidences of progress to funnel down.

The debate over the need for Black colleges accelerated after the entrance of Black students into predominantly White schools in the 1960s. The major question is whether having a dual system of higher education is philosophically and economically sound. There were those who called for an end to racial dualism, proposing that integration is the policy that should be adopted. But under prevailing conditions, campus communities have a long way to go to be both equitable and fair. The task of self-definition and identity can easily be compromised for Black students on a White campus. The period of early and late adolescence is when a young person learns who he or she is. It is a time when youths differentiate themselves from the culture in which they find themselves. When race is a factor, as it surely will be for Black students on a White campus, they will have to cope with more than their share of feelings of uncertainty and insecurity. The change from high school to college, in and of itself, is a difficult change; however, that difficulty can easily be compounded when students feel vulnerable and frustrated by a campus where they do not feel fully accepted.

We need to be reminded that Black colleges provide an atmosphere in which concerns about social consciousness are paramount. The drive for equal opportunity does not always have happy consequences on the traditional White campus. The climate of social conformity is more likely to be a part of the campus culture on campus, especially regarding issues of race; the result is often political apathy unless Black students take the lead in a challenge for justice. The history of the 1960s informs us that students on Black college campuses assumed the roles of rebel, reformer, advocate, crusader, and critic of the status quo.

It stands to reason that the Black college is equipped to help the Black student to restore himself to himself and herself to herself. This can occur only when an institution accepts the responsibility for helping students resist the social patterns to be found in contemporary American culture. Such a focus on resistance is the means by which the student may achieve a moral and intellectual maturity.

Black Education: A Parallel Response to Isolation

While Black colleges grapple with the demands for achieving academic excellence and for promoting the importance of teaching and research, they have made a distinctive contribution to the higher education community generally and to the African American community in particular. These institutions were designed to help Black students break through the walls of misguided opinions about themselves and then to challenge the system that has used abrasive strategies to incarcerate their spirits. Carter G. Woodson dares to be explicit in *The Miseducation of the Negro*[2]:

> The present system under the control of whites trains the Negro to be white and at the same time convinces him of the impropriety of his becoming white. It compels the Negro to become a good Negro for the performance of which his education is ill-suited.

Raymond Winbush, author of *The Warrior Method*, declares that the history of educating African American students about who they are is a history of struggle. Only limited glimpses concerning the history and contributions of Black people have been available in American historiography. This has been one way, consciously or unconsciously, to set the stage for Black students to be educated out of their Blackness. While ethnic groups, such as Germans, Italians, Russians, and the British and French, bring a rich reservoir of their history to the table of learning, for some reason, the issue for African-centeredness conveniently shifts when the education of Black youth is addressed.

Samuel DuBois Cook believes that the social and ethical role of Black colleges is directed at social change. It is not change for its own sake but for a continual challenge of the status quo in oppressive race relations and social behavior. The Black college has the positive element of opening students' minds, helping them become aware of their own capacities. In the process, they become aware of those issues that need to be addressed in order to im-

---

[2] Carter G. Woodson, *The Miseducation of the Negro* (The Associated Publishers, 1933), pp. 23–24.

prove and advance the lot of their own people. Such education opens them to their potential and the traditions that have fettered and impeded the aspirations of Black people.

Historically Black colleges have taken steps to succor and to protect the emotional well being of their students. These institutions are aware of the anxiety-producing conditions of provocation, discrimination, neglect, and exploitation that these students will have to face in society.

Sometimes in majority White colleges of higher education, Black students suffer from what remains of institutionalized discrimination in many ways, including curriculum bias, negative faculty and students' attitudes concerning their potential, and by insistence, consciously or unconsciously, that they be educated out of their blackness. Even more often they expect students to minimize or to step outside of their subculture rather than to change or modify the structure of the institution in a way that will accept, understand, celebrate, and learn from the perspectives of the diverse cultures on campus.

Like other reputable institutions of higher education, Black colleges and universities have concerned themselves with preparing their students with academic knowledge and the sophistication that ultimately will make them successful in their chosen careers. It is reasonable to presume then that the students who have attended these schools can look back upon them as the academic expressions of their own aspirations.

Dr. King V. Cheek, Jr., former President of Morgan State University, observed that "these institutions can help Black students to understand that when they enter the real world of competition, they will stand alone; their success or failure will depend on their adaptable intellectual tools . . ." Cheek continued, "Black colleges and their Black students helped Americans realize that the first step to freedom is to break the shackles of psychological bondage—to free oneself from the prison of self-hate and despair . . ." For many Black students, the Black college is the only environment in which their personal objectives can be accomplished. They have good reason to prefer the comforting climate of a Black campus with Black adult and peer model figures to one which may be cold, hostile and unfamiliar."[3]

To Be or Not to Be

The questions remain. Are Black institutions of higher education necessary? Now that most major institutions no longer have blatant racial discrimina-

---

[3] King Cheek, Jr., "The Black College in a Multiracial Society," in Dyckman Vermilye, ed., *The Expanded Campus* (San Francisco: Jossey-Bass, Inc., 1972), pp. 67–77.

tion policies, why are Black institutions necessary? Don't HBCUs promote segregation, the very thing that Black people have fought against? Aren't they avowedly exclusive and self-serving? Isn't there sufficient evidence to indicate that their contributions are only marginal within the community of higher education? Why should the federal government, a state, or community whose own resources are limited provide support for these institutions? Shouldn't financial resources be allotted to only the premier institutions with strong track records?

Dr. Benjamin E. Mays once articulated this powerful statement:

> No one has ever said that Catholic colleges should be abolished because they are Catholic. Nobody says that Brandeis and Albert Einstein must die because they are Jewish. Nobody says that Lutheran and Episcopalian schools should go because they are Lutheran or Episcopalian. Why should Howard University be abolished because it is known as a Black university? Why pick out Negro colleges and say they must die? Blot out these colleges: you blot out the image of Black men and women in education.[4]

It is both interesting and bewildering when sharp distinctions are made between Black colleges and the traditional White college. The truth is that no one recommends that all White colleges be on the same academic level as Yale, Harvard, Chicago, Princeton, or Berkeley. What Black colleges and universities propose is that they prepare students to live and make contributions in a competitive world and infuse them as well with a passion for social justice and a responsibility to use their training to provide liberation for the Black community.

It should be noted that Black institutions of higher education have always been open to students and faculty without regard to race, creed, or national origin. Gregory Kannerstein underscores the fact that "the dedication of Black colleges to openness and equal educational opportunity, which is no new development . . . is an expression of the belief that they can truly serve their people and preserve their culture while they offer an education and a unique experience to people of all backgrounds."[5]

I sometimes reflect upon the challenges that the events of the 1960s offered me when I served as a faculty member at Central State University in Wilberforce, Ohio. These events provided my classes with a provocative plat-

---

[4] Benjamin E. Mays, "The Black College in Higher Education," in *Black Colleges in America*, Charles V. Willie and Ronald R. Edmonds, eds. (New York: Teachers College Press, Columbia University, 1978), p. 27.

[5] Gregory Kannerstein, "Black Colleges: Self-Concept," in Black Colleges in America, Charles V. Willie and Ronald R. Edmonds, eds. (New York: Teachers College Press, Columbia University, 1978), p. 35.

form for students to do some very serious thinking on issues that were so vital to them and to explore ways of presenting their views among the following issues:

- Is non-violence productive in the long run?
- What is the best way to fight racial prejudice, segregation, and discrimination?
- Will White people ever willingly and equitably share the resources of this nation with Black people?

All the while, I was seeking additional ways in which I could give students at Central State an opportunity to learn and share in the historical and dramatic moments of the time. By early 1963, racial turmoil had driven American Blacks to such lengths that the voices of militancy were gaining momentum among the Black masses. Still, the non-violent middle-class voices of Black leadership sought to move in a disciplined and restrained way to capture the nation's attention. Martin Luther King, Jr., had written a most cogent and stirring expression of his philosophy of non-violence in his "Letter from a Birmingham Jail." By midsummer, the scope and details of racial unrest were immeasurable. The reverberations and the repercussions of the Birmingham bombings and riots had crisscrossed the country, triggering confrontations in the major cities of the North. A. Phillip Randolph convinced Black leadership that the March on Washington idea, first promoted in the early 1940s, was an idea whose time had come.

The intensity of the mass media promotion of this spectacular undertaking prompted me to seek the permission of Central State's president, Charles Wesley, to offer students the opportunity to attend and participate in this great convocation of national unity on August 28, 1963, in Washington, D.C., where major spheres of business, labor, religion, industry, the professions, and every other imaginable area of daily life were to be gathered. Students and faculty sprang most eagerly and vigorously to the opportunity, so much so that, in short order, we had a caravan of vehicles headed east and ready to converge on the nation's capital. As faculty and as students we were joining our "brothers and sisters" from around the country who were coming boldly to vent their indignation at the mindless dehumanizing indignities designed to crush the initiative, control the spontaneity, and impose senseless regulations on those who sought to gain the full freedom that most Americans were accorded at their birth. The March on Washington aided in the passage of the Civil Rights Act of 1964 and opened the doors of equal opportunity in many areas for Black people. The voices of Black students from many Black colleges, along with thousands of others, thundered with resonance and conviction that sent the walls of legalized segregation and discrimination tumbling down. Joshua, "who fit the battle of Jericho," wasn't standing all by himself.

Epilogue

White institutions of higher education, wittingly or not, are designed to make students replicas of their own image. I am fairly certain that in many instances they have been far too successful. Brainwashing is not a foreign idea in American education. The appeal to the young Black students is seldom to celebrate their culture; it is almost always to celebrate cultures other than their own. Being excluded from identifying with their own culture, they have reason to conclude that they have no power or position in their own right. Thus the assumption is that they can only achieve a sense of power and reality by identifying themselves with other cultures.

If people believe this loss of Black identity inevitable, I beg to differ. Upon accepting the position of associate dean of the graduate school at The Ohio State University in 1971, I began to make plans on how best to attract Black students to pursue graduate education at the university. Because I had sat on the Board of the United Negro College Fund and had been intimately associated with the presidents of those institutions, I was well aware of the wonderful record that many Black colleges and universities had in graduating students who later earned graduate and professional degrees at major institutions. I felt certain that the intellectual stimulation which they received at Black institutions was more than adequate to make them competitive students once they were admitted into the graduate programs at Ohio State.

The university agreed to fund the fifteen million dollar bank of fellowships which I requested, and then appointed me Chairman of the Graduate School Fellowship Committee in the autumn of 1971. I immediately initiated a Graduate School Visitation Days Program, a two-day event in which fifty Historically Black Colleges and Universities were invited to send their five highest-ranking seniors to The Ohio State University campus on the first weekend in November. During their stay, the 250 honor seniors attended an opening convocation to meet representatives from admissions, financial aid, housing, student services, and minority affairs. The next day they spent the morning meeting with departmental faculty in the areas where they wished to pursue graduate degrees. In the afternoon they met with Black students who were already pursuing graduate work at the institution. The hosting students were encouraged to tell it "like it is" on campus or in the departments where the honors seniors were seeking admission.

During my eight-year tenure as associate dean and as chairman of the Fellowship Committee of the Graduate School, nearly 1,600 fellowships were awarded to Black students. Approximately 1,200 of those students went on to earn masters' and/or doctoral degrees. During that period, Ohio State had a running head start on graduate schools nationwide. The positive effect of our success not only benefited Ohio State, it motivated other institutions to visit our campus, learn our strategies, and then return to their institutions to establish similar programs. By the late 1970s, Ohio State became the number one producer of Black Ph.D.s in America. Even though the competition became fierce, as the founder and forerunner of minority graduate recruitment on a massive scale, the Ohio State Program was perceived and labeled as the best, and many of my colleagues at other institutions have referred to me affectionately as the Dean of Diversity. Such a response was not only a recognition of our efforts at Ohio State, but it also acknowledged the endorsement and collaboration that we shared with the administrators and faculty at historically Black colleges. The real accolades should go to those marvelously, academically well-prepared Black students who are graduates from historically Black colleges. The salient factor is that Black students from Black institutions of higher education were ready for competition at major institutions long before those institutions had the courage to admit them.

The essays in this volume come from the pens of experienced champions of Black higher education. They build upon the unique and splendid contributions of the particular institutions where they have served. Their words intend to correct the misinformation regarding Black institutions of higher education. Their voices reinforce each other's positive messages. They have no other choice. They share and applaud the enormous and ennobling contributions of these towers of Black higher education.

Dr. Frank W. Hale, Jr.
Vice Provost and Professor Emeritus
The Ohio State University

Samuel DuBois Cook

Dr. Samuel DuBois Cook, president emeritus, Dillard University, has an outstanding record as a political scientist, scholar, educator, teacher, administrator, and civil and human rights activist. In addition to teaching, he has lectured extensively at colleges and universities throughout the country and in Africa, Asia, and Europe. Even while president of Dillard, he continued to participate in the world of scholarship through publications, lectureships, and professional organizations.

A native of Griffin, Georgia, and a Korean War veteran, Dr. Cook is a graduate of Morehouse College, and he earned his M.A. and Ph.D. from The Ohio State University. From January 1, 1975, until his retirement on June 30, 1997, he was president of Dillard University. Dr. Cook's contributions to the university's progress spanned academic improvement across the board, financial viability and management, enrollment growth, faculty development and productivity, information technology, the physical plant, alumni relations, student welfare, the institution of new programs, mutually beneficial relationships with The United Methodist Church and The United Church of Christ, and the regional and national reputation of the institution.

Dr. Cook has taught at Southern University, Atlanta University, the University of Illinois, the University of California at Los Angeles, and Duke University. He was not only the first African American professor at Duke, but he has the distinction of being the first Black to hold a regular (full-time and/or tenured) faculty appointment at any predominantly White college or university in the South.

Dr. Cook is the author or editor of many scholarly publications, including the recently published *Black-Jewish Relations: Dillard University National Conference Papers, 1989–1997*. He has also been a program officer in higher education and research at the Ford Foundation. President Jimmy Carter appointed Dr. Cook to the prestigious National Council on the Humanities, and President Bill Clinton appointed him to the historic United States Holocaust Memorial Council.

In 1997, Duke University established the Samuel DuBois Cook Society; in 1998, The Ohio State University inaugurated the Samuel DuBois Cook Young Scholars Summer Conference; and, in 2000, Ohio State's Department of Political Science established the Samuel DuBois Cook Fellowships to honor one of its "most distinguished graduates and African-American alumni." In 1998, Dr. Cook was elected to the Black College Hall of Fame.

HISTORICALLY BLACK COLLEGES AND UNIVERSITIES (HBCUs) IN THE OLD SOUTH AND THE NEW SOUTH

Change and Continuity

In the broad sweep and vivid landscape of Southern history and culture, and, indeed, in the total framework of the American experience since their general beginning in the tragic aftermath of the Civil War, it is difficult to overestimate the significance of historically Black colleges and universities (HBCUs).[1] Despite the endless challenges and obstacles to survival, success, and fulfillment; despite the general invisibility, marginality, terrible lack of appreciation; despite massive deprivation and the call for their death as identifiable institutions, they have, generally speaking, continued to be creative and productive in the universe of American higher education, diversity, and pluralism. A persistent, tireless, and endless question to this day is: How do you justify the existence of Black colleges and universities in this day of "desegregation" and "integration"? A wise, scholarly, and prophetic man, Bishop James S. Thomas of The United Methodist Church, has countered compellingly: "The question is not so much: 'How do you justify the Black college?' but 'When will America and the church face up to the debt they owe to institutions whose contributions to the society have far out-distanced investments made in them?'"[2]

After the Civil War, in no small measure because of the incredible intellectual eagerness and academic hunger of ex-slaves, the education of Blacks assumed great significance—at least in certain quarters. It was neither accidental nor an experience of minor and fleeting importance and relevance that virtually all of the educational institutions founded to educate freedmen were church-related. Indeed, the church-relatedness of their origin was of overwhelming and enduring significance, meaning, and value. Involved were a theological worldview, formal commitment to the fatherhood of God and the brotherhood of man, and a belief—however insufficient—that ex-slaves and their descendants were human persons endowed by God with intrinsic dignity, value, and worth and were equal in God's sight. Over the long haul of history and culture, the implications and consequences have been far-reaching. Whatever the shortcomings—and there were many—significant seeds of a common humanity and a minimum decency of human relations were planted and began to sprout, grow, and bear fruit and, in the long run, to help to improve the status and facilitate the progress of Blacks and change the course of Southern and American history and culture. Public institutions of higher education for Blacks had to await a later period, spirit, and historical context.

Various churches, through their denominational boards or other agencies, began the sacred work of establishing, financing, and operating academies, normal schools, and colleges across the South. Missionary schools flourished, and missionaries from the North trekked south to teach freedmen and their children who had insatiable intellectual curiosity. The American Missionary Association, the Freedmen's Aid Society, and the Freedmen's Bureau were especially active. Baptists, Methodists, Congregationalists, Presbyterians, Episcopalians, African Methodist Episcopalians, Christian Methodist Episcopalians, and African Methodist Episcopal Zions, in various degrees, became involved in the educational enterprise for former slaves by establishing colleges and universities that were often simply grade schools. Attaching to the names "colleges" and "universities" expressed more hope, ideals, and aspirations than reality.

Genuine excitement, involvement, enthusiasm, and passions were afloat. In conceptualization and fermentation, HBCUs were sensed and thought of as institutions of hope, self-help, progress, promise, growth, self-reliance, racial reconciliation and understanding, development, excellence, emancipation, transformation, dreams, aspirations, expectations, liberation, cultivation, fulfillment, and reverence for learning. They represented, intuitively for the freedmen, so much of the vitality, ingenuity, nobility, and higher possibilities of the human mind, heart, will, and spirit. They embodied the human imagination unbound, cruising the uncharted seas and frontiers of limitless, open, rich, soaring, unshackled, creative, and redemptive possibilities of human life and destiny against the tragic background and memory of the infinite evils of slavery. We should not forget that, after all, it was a crime to teach slaves to read and write—laws that were, in some situations, ignored. Perhaps only ex-slaves could be so free, daring, and innocent to dream of, and aspire to, so much. The freedmen had an inexhaustible passion for education and viewed it as the chief vehicle of liberty, justice, upward social mobility, self-realization, citizenship, wholeness and fullness of common humanity, and full participation in the mainstream of American life, culture, and destiny.

From their very inception, Black institutions of higher education were agents of empowerment—intellectual, economic, social, political, constitutional, legal, and cultural—with a vision of and commitment to social, political, constitutional, legal, and cultural change. This article of faith was inexplicit, an "inarticulate major premise" that, in terms of survival in a hostile and cruel racial environment, had to be concealed and suppressed. Freedom means, among other things, power. It is the power or capacity to do or not to do, to act or refrain from action. Activism is central to freedom and the quest for freedom. John Dewey asserted,

> [L]iberty is not just an idea, an abstract principle. It is power, effective power to do specific things. There is no such thing as liberty in general, liberty, so to speak, at large. If one wants to know what the condition of liberty is at a given time, one has to examine what persons *can* do and what they *cannot* do. The moment one examines the question from the standpoint of effective action, it becomes evident that the demand for liberty is a demand for power, either for possession of powers of action not already possessed or for retention and expansion of powers already possessed.[3]

Formal emancipation of the slaves had to be endowed with *material* content, the flesh and blood of empirical or substantive, objective reality, and meaning.

In talking about HBCUs as institutions of empowerment and social and historical change, let it be clear that we are not ascribing omniscience to their founders and other original constituencies in terms of what these educational vessels and incubators would become. We are dealing with the evolution and development of institutions, ideas, ideals, expectations, aspirations, and hopes. We are talking about the seeds planted, cultivated, and harvested in the gardens and fields of the continuum of human experience and adventure.

Triumph against Old South Racism, Dehumanization, and Degradation

In the post-Civil War era, when most HBCUs were established, the racist doctrine of slavery continued in the form of caste.[4] The South—and much of the North as well—viewed Blacks as subhuman and, therefore, biologically, intellectually, and morally inferior and beyond the realm of educability. They are thus unworthy of any claim to equality of consideration in terms of citizenship and humanity. As Dr. Benjamin E. Mays observed,

> There were at that time only a few persons who believed that the Negro was capable of doing college and university work. For a long time scientists, educators, statesmen, and even men supposedly called of God to preach, had been proclaiming the Negroes' inability to learn. Years before my day, a fellow South Carolinian, thinking that he was perfectly safe in making such a proclamation, declared that he would be willing to give the Negro citizenship when he mastered the Greek verb.[5]

Resources were meager: the southern White community was hostile, but faculties were competent and committed and comprised mostly missionaries from the North. Students were eager to learn and had a great passion for education.

Private Black colleges and universities, despite the heavy odds against them and persistent, painful financial burdens and woes, generally survived and succeeded. Many of them are well into their second century of service and contributions to better lives. They have made and continue to make basic and enduring contributions not only to the Black community but also to the South, the country, and the world.

Seeking to be suggestive rather than exhaustive, we want to note several major contributions of HBCUs.

First, Black colleges and universities have contributed mightily to the establishing, nurturing, cultivating, and strengthening of the Black intellectual tradition with its commitment to reverence for learning and life of the mind. They have also helped to bolster and enrich the American intellectual tradition. It is difficult to believe that, until relatively recently, with only a few, rare, and lonely isolated exceptions, HBCUs were the only institutions of higher education that provided employment opportunities for Black scholars; White institutions did not hire them, no matter how high the quality of their performance or how brilliant and promising and able they were to make contributions to the advancement of knowledge and the progress of society through teaching, research, publication, professional leadership, mentoring, role modeling, and community service. The door of professional access and participatory contribution was tightly closed. What did such an intellectual and professional tragedy do to the initiative, motivation, aspirations, and expectations of Black scholars? *Merit was irrelevant* to their employment at White colleges and universities.

Sadly and tragically, Black scholars were systematically, routinely, and automatically excluded from employment, not only by White colleges and universities in the South, but equally by the great White colleges and universities of the North, East, and West. Even the peerless W.E.B. DuBois with a Ph.D. from Harvard; philosopher Alain Locke, a Rhodes Scholar from Harvard; the gifted Ralph J. Bunche, a Harvard Ph.D. in political science; and until the mid 1950s, the incomparable John Hope Franklin, also a Harvard Ph.D., were restricted to employment at HBCUs. Exclusion of Black scholars from the professorate was the norm. What would have happened to them without HBCUs, with their comparatively meager resources? The world of scholarship and the divine adventure of life of the mind—both White and Black—would have suffered irreparable harm and deprivation.

In the historical context of the systematic, rigid, and race-conscious exclusion of Blacks from the professorate of White colleges and universities in America, one cannot avoid thinking of the current controversy over affirmative action, diversity, and equality of opportunity in American higher education. Remember when Blacks were systematically excluded solely due to the color of their skin? Remember the absolute irrelevance of merit?

Second, HBCUs have provided top local, state, national, and international leadership in education, business, science, the arts, medicine, civil and human rights, religion, politics, government, industry, the military, diplomacy, and world affairs. In time and because of progress, countless outstanding Black professionals did not attend HBCUs, but their parents and grandparents often did. Black institutions provided the stimulus, the bridge, the preparation, the foundations, the stepping-stones, the door opening, the initial test and proof of academic competitiveness and worth.

In a November 18, 1966, address at Shaw University, Dr. Mays said eloquently,

> Despite meager support and the conviction that Negro schools need less than White schools, Shaw and other predominantly Negro colleges have prepared Negroes for outstanding leadership. I am sure that 90 percent or more of all Negro college graduates graduated from predominantly Negro

colleges like Shaw and Morehouse. Easily 90 percent or more of all Negro doctors, lawyers, and dentists took their undergraduate work at schools like Shaw. I would wager that 95 percent of all Negro teachers in our public schools and colleges came from predominantly Negro colleges. The vast majority in business and skilled trades are graduates of our colleges.[6]

The statistics have changed, but the historical record has not and cannot change. It is immutable.

It is important to be reminded that

These colleges have given to America Booker T. Washington, Robert Russa Moton, Mordecai Johnson, John W. Davis, and Mary McLeod Bethune in education; Howard Thurman, Channing Tobias, James Robinson, and George Kelsey in religion; Charles Johnson, E. Franklin Frazier, and Ira Reid in social science; James Weldon Johnson, Walter White, Frank Yerby, and Langston Hughes as authors and poets; Louie Wright, T.K. Lawless, and Peter Marshall Murray in medicine and surgery; P.B. Young, Robert Vann, Robert Abbott, Carter Wesley, and the Scotts and Murphys in journalism; and James Nabrit, Thurgood Marshall, and Judge Stephens in law. At this very moment, graduates work in our leading universities, including Columbia, Harvard, Yale, and the University of Chicago.[7]

Dr. Mays delivered the above words fifty years ago on March 20, 1955, at a United Negro College Fund Convocation at the Metropolitan Opera House in New York. Just think how impressive an update would be of the graduates of private Black colleges and universities. It would include a Nobel Peace Prize winner, a recipient of the Nobel Prize in Literature, several winners of the Pulitzer Prize and recipients of the Presidential Medal of Freedom as well as Rhodes, Marshall, and Truman scholars and MacArthur "genius" fellowships. The current list would also include prominent scholars; authors; recipients of numerous honors, awards, and citations in science, business, medicine, literature, journalism, the arts, engineering, foreign affairs, elective public office; members of presidential cabinets; the governor of a Southern state and a significant number of Black elected and appointed public officials in Dixie—including several members of the U.S. Congress, several mayors—and members of the military and other professions. It would include faculty members and administrators at the nation's most prestigious colleges and universities and professional schools in the North, South, East, and West—public and private, large and small, church-related and secular, elite and mediocre. On the list would be the president of Brown University, an Ivy

League institution, the presidents of a few other predominantly White higher education institutions, and the chief executive officers and board members of "Fortune 500 Companies." Not a bad record of achievement and contribution for 246 years of slavery and another century of Jim Crow segregation, discrimination, and exclusion.

Third, HBCUs are largely responsible for the rise, development, and expansion of the Black middle class, with its corresponding educational, professional, economic, political, social, and cultural power, influence, prestige, and skills. The Black middle class has helped to change the landscape of the nation. It contributed to the transformation of the Southern economy and culture from agrarian to industrial, urbanized, technological, and scientific. It also contributed to the transformation of Southern culture from racist determinism, degradation, oppression, and dehumanization to, in large measure, a society of mutual respect, decency, progress, tolerance, nonviolence, and a significant degree of human equality and racial justice. Education, skills, goodwill, social activism, civic engagement, political involvement, and legal redress were essential.

It was well said by C. Eric Lincoln that a "major role of the Negro college, then, was to insure the moral acceptability of the Negro vanguard, which would in turn leaven the Black masses with teachers and clergymen—and at industrial schools like Hampton and Tuskegee, with farmers and artisans who by precept and example would lift the race by its bootstraps."[8]

Fourth, as Dr. Julius S. Scott Jr. has emphasized, HBCUs have been the chief custodians, preservers, and enhancers of the Black heritage and experience—so much a part of the American journey in the New World.

This essay, however, focuses on the unique contributions and legacy of HBCUs to the richness and vitality of the country's tradition and ideals of diversity, inclusion, equality, democracy, multiculturalism, multiracialism, multiethnicity, multifaith, and progress in the transformation and democratization of the Old South into the New South and, by extension, the country. The New South is, in no small part, the child of the genius, vision, integrity, and commitment of Black institutions of higher education. What a paradox! Former slaves and their descendants helped to free the South from the shackles and prison of the tyranny and universality of racism that desperately sought to keep them in bondage. They helped to free the South from the deadly self-defeating, self-imprisonment and albatross of brutal, overt, institutional racism and helped to bring about social and institutional change so that the South, except for sad nostalgic echoes of neo-Confederates, could overcome the Civil War, rejoin the Union, focus on the real issues of the

region instead of the diversionary, divisive philosophy and tactic Negrophobia, and play a key role in the election of three Southerners in the twentieth
century—Lyndon Baines Johnson, James Earl Carter, and William Jefferson
Clinton—as presidents of the United States. Old South racism would have
deprived them of "electability."

Private HBCUs and the Tradition of Integration, Diversity, Inclusion, and Interracialism in the Old South

It is a supreme irony of the history of the Old South that, in spite of 246
years of slavery, private Black colleges and universities were an island of freedom in a sea of racial tyranny and imperialism. Not only in principle, policy,
and moral authority, but also, in no small measure; in fact, HBCUs have
been, from their inception in the post-Civil War era, pioneers, trailblazers,
and models of integration, diversity, democracy, pluralism, interracialism,
freedom, integrity, and inclusivity in education. How strange! How revealing
of the higher possibilities of the human mind and spirit!

It is important at this point to make a distinction between *private* and
public HBCUs. More than history is involved, including propositions of
worldview, origin, ethos, independence, autonomy or freedom, financial
support, leadership, heritage, and accountability. A chief difference is that
HBCUs originated in church relationships or, in some cases, issued from
nonecclesiastical religious dimensions or visions. HBCUs were born of secular forces and vitalities and supported by them. It is important to remember,
however, that several public Black colleges and universities had their origin
in church relationships or other religious dimensions and were, for various
reasons, "taken over" by public agencies and instrumentalities. Complexities
abound. In some situations, for example, HBCUs carried on several religious traditions of private Black colleges and universities, such as chapel and
vesper services, Sunday school, Bible study, prayer meetings, baccalaureate
services, etc. So, in certain circumstances, there was considerable religious,
moral, and spiritual overlapping between private and public Black colleges
and universities.

As Earl J. McGrath observed,

> Of the Fifty-one institutions operated under public auspices . . . thirty-six
> are supported and operated by states, twelve by counties, and two by cities.
> About half of the thirty-four senior colleges under the auspices of public
> bodies evolved out of normal schools established to train school teachers,

the other half were brought into being by the Land-Grant Acts of 1862 and 1890 which encouraged instruction in agriculture and the mechanic arts. Sixteen of these fifty-one are two-year community colleges, most of them in Florida and almost all established since the Second World War.[9]

Of special significance in the differentiation between the legacy of private and/or church-related historically Black colleges and universities and historically public or tax-supported Black colleges and universities are precious, fundamental, enduring, and consequential values and issues of academic freedom; civic autonomy and engagement; and independence of thoughts, vision, and action. Black public institutions were subjected to political interference, pressures, controls, conflicts, tensions, threats, harassment, deprivation, and manipulation in the Old South. Their budgets, which came from state legislatures, governors, governing boards, and other political oligarchies and elites, meant life or death for them. In particular, prophetic, moral, social, ideological, and racial criticism, judgment, and construction were not tolerated.

Total conformity with the merciless racial caste system was demanded and built into the very survival and bloodstream of the institutions. The Old South brooked no deviation from or disloyalty to the racial laws, etiquette, and mores by its public institutions of higher education. Racial orthodoxy was the order of the day and the command of the power structure. Presidents, faculties, staffs, students, and others had to "toe the line." They were under the surveillance of political and racial "watchdogs." They had to accommodate to the racist agenda or invite reprisals and deprivation. The institutions were often called "plantations." However, to be sure, during the heyday of the Civil Rights Movement, at least some Black public colleges and universities, especially through student sit-ins and other demonstrations and forms of protest, made significant contributions. They were caught up in various pressures and counterpressures, tensions, torture, and trauma.

Above all, historically public Black colleges and universities were, in the very nature of the case in the Old South, encumbered with and circumscribed by racial restrictions to maintain segregation and discrimination. They had no real choice; racial restrictions were in some of their charters. In at least three institutions, racial designations were in the very names of the institutions for a limited period. Reference is made to North Carolina College for Negroes, now North Carolina Central University; Louisville Municipal College for Negroes, which, in 1951, was absorbed by the University of Louisville; and Colored Normal, Industrial, Agricultural and Mechanical College, which, in 1954, became South Carolina State College.

On the other hand, the private or church-related Black colleges and universities had academic and social freedom, flexibility, openness, cultural multidimensionality, and virtual independence in race relations. Generally speaking, they had the freedom and autonomy to engage in the process of expressing dissatisfaction with the racial status quo; the advocacy of social and institutional change, experimentation, and dialogue; and the quest for social and racial justice and equality. No small wonder Dr. Mays could proclaim in 1957 without fear of contradiction that "the private Negro colleges are the freest colleges and universities in the South."[10]

Private historically Black colleges and universities are primarily those institutions holding membership in the College Fund/UNCF, along with former members such as Howard University, Hampton University, Lincoln University in Pennsylvania, Morris Brown College, Allen University, and a few others with church affiliations. A few private HBCUs, which contributed so much to the rich and vital tradition, no longer exist, such as Bishop College, which closed, and Atlanta University, which merged with Clark College in 1988 to form Clark Atlanta University.

First of all, private Black colleges and universities were established with an inclusive, universalistic worldview rather than an exclusive, narrow worldview. Although founded primarily for the education of Black freedmen, they generally had no racial restrictions or barriers—not even "quotas" or the seductive norm of "tokenism." All "qualified" learners were admitted, enrolled, welcomed, and taught. Customs, prejudice, options, laws, and other considerations generally kept Whites from matriculation.

Perhaps private Black colleges and universities were America's first "affirmative action/equal opportunity" employers.

"Black colleges have never been 100 percent Black. They were integrated institutions at the very outset. Their first teachers and presidents were White. Although these student enrollments were predominantly Black, racial segregation clauses were never written into their charters"[11] and, as Dr. Benjamin E. Mays asserted, "By nature, they are without prejudice and bias. The teachers from the beginning were members of the White race. They, themselves, have never closed their doors to students of other races, the state laws have done this. The private and church-related Negro colleges have been segregated institutions but not segregating institutions."[12]

Faculties, administrations, and boards of trustees were integrated: "Custom made them segregated institutions. The charters of the thirty-one [UNCF] colleges were all-inclusive from the very start. And where circumstances made it necessary to designate restrictions in order for the colleges to be born, steps have already been taken to remove such restrictions."[13]

The private HBCUs were generally established in the aftermath of the Civil War; for example,

> Howard University was born to serve all nations, all races, and all groups. But the University was also founded to play a special role in bringing a larger degree of freedom to Black people: a role which if Howard University and other colleges similarly circumstanced do not play, will hardly be played. Located here in the nation's capital, where representatives of all nations converge, Howard is uniquely qualified to serve the nation and the world and besides to address itself to the peculiar needs of Black people.[14]

As already indicated, the church-related nature of most of the original Black colleges and universities had an enormous and continuing impact on their lives, ethos, moral values, integrity, leadership, curriculum, philosophy of education, and worldview:

> The vast majority of these colleges were interracial in origin. Devoted, competent, saintly church people, imbued with a sense of mission, graduates of the best colleges and universities in the land, left their comfortable environments of the North, went into the heart of the South and founded Hampton, Virginia Union, Bennett, Fisk, the Atlanta group, Talladega, and the rest. They lived with Negro students and taught them with great affection and love. They saw their students not as sons and daughters of slaves, but as human beings of intrinsic value, worthy of respect and a chance to develop to the status of full-grown men and women. The faculties soon became integrated, and these institutions have never lost their interracial character.[15]

These institutions established the model of the union of diversity, integration, and excellence—a combination with which many White colleges and universities grapple today. The daunting task for the precedent-setting Black institutions, as for their White counterparts today, entailed a convergence of idealism and rational institutional self-interest. Recognizing the critical significance of a first-rate faculty, Dr. Mays, legendary president of Morehouse College from 1940 to 1967, asserted that he gave priority, in hard competition, "to securing and maintaining able teachers."[16] "I knew this could not be done," he went on to say, "by relying wholly on Negro scholars. Morehouse has a strong, traditional policy of cutting across sex, national, ethnic, racial, and religious lines. I have boasted of building at Morehouse an ecumenical, interracial community. Then too, there were then, as there are now, so few Black scholars available."[17]

When he retired as president of Morehouse in 1967, he asserted in his final commencement address, "Today the Morehouse faculty has Jews, Negroes, Protestants, Catholics, Hindus, Africans, White Southerners, and White Northerners. We sought to hire men and women of high academic achievement and good character, teachers who had risen above prejudice. If they met these criteria, they were hired."[18] Indeed, it is interesting and significant that Morehouse, under Dr. Mays, made a special effort to employ White Southerners—feeling that their "bonding" with Black students had extraordinary meaning and relevance to racial understanding and healing: "During my administration, many Morehouse teachers were Southern White men and women. It has been my belief that it is good to bring together Southern White teachers and Black students, since the racial gulf which usually prevents meeting on the basis of equality is so wide—in fact, it is almost impossible to span."[19]

In recruiting trustees, Morehouse, like other private Black colleges and universities similarly situated, followed the same policy of inclusion, diversity, and integration as in recruiting faculty: "We sought good men [and women], and race and religion were no barriers. Among the twenty-four trustees, as of June, 1967, were women as well as men—Jews, Catholics, Protestants, Negroes, Southerners, Northerners, educators, ministers, lawyers, doctors, and businessmen. These deserve much credit for the strength and status that Morehouse developed during the twenty-seven years I was president."[20]

The College Fund/UNCF Board of Directors is perhaps the most integrated and diverse national corporate board in America. And no less an authority as Dr. Benjamin E. Mays has made a compelling case for Howard University, in terms of faculty and students, being the most democratic, diverse, and integrated university in the country:

> I make bold to assert that no university in America has been as free from religious and racial prejudice, and from ethnic bias, and as democratic in faculty and student operation, as Howard University. Even when the great institutions of the East and West were so narrow in their minds that they had a quota system of Negroes and starved them out socially and dared not hire a Negro professor—even one as brilliant as W.E.B. DuBois—this University was a living demonstration of democracy in education. It has never barred or restricted members of other racial, religious, or ethnic

groups. While White institutions of the nation are now being praised and even financed for their being "liberal" and "open-door" policies since 1954, do not forget that they are being praised and financed for doing what Howard University has been doing for a hundred years. In this one thing alone Howard University has made a contribution to the nation and to the world.[21]

The current writer's data, as an officer of the Ford Foundation in the late 1960s and early '70s, provided compelling proof of Dr. Mays's contention. In preparation for making grants to Howard University, I received hard statistical demographic information on the racial composition of the faculty and student body. In some departments, the faculties were overwhelmingly, almost exclusively, White. The same was true of the student population.

Significantly, in the Reconstruction and post-Reconstruction eras, some HBCUs defied racist laws and customs and admitted White students; this was done to the dismay, anger, and retribution of White authorities. Consider the case of Atlanta University. In May 1887, for example, the Board of Visitors, a state agency appointed by the governor of Georgia, filed its report after an inspection trip to Atlanta University. Although the report generally commended Atlanta University for its work, its authors were deeply troubled by integration at the institution and found the presence of White students not only a violation of the general policy of the state, but also a "misuse of public funds."[22] Atlanta University was receiving an annual appropriation from the state at the time.

A controversy over the matriculation of White students at Atlanta University ensued, resulting in widespread publicity. The institution gained national attention for its courage and integrity. In the end, however, decisions of the governor, the Board of Visitors (the agent of the governor), the state legislature, other political leadership, and the anti-integration climate of opinion resulted, the summer of 1887, in termination of the state of Georgia's annual $8,000 appropriation to Atlanta University. The state sought to impose conditions that the institution, in spite of its dire financial needs, was unwilling to accept—the exclusion of White students on the arbitrary, a priori, irrational, and immoral ground of race or color.[23]

Consider Dillard University and one of its ancestral institutions— Straight College; founded in 1869, Straight College had a strong tradition of integration, including among its student body. Dr. Geneva Handy Southall asserted,

> From its beginning, Straight College figured heavily in Blacks' campaign for integrated higher education. Because L.S.U. [Louisiana State Univer-

sity] adamantly refused to admit Blacks, the Black legislators and their friends in 1873 cut off funds to L.S.U. and delivered them to Straight. Throughout the Reconstruction era, Straight was an integrated college, with eight of its ten law graduates in 1878 being White and their first medical graduate a White alumnus of Queen's College, Dublin. Such serves to document the fact that even in its ancestral period of academic gestation, Dillard was never and is still not a segregation institution.[24]

So, in terms of faculty, boards of trustees, students, visiting speakers and other persons and participants, and administration, private Black colleges and universities have a strong, deep, and continuing tradition of, and commitment to, integration and interracialism. Integration and interracialism have not been peripheral or marginal or restricted to a narrow dimension but have encompassed the total life and process of private HBCUs.

In terms of perspective, it is important to bear in mind that it was well into the second and third quarters of the twentieth century before the vast majority of private Black colleges and universities shifted from White to Black presidents; there was, in fact, much opposition in certain quarters to selecting Black presidents of Black colleges. Some thought that the presidencies of Black colleges were a White prerogative and indispensable to leadership, fund-raising, and quality.

So, Morehouse College got its first Black president, John Hope, in 1906; Howard University got Mordecai W. Johnson in 1926; Atlanta University got John Hope in 1929; Dillard University got William Stuart Nelson in 1936; Lincoln University in Pennsylvania got Horace Mann Bond in 1945; Fisk University got Charles S. Johnson in 1947; Spelman College got Albert E. Manley in 1953; Talladega College got Herman H. Long in 1964; Tougaloo College got George A. Owens in 1965; Xavier University got Norman C. Francis in 1968; and Paine College got Lucius H. Pitts in 1971. Dr. Francis, who continues to serve Xavier University with great distinction, is perhaps the longest-serving college or university president in America.

Morehouse College, in Atlanta, Georgia, the heart of Dixie, gave me my first exposure to and contact with Whites as Americans, educators, Southerners, Northerners, and human beings in an atmosphere of equality, decency, mutuality, dignity, and common humanity. At Morehouse, and in the Atlanta University Center generally, White humanity and Black humanity shared a common cause, mission, and life on the basis of human dignity and equality. Whites and Blacks participated as equals in the sacred enterprise of learning, life of the mind, and the sense of wonder.

For what it is worth, let me be open and honest and note that Whites constituted a small minority. Over the long haul of history, going back to the post-Civil War era, private Black colleges and universities served as centers of interracial contact, vigorous and candid discussion, social and moral light, opportunity, caring, sharing, understanding, and goodwill and as unique places of meeting, conferences, dialogue, communication, exchange, uplift, humanism, and idealism. They played a magnificent and special role as an oasis of democracy, diversity, fraternity, human brotherhood, and liberty for the human mind, spirit, and soul. In the South, where nearly all of them were located, Black colleges were the only places where White and Black human beings could meet and share as brothers and sisters, citizens, equals, and children of God. Such meetings could not take place on White college campuses—private or public. The Black church, the freest institution in the Black community, was secondary to Black institutions of higher learning in terms of racial integration, conferences, and centers of discussion of sensitive and "controversial" issues and problems of social change, institutional reform, and the promise of America. During the Civil Rights Movement, this great tradition of Black colleges and universities gained a new and special prominence, vitality, and significance.

No one has put the matter more succinctly and eloquently than Dr. Benjamin E. Mays. Almost fifty years ago, he asserted,

> For more than three-quarters of a century the Negro private and church-related college has been virtually the only place where Negro and White people could meet together on the basis of equality without fear and trembling. When church doors, White schools and hotels have been closed as if the doors were locked in steel, the Negro private and church-related college has been a citadel of interracial fellowship and good will.
>
> Even in 1960, it is only the Negro institutions in Atlanta and Augusta, Georgia, where true interracial freedom exists. On the campuses of the six Atlanta institutions . . . and in Paine College in Augusta, dozens of interracial meetings are held annually. This could not obtain on the campuses of private White institutions of Georgia. Nor could this happen in the White churches of Georgia. The freedom inherent in the Negro private and church-related college guarantees not only academic freedom not inherent in White institutions but it provides the opportunity to develop interracial understanding and good will which are sorely needed in times like these.[25]

The first interracial conference I attended was an annual religious-sponsored event at Paine College, a church-related institution in Augusta,

Georgia, during my student days at Morehouse in the spring of 1947. It was called the "Paine Conference." I met students—White students, of course—from Emory University, the University of Georgia, and, I believe, Agnes Scott College. The highlight was a discussion of the landmark report of President Truman's Committee on Civil Rights, entitled *To Secure These Rights*. The "Paine Conference" opened a whole new world to me. It was an epiphany.

Private Black colleges and universities were the only places that not only tolerated but encouraged discussion of timely and relevant, "controversial," and "hot button" issues of race relations: lynchings, the need for anti-lynching laws, desegregation, segregation, and integration of "race-mixing" in the heady context and powerful framework of the Declaration of Independence, the Constitution of the United States, the Christian faith, and the American dream. There were vigorous discussions of the responsibility of the President of the United States, the U.S. Congress, and the federal judiciary in promoting and protecting the civil rights of Negroes. Civil disobedience was discussed, as were "states' rights" and federalism.

The South has a very strong tradition of violence, intolerance and suppression of dissent, criticism, and civil rights and liberties as well as the enforcement of orthodoxy and conformity and contempt for free, rational, and vigorous discussion of sensitive social, moral, and religious issues. This has been especially true of "race matters" involving slavery, Jim Crow, segregation, discrimination, etc. These issues are discussed in texts such as W. J. Cash's *The Mind of the South*, James W. Silver's *Mississippi: The Closed Society*, Russell H. Barrett's *Integration at Ole Miss*, and Clement Eaton's *The Freedom-of-Thought Struggle in the Old South*, which in 1964, pointed out, "The Old South went to war rather than risk any basic change in its social order. Recently Mississippi and Alabama as well as other parts of the South have violently resisted any significant change in race relationships, both the old and the new societies have suppressed freedom of speech and forced their moderate citizens to acquiesce or to silence."[26]

Historically White public and private colleges and universities have operated in a repressive and oppressive climate and environment in terms of race relations. Oddly, historically private Black colleges and universities have been much freer, more tolerant, inclusive, diverse, democratic, and humanistic in the grand liberal arts tradition. Interracial conferences and discussions were centerpieces of their institutional and professional lives and fortunes:

> The Negro private and church-related colleges are significant in the same sense that private and church-related White colleges are significant. By and

large they are free of political domination and control. The White colleges of the South, whether private and church-related or tax-supported are not as free as the Negro private and church-related colleges. Since May 17, 1954, the year the United States Supreme Court declared segregation in the public schools unconstitutional, most of the White teachers in the South have been afraid to stand up and say in their classrooms that they believe in the May 17, 1954, Decision of the Supreme Court and that that Decision should be implemented.

There are campuses, both Negro and White, tax-supported and White private colleges, where one dare not discuss the Court's Decision and dare not express himself as being against segregation. Academic freedom has been completely stifled in this area. In most tax-supported colleges of the South, Negro and White, and in many of the White private and church-related colleges, fear permeates the faculties. There have been no such fears in the private and church-related Negro colleges. The administration and faculty of some private and church-related colleges have been cautious but there have been no great fears such as we find in the publicly-supported institutions.[27]

Not only were historically private and church-related Black colleges a haven for interracial conferences, dialogues, and conversations on vital issues of the day in the Old South, but they were also routine places for desegregated audiences for intellectual, cultural, social, and athletic events. Whites and Blacks sat freely in the seats of their choice. In 1957, it could be asserted without fear of contradiction, "Only in private Negro colleges in Atlanta can we have Christmas Carol Concerts where all races come and sit where they can find seats and stand where they can find room."[28]

In the economy of time and space, let us note in passing six other contributions of historically private Black colleges and universities to the transformation of the Old South into the New South and, by extension, to the birth of a new America, with genuine progress toward the equality of Blacks as citizens and human beings.

First, HBCUs contributed mightily to undermining the intellectual and moral underpinnings and foundations of White supremacy and the tyranny and totalitarianism of racism. Teaching in the classroom and outside was of immeasurable significance. But also of critical importance cumulatively and over the long haul was scholarship in the form of research and publication—the dissemination of knowledge in a stream of books, articles, essays, monographs, and pamphlets. Public lectures and speeches also played a significant role.

Of infinite significance were prophetic and relentless analyses and searching criticism of the evils of segregation. A long line of intellectuals challenged and refuted in no uncertain terms the defenses of racism and Jim Crow. The process was slow but steady. Black scholars and other thinkers kept chipping away at the foundations, the core values, the bedrock institutions of the Old South. Individuals such as W.E.B. DuBois, Booker T. Washington, Mary McLeod Bethune, George Washington Carver, Joseph T. Robert, Carter G. Woodson, Rayford W. Logan, Benjamin E. Mays, Mordecai Wyatt Johnson, Howard Thurman, John Hope, Ralph J. Bunche, John W. Davis, Vernon Johns, E. Franklin Frazier, Charles S. Johnson, Anne Cook, Alain Locke, Ira DeA. Reid, John A. Davis, Willa B. Player, Benjamin G. Brawley, William Stanley Braithwaite, William H. Crogman, Willette R. Banks, Charles H. Wesley, John Hope Franklin, Benjamin Quarles, James M. Nabrit, Samuel M. Nabrit, Horace Mann Bond, Rufus E. Clement, Rushton Coulborn, Harry V. Richardson, Felton G. Clark, Charles DuBois Hubert, Florence M. Read, Gordon Blaine Hancock, Henry C. McBay, William M. Boyd, James E. Shepard, Nathaniel P. Tillman, Frank Cunningham, C.V. Troup, Franklin L. Forbes, B.T. Harvey, Daniel C. Thompson, Samuel L. Gandy, W.J. Trent, William H. Hastie, Charles Drew, Samuel D. Proctor, George D. Kelsey, Richard I. McKinney, Jewel L. Prestage, James P. Brawley, Martin D. Jenkins, Elgon C. Harrison, Albert W. Dent, Hugh M. Closter, Albert E. Manley, Norman C. Francis, Emmett E. Dorsey, J. Neal Hughley, C. Eric Lincoln, William Stuart Nelson, Virginia Lacy Jones, Edward A. Jones, G. Lewis Chandler, Edward B. Williams, Robert H. Brisbane, Clarence A. Bacote, Vivian W. Henderson, Herman H. Long, Samuel W. Williams, B.R. Brazeal, Howard Zinn, Mack H. Jones, and countless others rush to mind. They were great teachers, role models, mentors, and benefactors. They educated, trained, inspired, motivated, and mentored generations of students not only in critical thinking, topflight preparation, and professional excellence, but also in the vision, ways, structure, and content of social and racial justice and equality and created in them radical dissatisfaction with racism and a sense of outrage at racial injustice. The planted seeds of rebellion—many times unconsciously and subconsciously—which, in their own good time, bore fruit. These giants established an imperishable and rich legacy and immortal foundation for HBCUs—both private and public.

A special word must be said about the faculties of HBCUs. Faculty members—both White and Black—were generally deeply dedicated, hard working, competent, sacrificial, and imbued with a heightened sense of vocation. This explains the seeming paradox: "Salaries were miserably low, but devotion was correspondingly high."[29] Teaching was a way of life, a "calling," a sacred commitment, and, to no small degree, a self-rewarding and self-fulfilling experience. Teachers cared deeply about their students' success and excellence. Individual success and excellence meant the advancement of the race. They knew what racism had done to the nerve of striving and self-respect of Black people. Hence they desperately sought to instill self-respect, self-esteem, self-confidence, dignity, pride, self-worth, and hope in their students since, "systematic undermining of self-confidence has done damaging things to Black people."[30]

The leadership of private HBCUs in the Old South displayed various degrees and kinds of courage and caution. Many presidents felt it necessary to walk a racial tightrope, but some institutions had a strong, powerful, and consistent tradition of courageous leadership and prophetic criticism of the status quo in race relations. They were characteristically critical and always protesting and expressing dissatisfaction with the "Southern way of life." "The leadership of Morehouse College," proclaimed Dr. Mays, "never accepted the *status quo* in Negro-White relations . . . . Throughout its history, Morehouse's leadership has rebelled against racial injustice."[31] Dr. Mays was especially forceful, effective, and brilliant in attacking racism and segregation head-on. He was relentless. At the twenty-first annual meeting of the Southern Historical Association, November 10, 1955, at the Peabody Hotel in Memphis, Tennessee, Dr. Mays joined Nobel Prize-winning novelist William Faulkner and attorney Cecil Sims shared the spotlight. Dr. Mays delivered a powerful, eloquent, and unforgettable address to the large audience of historians, writers, researchers, students, and other guests, entitled "The Moral Aspects of Segregation." The address has been widely read, circulated, and reprinted. No one surpassed or even equaled Benjamin Elijah Mays in beating down the walls and skillfully undermining the arguments for segregation, which he called "god" for the racists and segregationists. He relentlessly and powerfully attacked and refuted the major arguments—theological, moral, intellectual, psychological, sociological, philosophical—and exposed, in their ultimate nakedness and emptiness, their fallacies and treacherous illusions.[32] He had no equal. True, his colleague and friend, Mordecai W. Johnson, and his former student and dear friend, Martin Luther King Jr., came close, but Mays was peerless in his prophetic criticism of segregation, discrimination, and other forms of racism.

Third, private historically Black colleges and universities and selected community representatives played a significant role in the organization of

Black-White alliances and interracial organizations to challenge the tyranny of racism and segregation in the Old South and create the New South. A landmark example is the venerable Southern Regional Council, with its noble legacy of being in the forefront of the movement to democratize and humanize the South by extending civil and human rights to Black people. From groundbreaking and timely research, to massive interracial fellowship and cooperative planning and leadership, to widespread publications, to voter registration and education, to something of a "think tank" in strategizing for social change, the Southern Regional Council was a timely, prophetic, innovative, and visionary organization. It was, in a quiet, courageous, dignified, thoughtful, and largely behind-the-scenes operation, a powerful voice of decency in the Old South and its transformation.

"Up to 1942 Southern Negro Leaders in a body had never spoken their mind to the White South," observed Dr. Benjamin E. Mays. "Now the time had come. The aftermath of World War I was fresh in the memory of many of us. We had seen the birth of the Commission on Interracial Cooperation, which was brought into being primarily to ease racial tension that was mounting even before the First World War ended."[33] Deeply disturbed by the race situation, Dr. Gordon Blaine Hancock of Virginia Union University in Richmond, Virginia, in 1941, "released an article to the *Associated Negro Press* entitled 'Interracial Hypertension.' The article was on the gloomy side and aroused the concern of Mrs. Jessie Daniel Ames of Texas and Atlanta who was an official of the Commission on Interracial Cooperation."[34] Dr. Mays goes on to say that the article "was so important in the history and organization of the Southern Regional Council . . ."[35] On October 20, 1942, a group of Southern Negro leaders met at the North Carolina College for Negroes in Durham. Dr. Mays, who was a member of the drafting committee explains, "Gordon Blaine Hancock might well be called the father of the Southern Regional Council. Beside him as founder stands Jessie Daniel Ames, who was disturbed by Hancock's article, 'Interracial Hypertension.' "[36]

The Continuation Committee met at another historically Black institution, Atlanta University, on August 4, 1944. Dr. Howard Odum of the University of North Carolina was elected chairman of the meeting, where an agreement was made to establish the Southern Regional Council. Dr. Rufus E. Clement of Atlanta University, Dr. Charles S. Johnson of Fisk University, Dr. Howard Odum of the University of North Carolina, Mr. Ralph McGill of the *Atlanta Constitution*, and Bishop Moore applied for a charter for the organization. The board and executive committee were, of course, interracial. Dr. Guy B. Johnson of the University of North Carolina and Dr. Ira DeA. Reid of Atlanta University were named staff directors.[37]

Thus the organizational meeting of the Southern Regional Council was held on a Black college campus and involved leaders from Black colleges and universities: Gordon Blaine Hancock of Virginia Union University, Charles S. Johnson of Fisk University, and Rufus E. Clement and Ira DeA. Reid of Atlanta University. Dr. Benjamin E. Mays of Morehouse College, although apparently not at the organizational meeting, had input as a member of the drafting committee established by the Durham meeting of Negro leaders. This is a classic example of the involvement of HBCUs in Southern change.

Fourth, a major contribution of private HBCUs to diversity, desegregation, integration, democracy, inclusion, and pluralism and to the movement to equalize and humanize the South and the country was in the legal field of jurisprudence. Reference is made primarily to Howard University and its School of Law. Their great achievement was the legal and constitutional undermining of segregation as public policy in the United States. Involved is the historic landmark case, *Brown v. Board of Education*, of May 17, 1954, which declared segregation in public education unconstitutional because it violated the equal protection clause of the Fourteenth Amendment. Important, too, were the cases that laid the groundwork and foundation for the *Brown* decision. Dr. Mays put the matter in compelling and eloquent terms:

> This god, Segregation, had to be dethroned first in the federal courts. The cases designed to dethrone this god, Segregation, were developed not in the law schools of the University of Chicago, Columbia, Harvard, Yale, but in the law school of Howard University. It is not an accident that a university born with an interracial worldview would take the leadership in this field rather than the universities named above, which at that time had no concern in abolishing segregation. It is conceivable that if there had been no Howard University we would not have had the May 17, 1954, decision of the United States Supreme Court, declaring segregation in the public schools unconstitutional. That decision was and is one of the most historic documents in the annals of American law. It is most significant that the decision was argued and won by a Howard University Law School graduate, Thurgood Marshall. It is equally history-making that the District of Columbia case was argued and won by the present president of Howard University, James M. Nabrit.[38]

It is hardly an accident that the first Black member of the Supreme Court, Thurgood Marshall, a "liberal activist" jurist, graduated from a historically

Black college and law school, Lincoln University and Howard University, and the second Black member of the Supreme Court, Clarence Thomas, a "conservative activist" jurist, is a graduate of a historically White college and law school, Boston College and Yale University. Is the opposite inconceivable? Did their college and law school experience make a qualitative difference in their judicial philosophies, visions, perceptions, worldviews, and values? What if any difference did their educational experience, their total learning environment—classroom, residential, informal encounters—make? The mind cries out for an answer.

In any event, the Howard University School of Law made a unique and enduring contribution to American democracy. The *Brown* decision catalyzed, energized, and inspired the Civil Rights Movement and dramatized the great debt that our country owes to HBCUs. Reflect on the following observation made by Dr. Mays in the centennial address at Howard University, June 1967:

> If Howard University had done no more in these one hundred years it would have justified the millions the federal government has spent on this university. It is quite likely that the cases against discrimination prior to 1954 and the 1954 decision itself paved the way for Montgomery and the sit-ins, and the Freedom Riders, and these led to congressional legislation making the court decision the law of the land.[39]

Finally, HBCUs—primarily the private ones—provided the major, but by no means the exclusive, leadership of the Civil Rights Movement on national, regional, state, and local levels. They also provided other forms of support to change the Old South and the American commonwealth. The names of Martin Luther King Jr., Walter White, James Farmer, Jesse L. Jackson, Whitney M. Young Jr., Andrew J. Young Jr., John Lewis, Marian Wright Edelman, Julian Bond, Joseph E. Lowery, Floyd McKissick, Stokely Carmichael, C. T. Vivian, Donald L. Hollowell, Kelly Miller Smith, Samuel W. Williams, C. K. Steele, and countless others leap from memory to instant recall.

On February 1, 1960, a new kind of civil rights method and revolution began—direct student social activism and leadership by young dreamers and visionaries, female and male. Four freshmen at North Carolina A&T College in Greensboro took their seats at a local lunch counter. They were refused service and arrested. The sit-ins began spontaneously and quickly spread, not only to various communities in North Carolina, but to Virginia,

Georgia, Florida, Tennessee, South Carolina, and other Southern states as well. Students from HBCUs throughout the region got involved in sit-ins and other forms of demonstration and protests—joined, in some situations, by White students from the North. Student activism became a vital part of the Civil Rights Movement and helped to change the racial landscape of the Old South. It generated organization of the Student Nonviolent Coordinating Committee (SNCC) and a new dimension, energy, emphasis, perspective, and challenge of the Civil Rights Movement.[40]

The old order changeth! The Old South has "gone with the wind" of historical and social change—thanks to a variety of social, economic, cultural, and historical forces, impulses, and vitalities. New structures of meaning and value emerged. HBCUs have been vital agents of social, racial, and historical transformation of the Old South into the New South. The monumental Supreme Court decision in *Brown v. Board of Education* in 1954 was a revolutionary act and affirmation. It said, after all, that the Constitution of the United States applied equally to Blacks and Whites as citizens and as human beings. The Civil Rights Act of 1964, in effect, reinstituted the Fourteenth Amendment. The Voting Rights Act of 1965, in effect, reinstituted the Fifteenth Amendment. Other acts and patterns of progress—government and nongovernment—have disclosed something of the concrete, institutional, existential, behavioral, and attitudinal change and progress of the great promise of America.

Whatever other characteristics and qualities may be involved, the defining property and uniqueness of the historic South, all kinds of illusions, pretensions, rationalizations, and hypocrisies notwithstanding, have been race and racism and their tyranny, universality, and totalitarian authoritarianism. The "bottom line" has been racism and race.

It is part meaning and part mystery that institutions have a life apart from and independent of the limitations and possibilities of the finitude of individuals. Institutions have a "survivability," an endurance denied to individual human lives. Thus HBCUs have survived against the great odds of history and culture. They survived the tragic challenges of the post-Civil War era, Reconstruction, the nadir of post-Reconstruction, the anguish and pain of the era of "separate but equal" hypocrisy, and the terrible age of demagogic racism and Negrophobia of Ben "Pitchfork" Tillman, Cole Blease, the Talmadges, Bilbo, Ranking, J. Strom Thurmond and the Dixiecrats of 1948, George Wallace in his arrogant and simplistic heyday, Lester Maddox, and lesser racist demons. They somehow survived the racist dogmas of scientists, theologians, and Christian ministers who proclaimed, with the cocksureness of Thrasymachus, that Blacks were not only biologically, intellectually, morally, and otherwise inferior to Whites, but really subhuman, really animals, beasts. Nature and God had excluded Blacks, of course, from educability, but somehow, in some way, Blacks survived and progressed and made major contributions to American life and world civilization. A major contribution was to refuting and burying racist dogmas, institutions, and habits in the cemetery of human folly and tragedy.

Indeed, it would be a tragic mistake to assume or assert the death of racism and the birth of a colorblind society in the New South. While legal segregation is dead, and the rabid, public, and demagogic racism of the past is no more, racism continues to be alive and well in various forms. It is more subtle, covert, sophisticated, visceral, and often couched in "code words." It is latent, beneath the surface, subterranean. It sometimes takes a nostalgic turn in certain individuals—as in the recent case of Senator Trent Lott, the former majority leader of the U.S. Senate, who gushed warmly about J. Strom Thurmond's Dixiecrat campaign of 1948 and sorrowfully about its smashing defeat because its victory would have avoided certain problems. There is in some quarters a terrible nostalgia about the Old South and its myths and way of life, hypocrisy, and vain claims to virtue.

In the New South, HBCUs—private and public—have a continuity of responsibilities and challenges that they had in the Old South, as indicated in the early part of this essay. Reference, in particular, is made to preserving the tradition of commitment to diversity, pluralism, integration, interracialism, academic excellence, social relevance, the intellectual tradition, the unique mission to serve low-income students who otherwise would probably not have the opportunity to receive a college education, provide a nurturing and supportive learning environment, the cultivation of leadership, etc.

To meet the contemporary challenges, HBCUs must first attract and retain first-class administrative leadership with superb credentials, managerial skills, bedrock integrity, and imaginative vision. Second, essential are boards of trustees whose members are knowledgeable, vigilant, hard-nosed, generous, wise, effective, and prudent in exercising oversight, who will hold the presidents' "feet to the fire" and establish broad policies but avoid micromanagement. Third, indispensable are able and productive faculties deeply committed to teaching, research, scholarship, and community service and who love the divine art and enterprise of teaching and care profoundly about students and their development, future, and lives. Fourth, imperative are promising students who are serious and willing to work hard and "burn the midnight oil." Fifth, there must be adequate financial resources to support and sustain institutional priorities, programs, and mission. Competition in the marketplace for faculty, students, and funds is increasingly fierce. Wise fiscal management, rigorous accountability, and exacting responsibility for all institutional funds are crucial. Deficit spending is an invitation to institutional disaster, especially for private colleges and universities, and mismanagement of funds is simply and totally unacceptable and intolerable.

Increased competition for students in the marketplace is a special problem—not merely for "the best and the brightest" but for students in general, covering the whole range of quality. In the Old South, HBCUs simply competed with each other for the rich pool of Black students. Today, however, they face vigorous and sustained competition for Black students. Competition comes from all kinds of historically White colleges and universities—elite and mediocre, wealthy and poor, public and private, large and small, independent and church-related, North and South, East and West. There is also competition from public community colleges.

As in the Old South, HBCUs face enormous financial challenges and burdens. With meager endowments and lacking well-heeled alumni (though alumni can, should, and must be more generous in their support), private Black colleges and universities are strapped for cash: "The total endowment figure for all 103 historically Black schools, including 41 public institutions, is about $1.6 billion, according to Gray [President of the College Fund/UNCF]. Four schools—Atlanta's Spelman and Morehouse Colleges, and Hampton and Howard Universities—account for nearly 45 percent of that amount."[41] Since endowments are so important to the financial health, viability, self-confidence, and future of institutions of higher education, and especially those that are private or independent, the consequences of the above figures are immediate and far-reaching.

Instead of a level playing field, there are grave racial inequalities in the New South, as there were in the Old South from the perspectives of wealth, income, education, health, housing, unemployment, underemployment, life expectancy, and other vital indicators of socioeconomic status and well-being.

The Challenge to Make Amends and a Redemption of Southern History: The White South and Southern Philanthropy

In terms of Black Americans, and Black colleges and universities in general, the New South has an obligation to do its best to make amends for the tragedies, suffering, neglect, exclusion, and deprivations inflicted on Black people during 246 years of slavery and another century of Jim Crow segregation, exploitation, and discrimination. "America owes my people some of the dividends," cried Sojourner Truth, an illiterate former slave, fearless social activist, and crusading abolitionist. "I shall make them understand that there is a debt to the Negro people which they can never repay. At least they must make amends."[42] What she said about America applies with special force and meaning to the South. The New South ought to accept the challenge and the opportunity to make amends.

Whites, with all their vast economic advantages, did not provide financial support to struggling private Black colleges and universities in the Old South. They said, in effect, that the Yankees and Blacks established the institutions, let them support them. Even in a city like Atlanta, Whites have not historically supported HBCUs in spite of their great contribution to the economy, culture, civic, and political life of the community. In his final commencement address at Morehouse on May 30, 1967, Dr. Mays made the following sobering, sad, and almost incredible comment about how White citizens of the great progressive city of Atlanta had failed miserably to give financial support to the institutions of the Atlanta University Center, one of the nation's leading treasures in higher education:

> We believed that Morehouse, a Georgia institution for one hundred years and an Atlanta institution for eighty-eight years, would be able to get someone to head a campaign for at least a million dollars in recognition of one hundred years of valuable service to the city, state and nation. We were sadly mistaken. The colleges of Atlanta are not considered part of the parcel of the life of the community. My guess is that in a hundred years the six institutions of the Atlanta University Center have not received a million and a half dollars from the Atlanta community. It has accepted no responsibility for the financial health and development of these colleges, despite the fact that we spend millions here each year and provide leadership for the South and for the nation.[43]

What Dr. Mays said about the historic failure of Atlanta applies with equal force to private HBCUs in the South. According to the dogmatic historic record, there was not a single exception. Whites in the local cities and towns simply ignored Black institutions in terms of financial support. In fact, these institutions were often resented and forced to operate in a hostile environment.

Dr. Mays could not understand and rebelled against the idea that it took less money to support quality Black education than it did to support quality White education, just as he could not understand and rebelled against the idea that what was White was *intrinsically* and *automatically* superior, and what was Black was *intrinsically* and *automatically* inferior. This assumption means the complete denial of human equality and justice. This wise man and prophet went on to say,

> Desegregation, won through court decisions, congressional legislation, and demonstrations, has not changed the basic philosophy of inequality. So to use a good Methodist phrase, Negro colleges have been by design kept on short grass! For the health of Morehouse and other colleges similarly circumstanced, the philosophy must be accepted by philanthropic America and governments that a good college, whether it is predominantly Negro or predominantly White, deserves equal consideration in bidding for the tax and philanthropic dollar. If this philosophy cannot be developed, there will exist under the guise of desegregation and liberalism a form of discrimination as rancid and foul as anything that existed under legal and de facto segregation.[44]

Sadly and tragically, there was racial discrimination not merely by Southern Whites but also by White philanthropy in general as well as by the national and state governments when it came to the distribution of funds for colleges and universities. HBCUs were generally ignored:

> Although the Negro has helped to make the wealth of the nation, he has not been allowed to help shape the policies of how that wealth is to be distributed. And this inequality is largely true, too, in the use of government funds. Negroes constitute ten percent of the population of the country. It is my considered judgment that not one foundation, not one government agency, national or state, has ever thought in terms of allocating ten percent of all monies given for education to the support of Black institutions or for the education of Blacks. The heads of Negro institutions appreciate the support which White philanthropy and state and federal governments have given to predominantly Negro colleges and universities, but White philanthropists and government agencies are bound to know—as we know that Black institutions have been heavily discriminated against and still are.
>
> If McGrath's book . . . had been taken seriously, the foundations would have gotten together to do something substantial about the problem of Negro higher education. When it comes to the support of Black institutions, it takes philanthropy a long time to make up its mind, even when

the appropriation is relatively meager. Simply put, neither White philanthropy nor state governments, have decided what should be done with the Black colleges and universities. For good or ill, the White people have in their hands the power of life and death for Black colleges, but they do not have the wisdom to determine whether to sustain or to kill. . . . White philanthropy has an obligation to make amends for its hundred years of neglect of Negro colleges. It is odd indeed that after a war, a country should willingly make reparations to the enemy and yet feel little or no moral obligation to compensate its own citizens for decades of shameful and savage treatment.[45]

Dr. Mays goes on to say that, unlike in the Old South, discrimination in the future will be done by "good," "decent," and "respectable" Whites masquerading under the guise of liberalism, progressivism, allies, and friends:

Discrimination in the future will not be administered by poor Whites and the people who believe in segregation, [but] by the "liberals" who believe in a desegregated society. If this battle can be won, Morehouse will have an equal chance to develop like any other good college in America. If discrimination against Negroes is directed now against the predominantly Negro institutions rather than against the individual, the future will be difficult indeed. The Negro's battle for justice and equality in the future will be against the subtlety of our "liberal friends" who will wine and dine us in the swankiest hotels, work with us, and still discriminate against us when it comes to money and power.[46]

White Southerners and Southern philanthropy—not only because of past discrimination, neglect, and insensitivity to Black institutions of higher learning, and not only because of their abject failure to recognize the enormous contributions of these institutions to the development and transformation of the South from the old to the new, and not only because simple justice and fairness demand it but out of rational, enlightened, and long-term self-interest—should generously and consistently support and nurture HBCUs—private and public. These institutions are a vital and integral part of their communities and are making a continuing basic contribution to the region and to the nation.

We derive no joy or satisfaction from saying that despite significant progress in recent years, Blacks are, and are destined to be for the foreseeable future, a significantly disadvantaged economic group. Wealth and privilege are in the hands of Whites and are destined to be so for the indefinite future. No colorblind society and no level playing field are on the horizon.

As Dr. Mays concludes about continuing discrimination,

> The battle must be won because, for a long time, the wealth of this nation will be in the hands of White Americans and not Negroes. The abolition of economic, political, and philanthropic discrimination is the first order of the day, not for the good of Negroes alone but for the nation as a whole. The future of Morehouse will depend upon the ability to "buy" the intellectually talented students, just as many of the predominantly White institutions are able to do with finances given for that purpose. To finance White schools for this purpose and not Negro schools is gross discrimination, not by the admittedly prejudiced but by our "liberal friends."[47]

Since race was consciously used as principle and strategy for more than a hundred years for the exclusion and neglect of Black colleges and universities, it seems that simple justice and fairness require the use of race consciously for the inclusion and support of Black colleges and universities. If race was used for a century to establish and perpetuate the principles of inequality of opportunity, consideration, and self-realization, then there is moral and rational justification for the use of race to establish and perpetuate the principles of equality of opportunity, consideration, and self-realization. Equality is the cornerstone of justice.

History, the order of time and temporal succession and priority, is irreversible. The continuum of time flows only one way—forward. Southern history cannot be wiped out, changed, or reversed. It has been argued that while the historical process is creative, it is not redemptive. But there are redemptive dimensions, elements, or experiences in history. Human beings have the freedom, power, and moral creativity—to a large degree, at least—to redeem historical events and make amends for past wrongs, omissions, and failures. Through critical intelligence and reflection, bringing what is out of sight into view, conscience, empathy, commitment, humility, goodwill, and decency, it is possible to make amends. In terms of Blacks in general and HBCUs in particular, the White South has a unique opportunity and challenge to "make amends."

The harsh moral truth is that because of the Old South's terrible, shameful, disgraceful, and tragic legacy of brutal racism, social injustice, and particularly the painful neglect, exclusion, and lack of financial and other support of HBCUs, and because of these institutions' survival against great odds, their sustained excellence, rich traditions, and significant contributions to the region, the nation, and the world—in spite of the Old South's bankrupt leadership, ethical insensitivity, and humanistic failures—the New South ought to take the initiative and lead America in generously supporting and enhancing—especially in financial terms—historically Black colleges and universities and in ensuring that they offer for generations to come first-class quality education, in faithful obedience to their heritage, for all students beyond race, creed, color, ethnicity, nationality, gender, religion, sexual orientation, class, and culture.

Endnotes

1. However, two Black colleges were established before the Civil War—Lincoln University in Pennsylvania in 1854 and Wilberforce University in Ohio in 1856; see Earl J. McGrath, *The Predominantly Negro Colleges and Universities in Transition* (New York: Bureau of Publications, Teachers College, Columbia University, 1965), 15.

2. Introduction to James P. Brawley, *Two Centuries of Methodist Concern: Bondage, Freedom and the Education of Black People* (New York: Vantage Press, Inc., 1974).

3. John Dewey, *Problems of Men* (New York: Philosophical Library, Inc., 1946), 111–112

4. Benjamin E. Mays, "A Crisis and a Challenge," in *Dr. Benjamin E. Mays Speaks: Representative Speeches of a Great American Orator*, ed. Freddie C. Colston (Lanham, MD: University Press of America, Inc., 2002), 156–157, also p. 146.

5. Benjamin E. Mays, *Born to Rebel: An Autobiography* (New York: Charles Scribner's Sons, 1971), 187.

6. Benjamin E. Mays, "Desegregation: An Opportunity and a Challenge," in Colston, 93.

7. Benjamin E. Mays, "Our Colleges and the Supreme Court Decision," in Colston, 47.

8. "The Negro College and Cultural Change," *Daedelus* (Summer 1971): 612.

9. McGrath, *The Predominantly Negro Colleges and Universities in Transition*, 20.

10. Benjamin E. Mays, "The Advantage of a Small, Christian, Private, Liberal Arts College," in Colston, 89.

11. Daniel W. Wynn, "Higher Education for Blacks," in *Church Colleges Today, Perspectives of a Church Agency on Their Problems and Possibilities*, ed. Woodrow A. Geier (Nashville: Board of Higher Education and Ministry, The United Methodist Church, 1974), 24.

12. Benjamin E. Mays, "The Significance of the Negro Private and Church-Related College," *The Journal of Negro Education* 29 (1960): 246.

13. Benjamin E. Mays, "Our Colleges and the Supreme Court Decision," in Colston, 45.

14. Benjamin E. Mays, "An Impossible Dream Comes True," in Colston, 99.

15. Benjamin E. Mays, "Our Colleges and the Supreme Court Decision," Colston, 45.

16. Mays, *Born to Rebel*, 178.

17. Ibid.

18. Ibid., 179.

19. Ibid.

20. Ibid., 181.

21. Benjamin E. Mays, "Higher Education and the American Negro," in *What Black Educators Are Saying*, ed. Nathan Wright Jr. (New York: Hawthorn Books, Inc., Publishers, 1970), 106.

22. Clarence A. Bacote, *The Story of Atlanta University, A Century of Service, 1865–1965* (Princeton: Princeton University Press, 1969), 87–88; "It is inconceivable," asserted Dr. Bacote, "that the Board of Visitors had been unaware of the presence of White people in Atlanta University before 1887, for ever since Professor Chase had enrolled his daughter, Mary, in the primary department when the University opened in 1869, the children of White teachers had attended the institution along with the Negro pupils. This was a natural practice: it was convenient, the institution's program was superior to that which was available in the public schools, and the children were shielded from insults on the part of the White populace who resented their parents for teaching in a Negro institution. Furthermore, many of the students at that time were very fair in complexion, making it extremely difficult for the Board of Visitors to distinguish them from those children of pure White ancestry" (p. 88).

23. Ibid., 86–102.

24. "The Real Meaning of Academic Excellence," *Dillard University Alumni Bulletin* III (Winter 1978): 16.

25. Mays," The Significance of the Negro Private and Church-Related College," 247.

26. Clement Eaton, *The Freedom-of-Thought Struggle in the Old South*, revised and enlarged ed. (New York: Harper Torchbooks, 1964), Preface, vii; see, in particular, ch. IX, "Academic Freedom Below the Potomac."

27. Mays, "The Significance of the Negro Private and Church-Related College," 247. In 1957, Dr. Mays asserted that "there is not one publicly supported institution in Georgia where there can be held a meeting to discuss desegregation in the public schools, unless the meeting is to condemn integration and praise segregation. No teacher in a tax-supported institution in the deep South could openly advocate the implementation of the May 17, 1954, decision of the Supreme Court and hold his job" ("The Advantage of a Small, Christian, Private, Liberal Arts College," in Colston, 89.

28. Ibid.

29. Mays, *Born to Rebel*, 173.

30. Ibid., 140.

31. Ibid., 186; "The first president of the college, Joseph T. Robert," Dr. Mays goes on to state, "was a white South Carolinian who left the South because he did not want to rear his children in the section of the country where slavery existed. After Emancipation, Robert was persuaded to return to the South, and he became the first president of what is now known as Morehouse College" (ibid.).

32. See for example, Benjamin E. Mays, "The Moral Aspects of Segregation," in Colston, 60–66; see also *Seeking to Be Christian in Race Relations*, rev. ed. (New York: Friendship Press, 1964).

33. Mays, *Born to Rebel*, 213; Dr. Mays proceeded to say, "We remembered the

race riots which followed that war. We had noted that the number of Negroes lynched increased in the years immediately following the war. In 1942 we were engaged in the Second World War. Interracially things looked gloomy, and Negroes did not want the tragedies of the aftermath of World War I repeated after World War II" (ibid.).

34. Ibid., 213–214.

35. Ibid, 214.

36. Ibid, 319.

37. Ibid., 219–220; for a more extensive account, see John Egerton, *Speak Now Against the Day: The Generation Before the Civil Rights Movement in the South* (New York: Alfred A. Knopf, 1994), 301–316.

38. Mays, "Higher Education and the American Negro," in Wright, 107.

39. Ibid.

40. On student activism, sit-ins, demonstrations, and other forms of direct action, see, for example, the special issue of *The Journal of African American History* 88 (Spring 2003), especially V.P. Franklin, "Introduction: African American Student Activism in the 20th Century," and V.P. Franklin, "Patterns of Student Activism at Historically Black Universities in the United States and South Africa, 1960–1977," particularly 204–09, and Howard Zinn, *SNCC: Student Nonviolent Coordinating Committee, The New Abolitionists* (Boston: Beacon Press, 1964).

41. Andrea Jones, "Hard Times Harder on Black Colleges," *Atlanta Journal-Constitution*, June 22, 2003.

42. Quoted in Henrietta Buckmaster, *Let My people Go: The Story of the Underground Railroad and the Growth of the Abolition Movement* (Boston: Beacon Paperback, 1959), 314.

43. Benjamin E. Mays, "Twenty-Seven Years of Success and Failure at Morehouse," in Colston, 170.

44. Ibid., 171.

45. Mays, *Born to Rebel*, 193.

46. Mays, "Twenty-Seven Years of Success and Failure at Morehouse," in Colston, 171–172.

47. Ibid., 172.

Frank L. Matthews

Frank L. Matthews has devoted his professional career to Black and minority concerns, primarily in higher education. He is cofounder and publisher of *Black Issues in Higher Education* and *Community College Week*. He also cofounded Cox, Matthews and Associates, Inc., a Fairfax, Virginia–based communications company. In January 1999, the company successfully launched the *Black Issues Book Review*.

Mr. Matthews has been affiliated with George Mason University for twenty-nine years, teaching in both the Law School and the School of Business Administration. As assistant senior vice president and legal advisor for George Mason, he was responsible for employment and regulatory matters during the university's period of rapid expansion.

Mr. Matthews received a BA in political science from Clemson University, and a JD and MBA from the University of South Carolina.

B. Denise Hawkins

After earning her master's degree from Pennsylvania State University, B. Denise Hawkins began her journalism career writing about religion for the Syracuse (New York) *Post-Standard*. She works full time as a public relations executive in Washington, D.C., and does freelance writing. Her stories have been published by Religion News Service and have appeared in the *Washington Post*, the *Baltimore Sun*, *Black Issues in Higher Education*, *Christian Reader* (now titled *Today's Christian*), and the *Howard University* magazine.

As director of communications for the Baltimore Urban League, she spearheaded advocacy campaigns and branding strategies that raised awareness of the Baltimore Urban League's education, teen, and employment programs. She has worked as a news editor and senior writer for *Black Issues in Higher Education* magazine and *Community College Week* newspaper and as an assistant vice president at Widmeyer Communications. Most recently, Ms. Hawkins was a vice president at Hyde Park Communications, where she worked on health and health care issues, including HIV/AIDS, health disparities, and oral health.

Ms. Hawkins graduated from Howard University in Washington, D.C., and is a member of the Alpha Kappa Alpha Sorority, Inc.

2

BLACK COLLEGES
Still Making an Indelible Impact with Less

As the founding publisher and editor-in-chief of *Black Issues in Higher Education*, my experience, perception, and, most important, appreciation for critically needed education provided by historically Black colleges and universities (HBCUs) probably reflect that of many African Americans who did not attend one of these remarkable institutions. Like my colleagues who matriculated at traditionally White institutions (TWIs), the indelible impact and influence that HCBUs had on our lives has nonetheless been profound and extremely beneficial.

To understand this indelible impact on my life in particular you have to go back over a half-century. It was then that a young man returned from World War II to an impoverished, rural environment in a small hamlet near Florence, South Carolina. Even though he had participated in theaters of war in both Northern Africa and Italy, he, like most African American veterans, would return to rampant economic and social discrimination. In the tradition of male ancestors before him, he began the life of a sharecropper on the vast farm of West Gause, one of the communities of well-to-do land owners. Realizing the dim prospects that he and his emerging family faced, he soon decided to improve his skills and earning capacity by seeking to take advantage of a Federal Farm Bureau program under which veterans who were farmers could learn a trade if they enrolled in a night school program. An additional enticement was the $100 a month bonus during the one year the program would run. The main barrier to enrollment was that he had to own the farm you worked. Lacking such ownership he had to get West Gause's permission. Gause not only refused to grant permission but also enlisted the young man's father as an ally in an effort to dissuade him from pursuing the "foolish" idea of getting additional education and training.

After all, with a young wife and a growing family, the young man needed to be realistic about what was in his, as well as all parties concerned, best interests. His seeking to be educated beyond high school was an unprecedented and audacious act in the little hamlet.

It was while walking back from the fortuitous meeting with Gause that the young man made a very important decision. "I never want to be in this position again," he thought to himself. Being strong-willed and determined, the young man left the farm and enrolled at Morris College, a small HBCU in Sumter, South Carolina, some thirty-five miles away. Through a combination of the GI bill, support from his wife and other family members, and part-time employment, not only did he graduate from Morris College, but his wife did as well.

Wheeler and Lottie Matthews went on to become elementary school educators and, through a combined tenure of almost eighty years of teaching, service, and leadership, had a positive impact on the lives of thousands of students and family members. They also raised five sons.

The oldest son is finishing a stellar career as a chemical engineer with ExxonMobil Corporation. The second retired from an outstanding career as a military officer. The third is a well-respected electrical engineer with Duke Power Company. The fifth, after retiring from a career with the United States Air Force, is living near and looking after his parents in their advanced age. And the fourth son? He became a college professor and magazine publisher who gets to share the preceding story in speeches and in contributions to books like the one you're reading. Succeeding generations of Matthews would become M.B.A.s, medical professionals, and, of course, engineers, to name a few of the career paths facilitated be the family's educational legacy.

We can only imagine the alternatives for the young man and his family and heirs had he yielded to the pressure to remain a sharecropper and had not the little Black college been available to him.

So when we talk about the role and plight of HBCUs, we should never believe the statistically based efforts to marginalize such schools or believe incorrect tales about their lack of rigor or contemporary relevance. Capable people like Wheeler and Lottie Matthews are still out there. And even as these colleges continue to do more with less, the true nature of their impact on the lives of thousands of students and their heirs transcends these questionable barometers of their importance.

Since their founding in segregation, the nation's HBCUs have been studies in resourcefulness, contrasts, resoluteness, possibilities, and miracles. But have the past twenty years marked the worst of times for these venerable public and private institutions? Despite their problems—fractured budgets, ailing and aging infrastructures, and revolving door leadership—they continue to do more with less while managing to outpace majority institutions in training and producing the majority of the nation's Black teachers, preachers, social workers, lawyers, doctors, journalists, engineers, and scholars.

For the first time in their history, a record number of HBCUs are embroiled in fiscal mismanagement or confronting serious financial problems. Among them, Grambling State University, Texas College, Wilberforce University, Fisk University, Central State University, Atlanta's Morris Brown College, and nearly a dozen other HBCUs since the mid-1970s have received warnings or been placed on probation by accreditation agencies, mostly for financial problems, or have had to close their doors—permanently.

"The point is not to lose any of us," says Dr. Norman Francis, who has been president of Xavier University for thirty-five years. "Unless we all can compete, we are all at risk of closing. And every day that we open our doors it's a miracle because we are doing extraordinary things with so little resources," Francis says.

Xavier University in New Orleans, the nation's only Black Catholic university, was among a handful of HBCUs in the 1980s that began to set the standard by which other Black colleges and universities would be measured, not by Blacks but by Whites. Some HBCUs are enjoying unparalleled prosperity and major corporate and foundation gifts, boosting endowments, and successfully recruiting the best and the brightest applicants. In a recent address to United Negro College Fund (UNCF) members, Francis offered a lesson in "Marketing 101" and in staying competitive as a Black college: "Make sure that leaders in industry, business, state and local officials know what you do, and what you contribute. . . . This is a quid pro quo society. "If it is thought that you have no contributions to make, then you must be a liability," says Francis, whose small university has been the nation's leading producer of Black medical students and pharmacists. Today, it attracts competitive research and science dollars.

Dr. Johnnetta Cole, president of Bennett College, agrees: "There is enormous diversity among HBCUs, and there is a core of similarities among us. A large HBCU like a Howard has a string of differences from a small women's college called Bennett and yet, at the center of each of these institutions is a shared vision," says Cole, who led a successful $113 million capital campaign during her fourteen-year tenure as president of Spelman College in Atlanta. In 1987, Cole snagged a $20 million gift from Bill and Camille Cosby, still the largest amount ever donated to a Black college.

But the reality is that some HBCUs won't be able to compete and will be left behind, Francis predicts. "None of us is safe because none of us has a huge [fiscal] safety net." Record low numbers of Black students applying to HBCUs in the 1980s also left these institutions vulnerable, researchers say.

In the past quarter-century, the number of Black college students in the nation has increased nearly 60 percent to more than 1.6 million. HBCUs watched, unable to compete as academically prepared Black students were being lured away by majority institutions bearing scholarships and grants—not loans—earmarked for them and for other racial and ethnic minorities, says Dr. Leonard L. Haynes III, director of the U.S. Department of Education's Fund for the Improvement of Postsecondary Education.

"At the same time that these better-prepared Black students were enrolling in White southern schools, HBCUs were starting to enroll more and more students with education deficits," said Haynes, former president of Grambling State University. The result was an "explosion" in the early 1980s in remedial education on Black college campuses. "Twenty years later we know how to handle remedial students, but their high numbers remain an issue for many HBCUs," Haynes adds. Today, HBCUs graduate about 23 percent of all Black students who earn college degrees.

Leading HBCUs in the Next Twenty Years and Beyond

Tough times and financial woes, while not a new phenomenon at HBCUs, especially in the past two years, have contributed to the departures of nearly a quarter of the presidents of these institutions. Leadership is the key to HBCU survival in the next twenty years and beyond, declare some of the longest-serving HBCU administrators and CEOs. For them that means strengthening existing leaders and identifying new ones who bring experience and commitment to students and Black colleges.

Dr. Ernest L. Holloway, president of Langston University in Oklahoma, stops short of calling the union between a new Black college president and his institution a marriage that demands responsible leadership bound by vows of for better or for worse. "What I've observed about many new presidents is that they think that their institution began when they took office." Not so, says Holloway, "When you take office, you take the responsibility for the university—if that university is in bad shape when you arrive, it is now your problem. You are not going into a perfect environment."

One of the most troubling leadership shake-ups to rock the HBCU community occurred in early May 2004. Dr. Frederick S. Humphries, then-president of the National Association of Equal Opportunity in Higher Education (NAFEO), was forced to step down, along with several other senior administrators of the umbrella association for the nation's public and private Black colleges, after the NAFEO board cited a need to move in "another direction" (see Cassie Chew, "NAFEO Board Cites Need to Move in 'Another Direction': Humphries Out; Washington-Based Attorney to Serve as Interim President," *Black Issues*, May 20, 2004, p. 8).

NAFEO's leadership has been annihilated," says Dr. James E. Cheek, president emeritus of Howard University, who helped found the association in 1969. Cheek, like other HBCU experts and observers, wonders what the future holds for NAFEO and who will be the voice for these institutions. Thirty-five years ago, NAFEO was created to be that voice and that face to the government, to corporate America, and to the public, aggressively promoting HBCUs as necessary institutions for ensuring a Black presence in American higher education.

Cheek says that voice and the vision he and other educators had for NAFEO more than three decades ago blazed until the early 1980s. Today, he says, they have smoldered and are noticeably missing from the Black college landscape. "Ours is neither the time nor is the historically Black college and university the place for those of faint heart, feeble courage, weak commitment, confused and purposeless ambition or selfish motives," admonished Cheek in a 2003 address to usher in HBCU Week in the nation's capital. Langston's Holloway agrees. "This is not the time to be headless," he says of NAFEO and the impact the leadership void will have on an HBCU community that is reeling from the problems of two recent decades.

"It's a tough time to be a college president. This is a heck of a job whether you are Black or White, male or female," says Bennett's Cole with laughter and exasperation. She should know. The retired anthropology professor came out of retirement two years ago to head Bennett College, the historically Black women's college in North Carolina, when its buildings were eyesores, its leadership was shaky, and its enrollment totaled less than five hundred. In addition, it had a $2 million deficit, and its accreditation was in peril.

Other Black women are also up for the leadership challenge, says Cole, who is cautiously heartened by the modest gains in the number of female chief executives of UNCF's private Black colleges and universities. In 1999, there were eleven female UNCF presidents. Today there are twenty-three: "That is change, but we are far short of where we need to be," she says.

According to UNCF, African American women hold presidencies at less than 10 percent of HBCUs and minority-serving institutions. In late April, the sixty-year-old UNCF took its first steps to mentor and develop future female presidents. Cole, in her keynote address at the inaugural meeting of the Mable Parker McLean Women's Leadership Development Forum in Miami, issued an urgent message to her sister presidents and those aspiring to ascend to their ranks at HBCUs. "We want to avoid living out the Ethiopian proverb that says, 'If you wait long enough, even an egg will walk.' As women in higher education, we can't just sit around waiting for more African American women to move into the presidencies and academic and administrative leadership posts," Cole said. "We need to be proactive. This conference is dedicated to mentoring—those who are already there must help others to get where we are."

Lawrence A. Davis Jr.

Lawrence A. Davis Jr., chancellor of the University of Arkansas at Pine Bluff, has three earned degrees: a B.S. in mathematics from AM&N College (now UAPB); an M.S. in mathematics from the University of Arkansas at Fayetteville; and a Ph.D. in engineering mechanics from Iowa State University. He has conducted additional studies in physics, mathematics, computer science, and administration at Brown University, Oak Ridge Associated Universities, University of Oklahoma, and Harvard University.

Dr. Davis was a classroom teacher of mathematics and physics over a period of thirty-three years in various institutions, including Mississippi Valley State University, AM&N College, Arkansas Baptist College, Iowa State University, and the University of Arkansas at Pine Bluff. His administrative experience includes serving as research assistant in the Engineering Research Institute at Iowa State University; administrative specialist for the National Aeronautics and Space Administration Office of Advanced Research and Technology; and chairman of mathematics and physics, dean of arts and sciences, dean of science and technology, and currently chancellor at the University of Arkansas at Pine Bluff (since November 1991).

A prolific writer of speeches and articles with several publications, Dr. Davis has received many awards in education, community service, and leadership.

An active community leader, his board memberships include Jefferson Regional Medical Center; Jefferson County Industrial Foundation; Southern Education Foundation; Southern Regional Education Board; and the Federal Reserve Board, Little Rock Branch. Dr. Davis was also appointed by the president of the United States to serve on the Board of Advisors on historically Black colleges and universities.

3

SUCCESS AGAINST THE ODDS
The HBCU Experience

Historically Black colleges and universities (HBCUs) are not traditionally White institutions (TWIs) with a suntan. Rather, they are higher educational institutions that were created and developed because of the racial divide of the era in which they were founded. Consequently, because of the general attitude and perceptions of the majority population, they were forced to use innovative methodologies to maximize outcomes for their students. The challenges, customs, and operational procedures of these institutions because of isolation and lack of support are distinct, but they all have made tremendous contributions to the human capital pool of the nation. Indeed, had these institutions not been created, the African American middle and upper classes would be considerably smaller.

Despite the lack of financial support, instructional resources, and, in general, the less well-prepared faculty of the past centuries, staff, and administrators, HBCUs developed alternative success pathways for thousands of their graduates. Without elaborating on what precipitated the HBCUs' founding, a cursory review of who initiated their creation, funding, and support indicates that producing African American professionals has not been a historical priority.

Because HBCUs did not document and publish a reference book on the "best practices" that enabled them to succeed against the odds, their practices are difficult to delineate. However, several categories appear to be characteristic.

Extended Family

A common adage is "it takes an entire village to raise a child." At HBCUs, it takes the entire institutional family to produce competent graduates. The administration, faculty, staff, alumni, and community people who take a personal interest in the individual student is that extended family. They provide encouragement and emotional support and, in many cases, financial assistance. Physicians, attorneys, educators, government officials, military officers, etc., who are graduates of HBCUs can attest that, at critical junctures in their lives, the extended family provided the support that enabled them to persist to graduation.

Cultural Immersion

Since a great percentage of the students who matriculated at HBCUs came with academic, social, and financial deficiencies, it has been a prevailing philosophy that programs be provided to meet the students where they are. However, it should be noted that the average standardized test results do not address the potential of the student but, rather, reflect their home and earlier educational environments. Also, the campus environment plays a major role in removing the deficiencies the students bring. Reinforcement of desired behavioral patterns and academic goals are provided by all of the campus interactions the students experience. The library, the dormitory, the classroom, and all other centers of activity are a part of the educational program, and this total immersion makes a difference.

Self-Esteem

One central characteristic of successful individuals is a positive attitude, which is developed through experiencing success. Consequently, HBCUs attempt to facilitate successes by enriching each student through activities that provide avenues for success. Therefore, participation in athletics, band, choir, clubs, sororities, and fraternities, etc., is essential. Statistics show that students who become part of a team experience successes and develop self-esteem, which culminates in a positive attitude. Additionally, these teams' interactions offer other leadership opportunities that inculcate self-esteem as well.

Universal Inclusion

Students who feel a part of the institution are able to interact comfortably with others facing similar challenges and coming from similar backgrounds. Concomitantly, the presence of classmates, administrators, staff, and faculty who share a common heritage with the student is a source of accelerated maturation. An African American student who has role models, professionals who are also African American, learn that they can do what others of their race have done. The existence of these role models is an imperative for the success of many African American students at HBCUs.

Individual Interaction

The presence of administrators, faculty, staff, and others who take the time to interact with the student in unstructured events is definitely essential. Many of HBCU graduates relate interactions that opened their eyes to what they were capable of. They were motivated, challenged, changed, and encouraged by a single individual who intervened at a critical time, so they attribute their success to a single individual.

Epilogue

Although the existence of HBCUs is considered unnecessary by some in today's society, it should be noted that culturally biased institutions have a place. Just as Notre Dame, Brigham Young, Brandeis, the military academies, Southern Methodist University, Texas Christian University, etc., are able to provide quality education, HBCUs can also provide quality education; thus they have a place. They are critical to the nation as long as race continues to affect educational opportunity.

Why HBCUs?

The Role of HBCUs

Brandeis, Brigham Young, Notre Dame, West Point, and Yeshiva University: what is their role? Are these institutions really needed? Relative to HBCUs, I cannot recall this question being asked during the separate-but-equal years. What is inherently bad about an institution that is predominantly Catholic, Jewish, or African American as long as it is open to all? It is only now, after other institutions have been blessed with resources that were denied to HBCUs for over a hundred years, that their role is in question.

The institution I represent is the University of Arkansas at Pine Bluff (UAPB), formerly Agricultural, Mechanical and Normal (AM&N) College; formerly Branch Normal College of Arkansas Industrial University, now University of Arkansas at Fayetteville (UAF). We were founded in 1873 as Branch Normal College to educate the poorer classes. Our sole purpose as a normal school was to prepare teachers for the thirsty-for–knowledge, newly freed slaves and their descendants. The initial mission dictated that the institution develop curricula programs parallel to those at Fayetteville. As the second-oldest public institution of higher education in Arkansas, Branch Normal never attained this objective. Indeed, as other institutions were created in subsequent years, UAPB, AM&N, or Branch Normal was neglected for the most part. The physical plant and curricula at the institution provided irrefutable evidence of an unequal allocation of resources.

In 1928, Branch Normal became AM&N College, a designation that expanded a teacher preparation institution into one with a land-grant mission; this mission is only now being acknowledged by the state as a result of federal mandates. UAPB receives $1.2 million in matching funds from the state for its land-grant programs, whereas UAF (also a land-grant institution) receives several million dollars. Concomitantly, AM&N was denied a Reserve Officer Training Corps (ROTC) unit as prescribed by law until the social revolution of the 1960s. This denial was predicated on the fear felt by Caucasians that training African Americans in warfare would threaten the status quo. Also, denying necessary resources precluded development of graduate programs and professional offerings. In 1973, after AM&N College became the University of Arkansas at Pine Bluff, the institution continued to be an afterthought. But in the 1990s, with new leadership at university system level, UAPB began to progress; tremendous change is currently in process. A three-phase master development plan has been implemented to address past neglect; however, the current economy has hindered completion, even of Phase I.

UAPB's contemporary role is to provide educational opportunities for its traditional clientele and to serve a broader population simultaneously. UAPB's productivity in terms of human capital over the years, considering the magnitude of investment, defines it as a "blue chip" institution. Its role is encapsulated by the rubrics that follow.

Leadership Development

It has and must continue to train leadership for the nation in general and for African Americans specifically. Other institutions prepare African Americans for leadership, but they do so in an atmosphere of diminished self-awareness and reinforcement. It should be noted that many of the leaders of the social revolution of the 1960s were students or graduates of HBCUs.

Access

Although nearly all institutions publicly espouse the desire for a diverse faculty and student body, statistics contradict this aspiration. In the state of Arkansas over the past three years, UAPB has graduated approximately 40 percent of all African Americans receiving baccalaureate degrees from state institutions. Obviously, UAPB, which only enrolls approximately 25 percent of all African Americans pursuing baccalaureate degrees, plays an essential role. Further, despite not having a monopoly on African American talent, we take less of the cream but churn out most of the butter.

It is also significant to note that the African American graduates of TWIs in Arkansas are concentrated in less competitive career paths. Further, as colleges and universities increase emphasis on questionable admission criteria and retreat from affirmative action, it is imperative that African Americans have HBCUs as an alternative access path to higher education and to careers in which they are not well represented. In the year 2000, an African American female graduate of UAPB earned a Ph.D. in physics. In fact, UAPB's graduation rate exceeds the total number of African American graduates of all other state institutions in Arkansas.

Quality Education

HBCUs, as is tradition, provide quality education with a personal touch. This implies that individuals, who may lack the intellectual and emotional maturity to compete in the impersonal environment of larger institutions, are exposed to mentors who intervene, even into the personal lives of the students, to motivate them to realize their potential. UAPB continues to serve many students who are the first in their families to attend college. Also, students are exposed to individuals in positions of authority who can identify with them and share a common background. In many of the larger institutions, there are still professors who cannot envision African Americans as attorneys, physicians, and university professors. For example, in 2005, five African Americans, all graduates of UAPB, will graduate from the University of Arkansas Medical School. No other institution in Arkansas can equal this number. Arston Jacks, art major, is one of three finalists out of nine thousand entries for design of the Arkansas state quarter. Many graduates of UAPB testify to the poor educational backgrounds from which they came only to be nurtured by us and, consequently, allowed to achieve success. These individuals, who are leaders and are working in such cities as New York, Los Angeles, Detroit, Dallas, Kansas City and Chicago, include Danny Davis (congressman from Illinois), Darwin Davis (retired as vice president of Equitable Life), Samuel Kountz (who helped develop the technology for kidney transplants), Charlie Nelms (who served as president of colleges in Indiana and Michigan), Gloria Anders, Ph.D. (chemistry degree earned from the University of Chicago), Dennis Davenport (Ph.D. in mathematics from

Howard University), and Ulysses Hunter (Ph.D. in mathematics from Purdue University). The examples are extensive.

Cultural Preservation

Because of their isolation over the years, HBCUs have developed a unique culture that revolves around such traditions as homecoming and football classics. These have special significance for our entire race and have great value as a part of the total American fabric. A cursory scan of the attendees at athletic contests—those of TWIs and those of HBCUs—demonstrates the importance of these events to African Americans, and HBCUs remain an alternate path to professional athletics. The contribution of HBCUs to professional athletics, even in a time when a majority of the better African American athletes are attending TWIs, is convincing testimony. Four UAPB players were drafted by the National Football League in 1999, surpassing many of major National Collegiate Athletic Association (NCAA) Division I institutions.

National Conscience

As long as HBCUs continue to produce African American graduates, other institutions will be discouraged from ignoring the talent pool. It is ironic that the same institutions that are able to fill their athletic squads with African Americans find it difficult to realize this same success in the academic arena. It is also revealing that a disproportionate number of African Americans who enter TWIs do not graduate. In fact, the graduation rate of African American athletes is deplorable.

Diversity Model

HBCUs generally have more diverse faculties than do TWIs. In our own institution, the faculty roster is international. We have generally been more receptive to diversity than many other institutions. This diversity enables our students to be exposed to the world as it actually exists, thus, better preparing them to adapt to the greater world after graduation. It should be noted that this diversity includes within-group assimilation. Students from urban areas, such as Chicago and Dallas, join students from the agrarian communities of Arkansas. Also, UAPB enjoys more than one hundred partnerships that include other universities, local school districts, businesses, community organizations, large companies, and government agencies.

Economic Engine

UAPB infuses the local economy at a level of $50 million per year. As with TWIs, HBCUs bring culture and intellectual stimulants to the community that would not be present otherwise. However, the past social environment has precluded the community from embracing UAPB, so our potential is not fully exploited.

Conclusion

For the foreseeable future, HBCUs will be compelled to continue to be the major developers of the African American talent pool as they simultaneously provide opportunities for others. The HBCUs' contribution to America is phenomenal, especially when one considers how limited support of them has been. It would appear that if this nation is serious about equal opportunity for all, it should invest in HBCUs as it invested in the NSG in the 1960s. Our underdeveloped physical plants, limited financial resources, and, in general, benign neglect have restricted our capacity to do more. It is frightening to think what UAPB would be like were it not for Title III, student aid, and other federal assistance provided over the years. Also, over the years, because of Title III support, several of our faculty have earned terminal degrees and served higher education in an exemplary manner.

HBCUs must be empowered to do more. Resources are needed to develop additional baccalaureate and graduate programs, as is the capacity to build support to enable us to participate fully in the enterprise of education. Empowerment includes resources to develop and maintain adequate physical plants; resources to purchase and maintain equipment; the ability to procure technology and remain competitive; the development of meaningful partnerships with government agencies to provide opportunities for students and faculty to engage in educational activities and research programs; and increased student aid to assist students in meeting the ever increasing cost of higher education. These objectives can be achieved through additional Title III support and support from other federal programs as well. At UAPB, we subscribe to the development of a *"NO EXCUSE UNIVERSITY."* If we are supported, we will compete without special considerations. We will increase the number of African Americans and others who contribute to the continued vitality of our nation.

Elaine Johnson Copeland

Elaine Johnson Copeland is currently president of Clinton Junior College, Rock Island, South Carolina, a private, two-year institution supported by the African Methodist Episcopal Zion Church. Clinton College has a stated mission of providing educational opportunities to students who may present deficiencies in their academic transcripts, while challenging those who present significant academic promise.

She is associate professor emeritus of educational psychology and former associate dean of the Graduate College and associate vice chancellor for academic affairs at the University of Illinois at Urbana-Champaign, where she taught counseling psychology courses. Dr. Copeland has also taught psychology courses and headed the Business Department at Clinton Junior College.

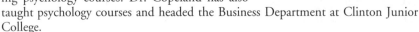

Dr. Copeland held the position of vice president for academic affairs and dean of the college at Livingstone College, her alma mater, in 2000–01. During her tenure there, she assisted in establishing a collaborative program with the University of Illinois that provides summer research experiences for Livingstone College undergraduates and lucrative fellowships for graduates who pursue graduate study at the University of Illinois that leads to academic careers.

Dr. Copeland attended the Harvard University Institute for Educational Management during the summer of 2001 and the Seminar for New Presidents in 2002. She is a licensed professional counselor and a national certified counselor. She also served as the first African American president of the National Association of Women in Education in 1989. Dr. Copeland has degrees from Livingstone College, (B.S. with honors), Winthrop University (M.A.T), the University of Illinois at Urbana-Champaign (M.B.A.), and Oregon State University (Ph.D. in counseling with high honors).

Nationally she serves on the Commission for the Transnational Association of Christian Colleges and Schools and on the American Council on Education Committee for the Advancement of Racial and Ethnic Equity. At the local level Dr. Copeland is a member of the Rock Hill Rotary and Chamber of Commerce boards.

4

CREATING A PATHWAY

The Role of Historically Black Institutions in Enhancing Access, Retention, and Graduation

The nation's Black colleges and universities have been a major asset in developing and educating minds for a large proportion of our society who otherwise might not have attended institutions of higher learning. Founded in the late 1800s and the early 1900s, these institutions served as a pathway to intellectual development, successful careers, and a better life for many of their alumni. Before the 1954 Supreme Court decision, *Brown v. Board of Education*, these institutions provided an education for most African Americans who pursued higher education. After the 1954 ruling and passage of the Higher Education Act of 1965, African American students had, in principle, access to predominantly white institutions. Yet, advocates of historically Black colleges and universities (HBCUs) have presented several justifications for continuing these institutions, including the development of citizens who assume leadership roles in society. HBCUs continue to graduate disproportionately more students than do their White counterparts if percentages of enrolled students are compared (Allen, 1992). Further, more students who graduate from HBCUs go on to pursue graduate and professional degrees, especially in science and engineering. It is essential that we examine the role of Black institutions in a contextual framework to understand the culture of such institutions, their histories, and their missions.

Historically Black Colleges and Universities, History and Mission

The first HBCUs were private rather than state supported. They were established to serve African Americans who had been denied admission, solely on the basis of race, to colleges and universities located in Southern and border states.

According to a 2004 report from the National Association for Equal Opportunity in Higher Education (NAFEO), there are now 109 HBCUs. There are fifty public and fifty-nine private institutions located in fourteen Southern states, three Northern states, three Midwestern states, the District of Columbia, and the Virgin Islands. The fifty public institutions, 46 percent of the total, include forty four-year institutions and ten two-year institutions. The fifty-nine private schools, 54 percent, include forty-nine four-year institutions and ten two-year institutions. Twenty states and the District of Columbia established separate institutions for Black students to avoid opening the doors of White institutions to this population. Twenty-one HBCUs are land-grant institutions.

The first institutions for African Americans were founded by religious organizations, sometimes with the assistance of wealthy philanthropists who understood the importance of a literate society and the need to educate all citizens. Most were established by denominations of Black churches or those that had large Black congregations. The first private historically Black institution, Lincoln University in Pennsylvania, was founded in 1854, prior to the Emancipation. Many other private Black colleges were founded during the thirty years following the Civil War. Some institutions now designated as HBCUs were assigned this status more recently because of the number of African American students they serve. State-supported Black colleges and universities were established to provide comprehensive training, including agriculture and science programs, or as institutions to train teachers. The comprehensive state institutions for African Americans were meant to provide similar programs and educations as those established much earlier; they became land-grant schools as a result of the Morrill Act of 1862. The primary object of the Morrill Act was, without excluding other scientific and classical studies and those related to military training, to offer programs related to "agriculture and mechanic arts, in order to promote liberal and practical education" (U.S. Statutes at Large, 12, 1862-508).

Historically Black land-grant institutions were created as a result of the second Morrill Act of 1890, which provided that historically Black institutions offer comprehensive programs, including agricultural and technical training, to a segment of the population that did not have access to institutions that had already established agricultural and engineering programs as a result of the first Morrill Act of 1862. Other public and private schools were established as two- and four-year liberal arts colleges with programs to educate teachers and "preachers" to provide the foundation for students who would eventually attend graduate and professional schools.

While all American higher educational institutions have had as a part of their mission research, teaching, and service, all historically Black institutions have, since their founding, stressed the importance of developing the whole person, intellectually, morally, ethically, and spiritually. Emphasis has been and continues to be on developing the mind, heart, and soul and a strong work ethic, along with social and civic responsibility. An examination of some of these institutions' mission statements reveals that, in addition to developing the mind, they are concerned with cultural values, ethics, character development, civic responsibility, leadership, and service to the community. Whether public or private, large or small, selective or with open admissions, these institutions continue to emphasize these ideals.

Some opponents have argued that HBCUs have now served their purpose, since predominantly White institutions are now open, in principle, to all. In *United States v. Fordice* (1992), the Supreme Court ruled that HBCUs were segregated institutions and should be eliminated or sound justification for their existence should be proposed. In many of the Adams states—those states that previously had segregated, state-supported higher education for Black students, so named because of the class action suit filed to integrate higher education—governing boards and legislators have attempted to dismantle state HBCUs. Others have supported mergers and have recommended continuation by suggesting that these institutions offer different courses and programs. The justification for closing these institutions is tied to concern for duplication of courses and programs and the need to more effectively manage state finances and resources. Yet, HBCUs continue to prepare a disproportionate number of students who graduate with undergraduate degrees and who go on to attend and complete graduate and professional schools.

Recent reports on the Status and Trends in the Education of Blacks from the National Center for Education Statistics (NCES) and the American Council on Education (ACE), Minorities in Higher Education Twenty-First Annual Status Report reveal that, while only 14 percent of African Americans attended HBCUs for the period 1999–2002, a total of 22.6 percent of the bachelor's degrees conferred in 2001–2002 to African Americans were from historically Black institutions (Hoffman, Liagas, and Snyder 2003). A further examination of "Doctorate Recipients from United States Universities" (Hill 2003) indicates that historically Black institutions continue to produce a disproportionate number of persons who obtain graduate and professional degrees and who pursue employment in the "academy" or in professional careers. These data indicate that African American doctorate recipients were not as likely to receive the undergraduate degree from the top twenty baccalaureate-granting institutions as were White students and or those of other racial/ethnic groups, with only 21 percent receiving their degrees from these institutions. Twelve of the top twenty institutions awarding the bachelor's degree to African American doctoral recipients were historically Black institutions, with Howard University being the alma mater of the largest number of recipients.

It is no accident that Jackson State University in Jackson, Mississippi, continues to graduate more students in chemistry than do many of its counterparts with larger science facilities and more research dollars, or that Xavier University of New Orleans produces a disproportionate number of students who attend and receive their degrees from medical schools. What is it about these schools and others like them that enhances opportunities and fosters success? There are numerous activities and programs that promote and encourage academic success as well as personal and professional development.

Barriers to Access, Retention, and Graduation

Successful programs incorporate activities to increase the pipeline, create the pathway, and aid in the transition to institutions of higher learning. Programs must serve as the bridge to support matriculation from one level of education (secondary education to the bachelor's degree and to graduate and professional training) to the next.

The National Center for Public Policy and Higher Education examined the critical factors that serve as major barriers to higher education. Its report, "Measuring Up" (2004), assessed the gains or declines of secondary school completion and matriculation beyond high school. The overall objective was to "gauge the educational health of each state population" in terms of five categories of college opportunity and achievement:

- Preparation: the extent to which high school students are equipped to pursue higher education
- Participation: the rate at which students attend higher education
- Completion: the rate at which students graduate, considering completion rates and time to attain a degree
- Affordability: whether higher education is affordable to all segments

of the state population, using median income of residence and college costs in individual states

- Benefits: The extent to which those who complete two or four years of further training contribute to the economic and civic well-being of each state.

These findings are disheartening, especially in terms of dropout rates, college enrollment, completion rates, and affordability. Many states with large African American and low-income populations have the largest dropout rates for degree attainment and low median income levels. Many HBCUs have developed activities and programs that recognize this dire need.

Increasing the Pipeline

It is apparent that many Black institutions provide a different milieu, an environment that promotes access and fosters retention and graduation. Efforts are made to remove barriers that impede academic success and foster a climate that promotes positive self-worth and development. Nearly all higher educational institutions now seek to improve their rates of access, retention, and graduation for underrepresented students, recognizing that changing demographics for such groups are necessary if the nation is to continue to educate all segments of society. If this issue is not addressed, society will suffer in terms of the economy and all of the other consequences caused by uneducated or undereducated members of the society. Programs that work include:

- General Equivalency Diploma programs at the college level and degree programs for nontraditional students. To address the problem of high dropout rates, some institutions have programs to create a path for students who did not receive the high school diploma. Clinton Junior College and some other two-year colleges offer General Equivalency Diploma (GED) programs that allow students to enroll in college course work while taking a course to prepare to pass the GED. This type of program increases the pool of students who can attend college. Other programs are necessary to reach nontraditional students—those who have completed high school but who are employed and need courses offered at times that fit their work schedules.
- Evening and weekend courses work for this population. These programs allow students to enroll in up to twelve hours per semester.

Strengthened Intellectual Competence and Personal Confidence

Many other academic courses and programs are needed to assist students once they do enroll (Hrabowski 2002; Hoffman, Liagas, and Snyder 2003). A list of such programs follows:

- Summer bridge programs are offered to high-risk students during the summer before they plan to enroll in college. Students are provided academic work, generally in mathematics and English, and receive counseling and advising services.
- Research seminars offered in the freshman year serve to build confidence for students who might not have had such experiences during their secondary school years.
- Summer research experiences and internships strengthen intellectual skills and build confidence. Two- and four-year institutions develop partnerships with research universities that offer the opportunity for students to engage in research with a faculty member and sometimes with graduate students as well. The benefits of such arrangements are many: students improve research skills, learn how to present papers, and develop networks with other students who participate in the summer research experience. Many of these students might not otherwise have considered graduate study.
- Legislative internships encourage Clinton Junior College students to participate in government in collaboration with the State Legislative Black Caucus of South Carolina. Through this effort, students learn how the political system works and begin to understand the importance of their participation.
- Community service learning programs require students to enroll in a course or courses that demand involvement in community agencies and schools. Students must complete a number of hours per semester in one or more community settings, which may include working at a soup kitchen, tutoring in a school setting, reading to senior citizens in a day care facility, or shadowing a city employee. The importance of such programs has been noted (Smith 1984).
- "Lunch buddy programs" are designed to have college students mentor students in the elementary schools. This type of activity mutually benefits the mentor and those who are mentored. A program that matches student athletes from Clinton Junior College with African

American third-grade male students from single-parent families proved to be beneficial for both groups. Spending two hours a week over lunch frequently results in continuous meaningful relationships.

- Lyceum or chapel weekly gatherings, offered by most private religious-sponsored colleges and universities, require students to attend. These activities serve numerous purposes: students are encouraged by presenters or speakers; student participation fosters leadership development and skills; and societal issues are addressed that often assist students in understanding their personal responsibilities to society.

- Participation in student government association activities at small colleges with a thousand students or fewer encourage all students to participate in extracurricular activities. Participation increases leadership skills and builds confidence.

- Student-alumni interaction also helps students to see positive role models. Events that foster these relationships contribute to students' understanding of the importance of setting goals; they begin to conceptualize their future roles in society in the workforce and as contributors to society.

College Affordability

Financial Barriers

The lack of financial aid can be a major impediment to college access, retention, and graduation. Various researchers have examined the effects of having sufficient financial aid at both the undergraduate and graduate levels on retention and graduation. The type of aid—loans, college work-study, need-based grants, or merit-based scholarships and fellowships—affects the progress or lack of progress toward graduation. Furr and Elling (2002) surveyed students at a predominantly White university to examine why African American students dropped out after the third and fourth semester. According to their data, the major reason for discontinuing educational pursuits was not having sufficient funds to pay tuition. These students did not have the personal or family income to subsidize support not available from the institution. In some HBCUs, as many as 85 percent or more of students are eligible for a full or partial federal Pell Grant. The following efforts can assist in bridging the financial aid barrier:

- The availability of other financial resources, such as institutional scholarships—both need based and merit—is essential.

- College work-study, work opportunities paid from institutional funds, and loans are essential for those who do not have the parental financial support or personal income to defray these costs.
- Before entering college, students and their parents must know how to apply for financial aid and understand the importance of applying for other scholarships such as those available from public service and civic organizations.
- Outreach is vital. Colleges must make special efforts to reach first-generation low-income students and their parents. Some students will not apply if they do not have the financial resources to attend. Providing information on how financial aid might be packaged tends to help both parents and potential students understand that college may be a viable option. Students with good academic records often receive additional financial assistance from sororities and fraternities, churches, civic clubs, and philanthropic groups.

Many HBCUs encourage prospective students to apply for all forms of aid and provide assistance to both students and their parents. To increase the probability that low-income students will pursue higher education, it is essential that they receive information on financial aid at various stages during their secondary school years. A number of methods are useful in distributing information: campus publications are mailed to prospective students and to local high schools, and workshops on applying for financial aid are beneficial for both prospective students and the parents.

Socioeconomic and Cultural Barriers

A number of studies have examined the major social and cultural factors that impact whether students are successful in obtaining a postsecondary education. Researchers (Allen, Bonous-Hammarth, and Teranishi 2002) have examined various factors that lead to student success and barriers that impede student progress. Many are due to socioeconomic factors, such as income status, parental educational level, and prior academic experiences and preparation, all of which influence student aspirations and achievement. These variables create differences in access to information, financial resources, and academic experiences and preparation. Many prospective students do not attend college because they do not aspire to careers requiring such degrees, often because they do not have information or financial resources, are not sufficiently prepared academically, and are not encouraged to pursue higher education or careers requiring such preparation.

Students who are the first in their families to consider higher education may not have mentors, parents, or other significant individuals to encourage them. When parental support is present, resources still may be limited. Specific demographics characteristics, such as income levels, family structure, and educational attainment of parents, can all affect the aspirations, academic achievement, and persistence rates of students. Other external forces, such as institutional size and climate, can contribute to or impede success. Some factors, such as financial resources, are obvious, while others, such as aspirations, persistence, and attitude, are more elusive. Even when students have adequate financial support and outstanding academic records—which are tangible and measurable variables—they may not have the nurturing and supportive environments that HBCUs have traditionally provided. The type of milieu in which students learn and develop can greatly influence retention and graduation rates.

When students are in environments where there is not a critical mass in terms of both culture and race, they may feel alienated and isolated. This situation may affect the self-esteem, confidence, persistence, and self-worth of students living in a "chilly climate." There are a plethora of activities and programs at HBCUs that contribute to creating a "warm" rather than a "chilly" climate on campus once a student enrolls; Tracey and Sedlacek (1987) examined some noncognitive variables that are indicators of academic success for nontraditional students. The ability to make positive and accurate self-assessments, to understand and effectively deal with racism, to set goals, to have a supportive milieu with individual mentors, and to show leadership and learn from nonacademic experiences have all been shown to relate to academic success. According to these researchers, students who realistically evaluate their strengths and weaknesses and who understand how to respond to their environments are more likely to persist. In environments where students do not have a "critical mass" of others who are culturally and racially similar, students who recognize and deal with racism are most likely to focus on their primary goals and not be adversely affected. Students with positive mentors and those who have developed leadership skills appear to persist where those without such traits may not be successful in negotiating the system.

Encouraging students to achieve academically must begin early. Grantham and Ford (2003) have examined the effect of racial identity on the academic achievement of gifted African American students. They relate psychological issues of Black students and theories of Black racial identity development to academic success. Institutions that recognize the value of interventions that support and nurture self-esteem can play a major role in increasing retention of all students.

Positing that administrators, faculty, and students greatly affect the improvement of student retention, Lau (2003) presents reasons for "dropout" and suggests effective methods to improve student retention. These recommendations relate to the need for financial and academic support to build self-esteem. The author recommends adequate funding, academic support, understanding and supporting cultural diversity, and using collaborative learning as tools that institutions may use to improve retention rates for underrepresented and physically disabled students. The following is a list with descriptions of some effective activities and programs:

- Students are assigned to mentors in addition to their academic advisors.
- Peer counseling and tutoring encourage team building and collaboration (McDonough 2004).
- Monitoring class attendance so that the importance of being in class is stressed; in some institutions students may not accumulate more than three unexcused absences.
- Students should be rewarded for academic and extracurricular accomplishments.
- Faculty should be recognized for outstanding teaching. Faculty encourage and promote student success through mentoring and support, and small class sizes, especially in some of the most challenging courses, allow students to have individualized instruction, encourage critical thinking, and promote learning.

Allen University in Columbia, South Carolina, has as part of its motto, to create "a mind to learn, hands to work, and a heart to love." While this mission statement might have been created over a century ago, it is relevant today. It is essential that education respond to needs of the "whole person." In this regard, historically Black institutions continue to play a vital and significant role.

References

Allen, W. R. 1992. The color of success: African American college student outcomes and predominantly white and historically black colleges and universities. *Harvard Educational Review, 62*, 26–44.

Allen, W. R., Bonous-Hammarth, M., and Teranishi, R. (2002). *Stony the road we trod . . . The black struggle for higher education in California.* Report funded by the James Irvine Foundation and the Andrew W. Mellon Foundation.

Furr, S. R., and Elling, T. W. (2002). African American students in a predominantly White university: Factors associated with retention. *College Student Journal,* 36: 188–199.

Grantham, T. C., & Ford, D. (2003). Beyond self-concept: Racial identity and gifted African American students. *The High School Journal, 24,* 18–29.

Hill, S. (2003). *Doctorate recipients from United States universities: Summary report.* Washington, DC: National Opinion Research Center.

Hoffman, K., Liagas, C., and Snyder, T. (2003). *Status and trends in the education of Blacks.* Washington, DC: National Center for Education Statistics (NCES 2003–034).

Hrabowski, F.A., III. (2002). Postsecondary minority student achievement: How to raise performance and close the achievement gap. *College Board Review 195,* 40–48.

Lau, L. K. (2003). Institutional factors affecting student retention. *Education* 124 (1):126–137.

McDonough, P. M. (2004). Counseling matters: Knowledge, assistance and organizational commitment in college preparation. In *Preparing for college: Nine elements of effective outreach,* ed. W. G. Tierney, Z. B. Corwin, and J. E. Coylar (pp. 81–103). Albany, NY: State University of New York Press.

National Center for Public Policy and Higher Education. (2004). *Measuring up: The national report card on higher education.* San Jose, CA: Author.

Smith, C. U. (1984). Community service and development in historically black colleges and universities. In *Black colleges and universities: Challenges for the future,* ed. A. Garibaldi, 24–47. New York: Praeger.

Tracey, T. J., and Sedlacek, W. E. (1987). A comparison of white and black student academic success using non-cognitive variables: A LISREL analysis. *Research in Higher Education* 27:333–348.

Stanley F. Battle has served as president of Coppin State University since March 2003. Among his first accomplishments was changing the name of Coppin State College to Coppin State University. Before assuming his post at Coppin, Dr. Battle served as vice chancellor of student and multicultural affairs at the University of Wisconsin-Milwaukee.

Pamela G. Arrington serves as chief of staff and associate vice president, planning and accreditation, and is a tenured associate professor of applied psychology at Coppin State University. She currently serves on the review board of the Society for College and University Planning Institutional Development and the Planning for Higher Education Editorial Review Board and as a reviewer for the Middle States Commission on Higher Education.

Ron L. Collins, Sr., is tenured in the Department of Humanities and Media Arts at Coppin State University in Baltimore, Maryland. Since 1998, he has served as dean of the Honors Division and director of the Ronald E. McNair Post-Baccalaureate Achievement Program at Coppin, where he secured two nationally competitive grants, totaling nearly $2.3 million, to support student preparation for graduate study.

Marcella A. Copes is a full professor and the dean of the Coppin State University Helene Fuld School of Nursing, where she has worked since 1999. She was an associate professor teaching parent-child nursing at Howard University College of Nursing in Washington, D.C., and assistant dean at Howard University College of Nursing and director of reaccreditation self-study.

Frances C. Gordon is an associate professor and assistant to the dean of Coppin State University (CSU) Helene Fuld School of Nursing, where she has worked since 1992. Mrs. Gordon is currently a doctoral candidate at Union Institute and University. She is a member of Sigma Theta Tau, International Nurses Honor Society, and the Mary Mahoney Honor Society.

5

A TRADITION OF ACCESS AND ACADEMIC EXCELLENCE

Coppin State University

Coppin State University is an HBI (historically Black institution) founded in Baltimore City in 1900. Nationally recognized for its innovative programs that empower achievement, Coppin State University offers excellence in academic programming, with fifty-three majors and nine graduate-degree programs. A national leader of excellence in higher education, Coppin State is named after the legendary, pioneering educator, Fanny Jackson Coppin. A fully accredited institution, Coppin State University offers a nurturing learning environment that helps primarily first-generation college students transform their lives and is a leader in educating Maryland's African American business leaders and workplace professionals.

As the institutional mission statement states, "Coppin provides educational access and diverse opportunities for students with a high potential for success and for students whose promise may have been hindered by a lack of social, personal or financial opportunity." Coppin State University embraces the particularly important mission of providing higher education to a significant number of students who historically have been underrepresented in higher education. This continuing legacy has posed some retention hurdles that the institution is overcoming.

This article gives an overview of selected Coppin State University retention and graduation-rate initiatives and discusses how a comprehensive campus retention focus, characterized by strong presidential leadership and coupled with varied campus programs supported by research-based teaching and learning practices, ongoing institutional studies, and the use of technology, coalesces to nurture the potential and transform the lives of Coppin State University students.

The Coppin State University Student

Historically, the student body has been characterized as predominantly African American, female, nontraditional, and commuter; the current student body reflects these characteristics. In fall 2004, 3,290 undergraduate and 585 graduate students were enrolled. The average age of the total student population is twenty-nine. Ninety-eight percent of the student population is minority and of this proportion, 93.6 percent is African American. Coppin State University is primarily an urban commuter campus[1] with two residence halls, totaling 642 beds. The majority of students (90 percent) are in-state residents who live in Baltimore (56 percent) and surrounding counties (44 percent). Of the 10 percent out-of-state student population, almost 3 percent are from foreign countries. Of the remaining 7 percent out-of-state students, most are from New York and the District of Columbia. For the fall 2004 cohort, 622 first-time, first-year students enrolled, of whom 589 are full time and 83 percent are in-state. Of this group, 42 percent are Baltimore city residents, 19 percent are from surrounding counties, and 39 percent are from out of state. The combined Scholastic Achievement Test (SAT) average was 780–910 (twenty-fifth to seventy-fifth percentile) with a range up to 1380.

The proportion of Coppin State students who need federal financial aid is the highest of any University System of Maryland campus. Fifty-six percent of Coppin State enrollees qualify for federal Pell Grants, a higher proportion than any other campus (average 21.6 percent) in the University System of Maryland, so Coppin State students are forced to strike a delicate balance between employment and continuing their education.

According to the most recent Cooperative Institutional Research Program (CIRP) Freshmen Survey results, almost half (42.7 percent) indicated that none of their first year's educational expenses (room, board, tuition, and fees) would be covered by family resources (parents, relatives, spouse, etc.). The majority noted that they are the first in their family to attend college. Over half (58 percent) live in a single-parent home, and most lived with their mothers (93 percent) during the last year of high school. Three-fourths (75 percent) graduated from a public school system. About a third (33 percent) of the first-year class indicated an interest in nursing as a major and as a career (30 percent).

---

[1] The university is located in a community that is 99 percent African American, in which women head more than one-third of the households, and in which 27 percent of the residents earn less than $15,000 annually. The neighborhood suffers from a crime rate that is among the highest in Baltimore. These factors intensify the university's mission—a commitment to access and academic excellence.

Administrative Conditions

Since the majority of Coppin State students are the first in their family to attend college, rely on financial aid, face tremendous socioeconomic and educational challenges, and have permanent addresses in Baltimore—a city plagued with a range of urban problems—the university has rallied to institutionalize a nurturing learning environment that will propel its students toward academic excellence. Student support staff members, working with the academic units, focus on such critical issues as premajor and general academic advising, a comprehensive advising plan, and training advisors. Establishing a nurturing learning environment by personalizing the academic experience for students has helped to ensure academic excellence for all students. This is a campus-wide goal that begins with robust presidential leadership and is communicated to every faculty and staff member of the university community. Subsequently, the president has recognized effective efforts at the unit level and has called for replication of those unit-level best practices.

Using ongoing institutional studies and posting the results on the campus Web site, as well as sharing information through campus workshops, a concerted dissemination campaign has been effective in communicating to the campus community the importance of retaining and graduating students. This practice accentuates the shared philosophy that every member of the campus community must play a role in this undertaking. The campaign has served to relay the successes and areas needing improvement concerning the university's retention and graduation goals. Continuous emphasis on these goals highlights the need for individual and collective institutional management, responsibility, and accountability. With each first-year cohort, the university collects retention data until graduation which are shared with the entire campus community.

Senior administrators were charged with educating the campus community, especially faculty, about how graduation rates are calculated.[2] With a better understanding of cohorts, faculty representatives across the academic majors routinely monitor students throughout the semester and academic year from predetermined cohorts. Faculty telephone and e-mail their majors who have exhibited a break in enrollment to assess how the university can facilitate their return to school. The cohort model provides a vehicle for faculty to follow students' progress. More important, the cohort-based model provides an effective means by which to identify those students at risk of leaving school.

[2] The number of first-time, full-time first-year students who matriculate in six years.

Another important element of the campus-wide dissemination campaign is the coming together of all constituencies to share the unit-level retention practices that are making a difference in students' completing their educational goals. Many data have been accumulated and disaggregated at the unit level so that progress in meeting retention and graduation goals is readily available. This ongoing conversation among campus groups has reinforced the university's goals of access and academic excellence as well as the need for improved strategies to ensure their accomplishment.

Campus forums and workshops where retention is the primary focus reaffirm these priorities. These campus events provide opportunities to recognize units with stellar practices in place and encourage others within the university to replicate the best of these practices. On the other hand, frank dialogue among faculty, staff, and administrators, facilitated through surveys and workshops, has prompted pointed recommendations for change that should be implemented, since data show that some current practices serve as barriers to students' academic success.

Surveys about how to best actualize student access and success are administered routinely. The results are the centerpieces for ongoing campus dialogue about improving retention and graduation rates, and these research-based discussions serve as catalysts for change in campus policies and procedures.

A final administrative condition benefiting the tradition of access and academic excellence at Coppin State is the university's advanced information technology infrastructure. The use of technology has been critical in maintaining a nurturing learning environment. The university has found that technology has significantly enabled its capacity for retaining students and values the use of technology to make learning more effective and its administration more productive. Use of technology as a tool for improving teaching and learning practices, client management, and student services is a highly valued principle on campus. Technology has helped faculty and staff to nurture students as they complete their educational goals and has aided students in registering for classes. With implementation of wireless technology on campus, students can connect to faculty and staff anytime, anywhere on campus, and the student-to-computer ratio was improved from 26:1 to 6:1. Given the large percentage of students who receive financial aid and the fact that most do not receive additional financial support from their families, a laptop ownership program was instituted for students. Additionally, by using technology and other appropriate strategies and tools, the university greatly enhanced the existing interactive learning environments conducive to learning. As a result, technology has dramatically changed the students' teaching and learning environment.

Data management systems have been developed for campus use, and faculty, staff, and administrators have been trained to use the systems to monitor student progress. The customized systems assist staff in identifying students in jeopardy of leaving school because of outstanding bills, mid-term deficiencies, or incomplete financial aid awards, to name a few red flags. Faculty can also use the customized data system to advise their majors about course requirements and course sequencing.

Each campus unit is responsible for determining its most appropriate retention activities, which are to be based on the national literature and the historical data for the campus and the unit. Best practices are recognized campus-wide, and units are encouraged to replicate elements from each other's activities that prove a best fit. Many units have followed the lead of the School of Nursing and the Honors Division, both of which have achieved many successes in retaining and graduating their majors. A brief overview of these retention initiatives follows.

A Nurturing Learning Environment: The Helene Fuld School of Nursing

The Coppin State University Helene Fuld School of Nursing credits its students' successes to its nurturing learning environment. The school mirrors the Coppin State commitment to academic excellence. The school values its students, and the learning environment is conducive to students' professional and intellectual growth. Learning occurs in a nurturing therapeutic environment where students are prepared to meet the challenges and demands of baccalaureate nursing education.

Nursing administrators and faculty are sensitive to the particular learning needs and issues endemic to the student population they serve. While possessing the potential to be successful, students are often confronted with myriad financial and psychosocial problems. Mirroring the Coppin State student profile, a typical nursing student is from a disadvantaged background, female with a mean age of twenty-seven years, African American, and the first in her family to attend college. More than 90 percent of nursing students are employed either full or part time, and many are single heads of household with one or more children. There is a constant struggle to manage multiple tasks, roles, and responsibilities, financial needs and worries are prevalent, and students' academic success is contingent on a holistic approach that addresses both academic and social variables.

Armed with this information, and with the fundamental elements in place, the School of Nursing devised a comprehensive academic support model to assist its students. The program is designed to increase retention rates and improve academic performance outcomes. Early diagnosis and intervention are major success strategies. Scores achieved on the standardized discipline specific tests provide baseline data regarding students' cognitive abilities and/or deficits. Early identification of existing deficits and implementation of appropriate remediation are hallmarks of the program. Emphasis is placed on learning and study skills, note taking, time management, goal setting, test taking, and critical thinking. Basic skills in math and reading are addressed in the Coppin State University (CSU) Academic Resource Center, which emphasizes mastery of course content.

There is compelling evidence in the literature that students are often reluctant to participate in "tutorial" programs because of the accompanying stigma. After much discussion, it was decided that the academic support program would be called the Nursing Student Enrichment Program (NSEP), and the "tutors" would be called NSEP specialists. The students responded favorably to these titles. Initially the program targeted students identified as at high risk academically; however, as the program expanded and realized success beyond projections, it was decided to approach academic achievement from a broader perspective. Nursing students at all academic levels and abilities are included. The criteria for participation now currently focus on at-risk students and the high achievers. Students are referred by faculty or may volunteer to participate, but students with a grade of less than seventy-five on a quiz or examination are referred by faculty and required to participate. Students who have consistently met with academic success are also encouraged to participate.

This eclectic mixture of students has proven beneficial for all of the participants. These heterogeneous groups serve as significant motivational factors, and peer support is stressed. Students functioning at a level of academic proficiency tend to lend support and assist their less proficient peers. The "scholars" serve as appropriate role models for their colleagues. Findings suggest that students who collectively explore and actively engage in the learning process improve their study habits and problem-solving skills. Critical thinking, time management, and test-taking skills are also enhanced. Students are encouraged to form small study groups that function outside NSEP sessions. While initially hesitant to participate in study groups, students have reported them to be highly beneficial. Higher achievers tend to realize even greater cognitive growth and accomplishments when positioned to offer peer support.

Academic support is provided in small groups of six to eight students, and intensive "enrichment" is provided on a one-to-one basis. This tactic has proven to be most effective for students who have demonstrated difficulty in grasping highly abstract and complex concepts. Teaching/learning strategies focus on the identified learning styles of students as derived from the test data. Students are assisted with clarification, reinforcement, and mastery of course work. Emphasizing the holistic approach to academic success, students are taught breathing and relaxation techniques as well as ways to deal with test anxiety.

Good communication is crucial to NSEP's efficiency and effectiveness; a close collaborative relationship must exist among faculty, students, and NSEP specialists. Input and contributions of all participants are expected. Of significance in the NSEP are the ongoing interactions and dialogue between faculty members and NSEP specialists, the goal of which is to maintain a monitoring system in which the academic status and progression of students are followed closely. Intervention strategies are enhanced and/or revised because of these evaluative measures. In addition, students are apprised of their performance and are included in the development of their individual intervention plans. Safer and Fleischman (2005) concur with this strategy: they maintain that tools developed for early identification of "students at risk academically" are extremely valuable/useful. They suggest, "instructional strategies be adjusted to better meet students' needs based upon findings extrapolated from the monitoring process." Findings can also be used to ascertain program effectiveness and determine the need for change or revision.

One tool the School of Nursing uses to monitor and determine the academic status of students is the "mid-term warning process," which readily identifies students at risk academically. This method of detection and diagnosis assists NSEP specialists in developing and implementing intervention plans that best meet the students' needs. The "mid-term" warning process has proven to be an effective tool. The literature supports the concept of early intervention tools; intervention after mid-term does not leave sufficient time to change poor study habits or resolve existing deficits. Students are usually not academically salvageable at this point. Most students demonstrate significant improvement and are able to progress to the next course and/or academic level when academic interventions are strategic and timely.

Data are collected and analyzed to ascertain that overall objectives have been achieved. Program effectiveness can only be determined by ongoing program evaluations. Data collected have clearly documented that NSEP has been successful.

A Nurturing Learning Environment: The Honors Division

The McNair Postbaccalaureate Achievement Program

In 1989, the U.S. Department of Education identified Coppin State as one of the original fourteen colleges/universities to develop a program that might prepare undergraduate students for doctoral study and for the professoriate. Currently, 179 McNair Programs exist at the more than fourteen hundred four-year colleges and universities in the United States, with only eleven McNair programs resident at HBIs. Coppin McNair graduates have earned 102 masters and six doctorates and have garnered Ph.D.s in pharmacology, education, criminal justice, higher education administration, and psychology from Duke, Harvard, Howard, Illinois (Champaign-Urbana), Lehigh, and Ohio State, respectively. In addition, fifteen Coppin McNair graduates are currently enrolled in doctoral programs.

Retention data for Coppin McNair participants from 1995 to 2004 reveal that 94 percent completed their undergraduate degrees in 4.4 years. These data are particularly interesting when compared to national data that suggest that only 63 percent of all U.S. college attenders complete their degrees in six years (Lotkowski, Robbins, and Noeth 2004). Structural elements of the Coppin McNair model may account for Coppin McNair students' persistence to graduation. In our view, students of color persist to graduation at higher levels when three program elements coalesce: (1) students regularly participate in required discipline-specific academic forums that include opportunities to present at research conferences and to visit leading graduate schools; (2) students receive academic and personal counseling on demand; and (3) students are guaranteed scholarship assistance sufficient to cover tuition/fees, book cost, and, whenever possible, paid summer-research opportunities at doctoral intensive or extensive universities. Coppin McNair Program components, therefore, include graduate school visits; travel to research conferences; fellowship workshops, graduate assistantships, and other forms of financial support available to graduate students; workshops on the graduate admissions process; a speakers' series featuring successful role models who have earned terminal degrees; preparation for graduate admissions tests; tutoring support; ongoing individual and group meetings with mentors; an eight-week summer research experience; a $2,800 summer stipend; and a tuition/fee scholarship during each semester of eligibility.

The guarantee of financial assistance, the assurance of intensive academic/personal advising, and the active involvement of students in discipline-specific learning community activities serve as the three critical institutional factors that encourage Coppin McNair students to graduate.

The Honors Program

Designed to prepare student achievers for graduate school or professional study, the Honors Program has attained an average yearly retention rate of 85 percent over the last ten years and a 94 percent year-to-year retention rate for students entering the university in fall 2003 and returning in fall 2004. Within the Honors Program, year-to-year retention is achieved through implementation of the following four strategies:

- helping students to identify and achieve personal, academic, and career goals;
- offering a challenging, accelerated academic track that complements personal, academic, and career goal achievement;
- providing opportunities for leadership development within both the program and the broader campus community; and
- committing to program support of student goals.

Students entering the program are enrolled in a common first-year track of accelerated, general education requirements. Small classes, taught by experienced faculty, allow for scholarly engagement among peers and between students and instructors. As students advance through their majors and begin the junior year, they are introduced to research methodologies in a series of honors-level research courses. Outside the classroom, students are exposed to current research by master's and doctoral students, they participate in graduate school entrance exam preparatory seminars, and they visit and apply to graduate schools across the nation.

Throughout each semester, an interventive system is available to help students experiencing academic and/or personal challenges. An "open door" policy within the Honors Program creates a relaxing, even familial environment where students are granted continual access to staff. Indeed, the Honors Program counselor extends on-call personal, academic, and career counseling. At mid-semester, progress reports identify students at risk for "stopping out," and scheduled counselor and instructor conferences follow for each student earning a grade of "C" or below. In addition, mandatory progress meetings with the dean are scheduled with each first-year student twice during the first semester—that is, during the fourth weeks of September and October.

Rounding out students' academic preparation are extracurricular activities. Throughout the year, honors students represent the program and the university in a variety of activities, such as student panels, educational and research forums, competitive national academic teams, and campus fundraisers. Of course, students also hone leadership skills as athletes and as members of various social organizations.

The Honors Program has been successful in marrying academic theory with "real-life" experiences through community service and summer internships. Honors Community Service is a one-credit, first-year course that provides a one-semester opportunity for students to assume the roles of mentor and tutor to elementary school-age children. This experience sets the stage for many character- and esteem-building service opportunities for students throughout their years in honors. Woven into the honors experience is the requirement that each student apply for one summer internship every year. These academic discipline-related internship positions allow students to develop as professionals.

Support for the Honors Program student actually begins before the onset of the academic year, with the Honors Division's First-Year Student Reception. This reception introduces students *and* their parents to university administrators, program staff and faculty, and current Honors Program students. This effort continues with a First-Year Student Orientation event at which new students are exposed to the operational aspects of honors education at Coppin State. Program goals are reinforced to upper-division students in the Continuing Student Orientation. In addition, athletes meet separately with the dean and representatives from the Athletics Department to discuss tactics to balance the demands of both programs so as to ensure student success.

As students settle into their academic routines, they encounter the one-credit, first-year course, "Honors Freshman Seminar," which assists in retention of students as it offers an orientation to campus life, provides a foundation for student success, and reinforces the goals of the Honors Program.

While most Honors Program students complete the first semester with grade point averages of 3.4 (on a 4.0 scale) or higher, from time to time, students require additional assistance. Program tutors provide mathematics/ statistics and writing assistance at students' request.

Financial support is also critical to maintaining a yearly retention rate of 90 percent or higher. Selection to the Honors Program guarantees a student one of six scholarships that are renewable each semester the student meets the eligibility criteria. Certainly, guaranteed funding is key to maintaining student retention levels from semester to semester; however, in many cases, student expenses may exceed scholarship provisions. As the departmental budget permits, students are supported with textbook stipends and graduate school entrance exam and application fees. Students are also exposed to external scholarship opportunities and paid summer internships and are required to attend workshops that address such topics as money management and federal and state financial aid sources.

Other units of the university, including the School of Arts and Sciences and the School of Professional Studies, have created nurturing learning environments by mixing program elements similar to those in nursing and honors, crafting a best fit for the student profile evidenced in these schools. How? By melding early warning tools, intrusive advising, tracking systems, high-quality faculty-student interactions, attendance-monitoring programs, and tutoring elements into academic support programs that best fit the needs of students majoring in a particular discipline, all campus units have instituted a nurturing learning environment for the advancement of access and academic excellence. There is campus-wide commitment to these priorities evidenced at all levels of operation; we have highlighted only two such initiatives here. These same elements can be seen at the individual academic program level and, collectively, at the institutional level.

In conclusion, a comprehensive campus focus on retention has aided the university in supporting its students to complete college (Nettles, Wagener, Millett, and Killenbeck 1999). Beginning with committed leadership, faculty involvement, and early diagnosis and interventions, followed by a nurturing and caring campus climate and supported by the use of technology and data, the university has made great strides along the access-to-academic-excellence continuum. This relationship among committed presidential leadership, administrative conditions, teaching and learning practices, ongoing institutional studies, and enrollment management procedures has coalesced to ensure access and academic excellence for students at Coppin State. Enhancing access and academic excellence even more, the university will embark on an aggressive fund-raising campaign for scholarships. Since the majority of the students enrolled at Coppin State must strike a delicate balance between employment and continuing their education, the university's capacity to increase need and merit scholarships will certainly help to increase its retention and graduation rates.

References

Lotkowski, Veronica A., Steven B. Robbins, and Richard J. Noeth. "The Role of Academic and Non-Academic Factors in Improving College Retention." *ACT Policy Report* (2004):vi.

Nettles, M. T., U. Wagener, C. M. Millett, and A. M. Killenbeck. "Student Retention and Progression: A Special Challenge for Private Historically Black Colleges and Universities." *New Directions for Higher Education* 108 (Winter 1999):51–67.

Safer, Nancy, and Steve Fleischman. "How Student Progress Monitoring Improves Instruction." *Educational Leadership* 6 (February 2005):5, 81–82.

Bibliography

Deno, S. L. (2003). "Development in Curriculum-Based Measurement." *Journal of Special Education* 37 (2003):184–192.

Freeman, K., and G. E. Thomas. "Black Colleges and College Choice: Characteristics of Students Who Choose HBCUs." *The Review of Higher Education*, 25 (3) (2002):349–358.

Fuch, L. S., and D. Fuch. "What Is Scientifically-Based Research on Progress? Monitoring?" (technical report, Vanderbilt University, Nashville, TN, 2002).

Hurd, H. "Staying Power: Colleges Work to Improve Retention Rates." *Black Issues in Higher Education* 17 (October 26, 2000):18, 42–47.

Hutto, C. P., and L. T. Fenwick. (2002). *Staying in College: Student Services and Freshman Retention at Historically Black Colleges and Universities (HBCUs)*. Washington, DC: U.S. Department of Education Office of Educational Research and Improvement (ERIC Document Reproduction Service No. ED468397).

Kirkpatrick, Denise. "Slowing the Revolving Door: Providing Academic Support for Distance Education Learners." Paper presented to Cambridge Open and Distance Education Conference, Cambridge, MA, September 2001.

Maryland Higher Education Commission. "Access and Success: A Plan of Action for Maryland's Historically Black Institutions." Annapolis, MD: Author, June 12, 1997.

Roach, R. "Battling for the Best." *Black Issues in Higher Education*. 17 (October 26, 2000):18, 36–41.

Shen, Jianping, Lu Duejin, and Joseph Kretovecs. "Improving the Education of Students Placed at Risk through School-University Partnership." *Educational Horizons* 82 (3) (Spring 2004).

Tinto, B. *Leaving College: Rethinking the Causes and Cures of Student Attrition.* 2nd ed. Chicago: The University of Chicago Press, 1993.

Tinto, V., A. Goodsell Love, and P. Russo. *Building Learning Communities for New College Students.* University Park, PA: The National Center on Postsecondary Teaching, Learning and Assessment, Pennsylvania State University, 1994.

Wagener, U., and M. Nettles. "It Takes a Community to Educate Students." *Change* 30 (1998):2, 18–25.

Charles V. Willie

Charles Vert Willie, Ph.D., is Charles William Eliot Professor of Education Emeritus at the Graduate School of Education, Harvard University. Before his Harvard appointment, he was professor of sociology, chair of the Department of Sociology, and vice president of student affairs at Syracuse University. Professor Willie has earned three academic degrees—a Ph.D. in sociology from Syracuse University, a master of arts from Atlanta University (now Clark Atlanta University), and a bachelor of arts from Morehouse College.

He is former vice president of the American Sociological Association, former president of the Eastern Sociological Association, and a member of the Association of Black Sociologists. Among his books on black students in higher education are *Black Students in White Colleges* (1972), *Black/Brown/White Relations* (1977), *Black Colleges in America* (1978), *The Ivory and Ebony Towers* (1981), *African-Americans and the Doctoral Experience* (with Michael Grady and Richard Hope, 1991), and *Black College Mystique* (with Richard Reddick and Ronald Brown, 2005).

6

A CONTRIBUTION TO HIGHER EDUCATION

Mentoring Methods and Techniques Developed by
Historically Black Colleges and Universities

Confidence, trust, and respect are preeminent mechanisms in the attainment of formal education. Teachers cannot educate students in whom they have no confidence, and students cannot learn from teachers in whom they have no trust. Reciprocity between confidence and trust generates respect—respect for teachers by students and respect for students by teachers. It is the mutuality of these two mechanisms—their reciprocity—that results in respect.

Respect, therefore, is a phenomenon that cannot be demanded either by dominant or by subdominant people of power; that is to say, "[it] cannot be [forced] by a single individual in a one-sided way" (Willie 2000, 261).

Sara Lawrence-Lightfoot conceptualizes respect as offering the "promise of symmetry" (2000, 4)—giving "good" for "good." Where there is respect, there is care, concern, and consideration. Thus, I conclude that "inspired teaching and useful learning are enhanced in school communities where there is [mutual] admiration and respect between teacher and student because of their confidence and trust in each other" (Willie 2000, 262).

This circumstance is frequently found in historically Black colleges and universities (HBCUs) in the United States and indicates why they have accomplished "so much with so little and so few" (Mays 1971, 170).

The late Benjamin Elijah Mays is one of the most esteemed Black educators in the United States. He was successful as a student, teacher, and administrator in HBCUs. A brief review of his educational odyssey and career is offered as a prototype of effective education in these kinds of schools.

In 1916, Mays enrolled in the freshman class at Virginia Union University in Richmond, Virginia. Virginia Union was and continues to be an HBCU. According to Mays, the student body was "serious-minded," and "a few students . . . were worthy competitors in the pursuit of academic excellence"; moreover, the faculty was "racially mixed" and "able." Mays discovered that "the [Black] professors were just as able as the white ones, . . . [which] presented a good image to the . . . [Black] students" (Mays 1971, 52).

At the end of his first semester at Virginia Union, half of his class had flunked college algebra, and the school chose Mays to teach mathematics to those classmates who had failed (Mays 1971, 52). This was an early example of peer consultation, later encouraged by Uri Treisman (1992), that was sanctioned by the school and must have been a confidence-building experience for young Benjamin Mays (Mays 1971, 52).

While studying for his first graduate degree at the University of Chicago, Mays was invited by John Hope (the first Black president of Morehouse College, an HBCU for men in Atlanta) to teach mathematics, psychology, and English and to coach the debating team (Mays 1971, 66). Mays said, "[He] made history at Morehouse by teaching the first course in calculus ever to be given there" (1971, 67). During his three years at Morehouse, Mays taught, served as acting dean, and was a pastor of Shilo Baptist Church, a small church with 125 members located three blocks from the Morehouse campus (Mays 1971, 97).

Mays later accumulated other useful experiences: as a teacher at South Carolina State College in Orangeburg, executive secretary of the Tampa Urban League, student secretary serving Black colleges with the National YMCA, and director of research for a study of Black churches sponsored by the Institute of Social and Religious Research. Although these were described as good jobs, Mays was determined to earn his Ph.D. in religion at the University of Chicago. This he did in 1935.

Seeing how close Mays was to obtaining his terminal degree, Howard University invited him to become dean of the School of Religion (for the next six years) in 1934. That same year, he was elected to Phi Beta Kappa by the Bates College chapter, the school where he matriculated after transferring from Virginia Union at the end of his freshman year.

In 1940, Mays was elected president of Morehouse College. Along with his letter of acceptance, Mays asked the board to upgrade salaries of faculty members and to include the president as a member of the board's Executive Committee. Mays's immediate goals after his election as president were to secure more money for Morehouse and increase the size and quality of the faculty (Mays 1971, 176). It was his belief that "a college is no stronger than its faculty" (1971, 178). This belief differs significantly from that of other leaders in higher education who evaluated the quality of their schools by the quality of students they attracted and enrolled.

Mays acknowledged that "in the final analysis, a college or university must be judged by the achievements of its alumni" (1971, 183). However, he considered alumni to be reflections of the educational experience provided by the school.

After fourteen years of continuous effort, Mays persuaded representatives of Phi Beta Kappa to visit Morehouse College to determine whether it qualified for membership. In January 1968, the Delta of Georgia chapter of Phi Beta Kappa was established at Morehouse College, and the first students to qualify for membership were initiated May 17 of that year. Mays considers this event to be one of his major achievements at Morehouse College.

Near the end of his twenty-seven years as president of Morehouse, Mays reported that "one of every eighteen [African Americans] earning doctorates [in the United States] had received the A.B. or B.S. degree from Morehouse." Mays considered this to be a marvelous figure because no more than four thousand men had graduated from Morehouse College at that time (1971, 184).

Mays explains the success of Morehouse this way: (1) the faculty was able and dedicated; (2) the trustees were loyal and gave him the freedom to do his work; (3) as president, he never ceased to raise his voice and pen against injustice; (4) Morehouse never accepted any grant with strings attached such as those designed to silence resistance to segregation; (5) students were invited to participate on the advisory committee with an equal voice with the faculty when a student was tried for some violation; and (6) daily chapel was a special institution where students could and did question the president about matters concerning the college (Mays 1971, 181–191). During his presidency, Mays taught the students who attended Morehouse, "if [one] is to be free in [one's] own mind and soul, [one] must forever be on guard against accepting conditions that will enslave [one's] spirit" (1971, 196).

Mays concludes the assessment of his presidency of Morehouse college with these words: "We believe that during our twenty-seven years, we helped instill in many a Morehouse student a sense of his own worth and a pride that thereafter enabled him to walk the earth with dignity" (1971, 199).

I conclude this brief report on the life and times of Benjamin Mays with comments from students who attended Morehouse during his presidency. George C. Grant (class of 1961) said, "There is no official record of the number of persons that Dr. Mays mentored. However, there were dozens." Grant described Mays as "the multi-dimensional man who provided academic and moral leadership . . . as a vision-setter and a personal role model."

Fred Lofton (class of 1953) recalls the activities of Dr. Mays during the Civil Rights Movement: "When students became involved off-campus in this struggle, Mays did not try to stop them; he stood by the students at Morehouse . . . and gave them guidance" (Lofton 2002, 49). Leonard Ray Teel, who prepared an article on Benjamin Mays for the October 1982 *Change* magazine, mentions that a number of the students who led sit-ins and protests in Atlanta, Georgia, during the early 1960s were enrolled in Morehouse; he shares with us Mays's response to this matter: "Far from being surprised that our students were 'getting into the act,' I would have been dismayed had they not participated in the south-wide revolution. . . . When one or two trustees requested me to stop the Morehouse students from demonstrating, I politely refused" (Teel 1982, 15).

Gathering up these and other actions in his own testimony, Samuel DuBois Cook (class of 1948) described Mays as "a powerful disturber of the human conscience and an implacable foe of every form of complacency, mediocrity, self-righteousness, moral conceit, and hypocrisy" (Cook 1971, xii). Martin Luther King, Jr. (class of 1948), called Benjamin Mays his spiritual mentor and "one of the great influences in my life" (King 1958, 125). Lerone Bennett, Jr. (class of 1949), declared that Benjamin Elijah Mays is "the last of the great school masters" (Bennett 1977).

Thus far, I have reported how others viewed Benjamin Mays's mentoring role. The next section demonstrates how I experienced his mentoring-in-action as well as mentoring by other professors at Morehouse.

I majored in sociology in college. During my senior year at Morehouse, Professor Walter Chivers, chair of the Department of Sociology at Morehouse College, took a special interest in me and my career. He advised me to enroll in Atlanta University (also, an HBCU) immediately after graduating from Morehouse to study for a master of arts degree in sociology.

After I won a tuition scholarship from Atlanta University, Professor Chivers approached the president of Morehouse College, Dr. Benjamin Mays, and convinced him to establish a teaching assistantship in the Department of Sociology. There was only one candidate for this position—me. The salary for my work that year was not negotiated; it was exactly the cost of room and board at Atlanta University, where I matriculated for my master's degree. I remember well the experience of picking up my check monthly from the business office of Morehouse College, signing it, and immediately turning it over to the university bursar. The job of teaching assistant was created especially for me; in fact, I was probably the first teaching assistant Professor Chivers ever had. President Mays was an accomplice in this arrangement. As president of the sophomore, junior, and senior classes and editor of the news magazine published by students during my third year of college, I knew that I was one of the president's favorite students because of the leadership responsibilities I assumed on campus. However, my grade point average when I graduated from college was good but not great.

My mentor, the chair of Morehouse's Sociology Department, had other plans for his protégé after graduation. Believing that I should continue graduate school for a doctoral degree, Professor Chivers again convinced Dr. Mays to provide him with sufficient resources to invite a guest lecturer to Morehouse College—the chair of the Department of Sociology at Syracuse University, whom Professor Chivers had met and befriended at national meetings. My mentor's strategy was to bring the Syracuse University professor to Morehouse College and introduce his protégé to him. The strategy was successful.

Honestly, I cannot remember the topic of the Syracuse professor's lecture. I do remember, however, that before he left the Morehouse campus, he had promised to intercede in my behalf with the Syracuse University Department of Sociology and urge it to grant me a scholarship, provided I applied and was admitted to the graduate school. After completing my master's degree, I had intended to seek employment, probably in a social service agency like the YMCA. But my mentor believed I had another calling. I trusted his judgment, so I left the South and traveled to central New York to enroll in Syracuse University—a region far removed from my hometown in geographical and cultural ways.

Syracuse University and I were a good match. I earned a Ph.D. in sociology eight years after enrolling in 1949. I served Syracuse University as a teaching assistant, faculty member, Sociology Department chair, and vice president. Two decades or more later, I received an honorary doctorate from Syracuse University as well as its highest alumni award. All of this, directly and indirectly, can be attributed to the efforts of my mentors, especially Walter Chivers and Benjamin Mays, who acted in my behalf to facilitate my entry into a Ph.D. program at Syracuse.

My experience is not unlike those of other educators affiliated with Black colleges and universities. John Hope, the first Black president of Morehouse College, approached the young Benjamin Mays in the library of the University of Chicago in 1921 and offered him a one-year job teaching college mathematics and high school algebra at Morehouse College. Mays had taken graduate courses in mathematics, but he did not have a master's degree and was leaning toward religion as the field of study for his Ph.D.

Because of the confidence that President Hope had in Mays, and because "[Mays] had no money and it was not clear . . . how he was going to be able to continue . . . [his studies] at the University of Chicago, Mays went to Atlanta" (Mays 1971, 66). President Hope was so satisfied with Mays's work that he extended the one-year contract for three years.

In telling this story, Mays marveled at "how fortuitous is the life of [a person]." He said that "a simple contact," like his meeting that summer day in 1921 with John Hope [in the University of Chicago library], "was probably decisive in determining his career" (1971, 66).

My traveling from Dallas, Texas, to Atlanta, Georgia, in 1944 for a college education at Morehouse College and, of course, to meet Professor Chivers and President Mays was accidental. It was the first act in the unfolding drama of my professional career, but I did not recognize it as such that year.

I was the middle child in a working-class family with five siblings. Our family had bread enough but not much of anything else to spare. My parents made great sacrifices to send us to college. My father, the chief breadwinner in our family, was a Pullman porter and traveled out of town each week. His formal education ended after the eighth grade, but his travels gave him a cosmopolitan point of view. My mother was a stay-at-home mom, because during the Depression the local school system in Dallas, Texas, would not hire a woman whose husband had a job. So my mother stayed home with her five children. This was hard work, especially in a single-income household. To exercise her special teaching gifts, my mother decided to operate a "home school" for her children and husband. Thus we got a "head start" on our public schooling long before the 1960s, when the federal government conceived such a program. My mother, with her B.A., was our private head-start teacher.

When Wiley College of Marshall, Texas, an HBCU from which my mother graduated, offered a scholarship to the ranking student in Lincoln High School's class of 1944, I, who was ranked second, lost out to a female classmate, Myrtle Reed, who was valedictorian. Because of limited family finances and the size of our family, I needed scholarship assistance. My band teacher and choral director, A. S. Jackson, was one of my mentors in high school. He advised me to apply for admission to his alma mater, Morehouse College, in Atlanta, Georgia. Since I was salutatorian of my high school graduating class, I was eligible for the scholarship that Morehouse offered to the ranking student in all Black high school graduating classes; Morehouse was a men's school and the highest-ranking student in my class was female. Based on this logic, I claimed the scholarship and left Texas to attend college in Atlanta.

My experiences at Morehouse were not different from those of Dr. John Hope Franklin at Fisk, and Dr. Kenneth Clark at Howard. These two gentlemen of color had experiences with mentors at their HBCUs that were very similar to mine.

At Fisk University in Nashville, Tennessee, where Dr. Franklin studied history, he met a young White professor, Theodore Currier. Professor Currier discovered that Franklin had some promise and advised him to attend Harvard for graduate study. Franklin described his teacher as a person with great charm who became his mentor and closest friend. Graduating magna cum laude from Fisk University when he was only twenty years old, Franklin applied to and was accepted for graduate study at Harvard. This was in the middle of the Great Depression, and his family could not finance his study. His father's law practice was crushed when the building in which its office was located was burned to the ground during the 1921 Tulsa, Oklahoma, riot. Returning to his home in Oklahoma after graduation from Fisk, Franklin wondered what to do.

When Professor Currier heard of Franklin's problems, he said, "Money will not keep you from going to Harvard" (Willie 1986). Since neither Franklin nor his mentor could find any funds to tap for graduate education, Currier, a thirty-three-year-old professor, went to the bank and borrowed enough money to pay for Franklin's first year. Franklin said that he would always remember Professor Currier's decisive remark about money and Harvard. Because his mentor would not let the absence of scholarship assistance become a stumbling block for his protégé, Franklin attended Harvard.

When Dr. Clark was a child growing up in Harlem, he admired his playground attendant, who was a medical student at Howard University in Washington, D.C. She described Howard to him as a place where Blacks were in control. Since he had never experienced a setting in which Blacks were in control of anything, Clark wanted to enroll in Howard as an undergraduate. He did in 1935 and studied for a bachelor's degree in psychology. One of his teachers who remained a friend until death was Professor Francis Cecil Sumner. Clark called Professor Sumner, for whom he reserved special praise, as "the key at Howard" for him (Willie 1986). Though soft-spoken, Professor Sumner, according to Clark, was uncompromising in insistence on high standards of the students worthy of his attention. Clark said that he admired Sumner and leaned on him, describing Sumner as his mentor and his friend. Clark remained at Howard for a year after graduating and studied for a master's degree in psychology while teaching part time as Professor Sumner's protégé. Clark said that he moved through Columbia University rapidly for his Ph.D. studies because there were no challenges more daunting than those of Sumner.

Clark said Sumner continued to be pleased with all that happened to him. In 1986, I wrote a book, called *Five Black Scholars, An Analysis of Family Life, Education and Career*, that included the stories of John Hope Franklin and Kenneth Clark, along with those of Matthew Holden, Jr., W. Arthur Lewis, and Darwin T. Turner. These last three gentlemen of color did not have mentors, not because they did not wish to have them, but because none volunteered to fulfill this role. It is interesting to note that the three scholars of color who did not have mentors received baccalaureate degrees from traditionally White institutions (TWIs).

In recent times, HBCUs like Xavier have demonstrated the value of mentoring for success in higher education. "Xavier [is] far out front of any other university in America in the number of Blacks placed in medical school" (Cose 1997, 57). This remarkable accomplishment, in part, has happened because "Xavier University realized [it] needed to start work even before students show . . . up for . . . freshman classes" (Cose 1997, 55).

A summer program, called Stress on Analytical Reasoning (SOAR), has been offered at Xavier since 1977. The university explains that SOAR is aimed at students not yet in college. "High school juniors and seniors . . . are put through . . . [an] academic boot camp" and "are in [summer] classes from eight in the morning until eight at night," which includes "required study sessions" (Cose 1997, 55). J. W. Carmichael, a chemistry professor at Xavier, said the program is "intense work . . . on reading skills, mathematics, vocabulary building and exercises in abstract reasoning" (Cose 1997, 55).

An academic advisor is assigned to each SOAR high school graduate who enrolls in Xavier for a program of college studies. Tutoring and other supports are rendered by the advisor, especially during the first two years of college (Cose 1997, 56). The program emphasizes working in groups (Cose 1997, 56), which is a way of increasing peer assistance and consultation, activities that Uri Treisman found to be useful. Professor Carmichael said his eyes fill with tears when he talks about SOAR students who "thank him for giving them [such an] opportunity . . ." (Cose 1997, 65). A first-year female student at Xavier attributed much of the university's success to the dedication of the faculty. She said, "they're there whenever you need them" (Cose 1997, 58).

Sarah Willie's comparative study of the adaptation of Black alumni in Black and White college settings reports the observations of Peter, who transferred to Howard from a predominantly White university: "My entire . . . years at Howard just stood out as extraordinary . . . . People believed in me and showed confidence in my ability" (S. Willie 2003, 91). Another student, Shirley, reflected on her time at Howard ten years after graduation: "Howard helped me because I had teachers who were very caring, who made me feel like I could do anything. They'd fail you in a minute; but yet . . . they were still behind you" (S. Willie 2003, 92). Finally, Karl (a member of the Howard class of 1989) said: "I developed some relationships with a couple of professors [at Howard] who really, sincerely seemed to care and were interested in me. [They gave] a lot of tips about how to deal with the world" (S. Willie 2003, 94). Sarah Willie presents these opinions in a section of her book, *Acting Black*, entitled "The Importance of Trustworthy Professors." She concludes that "the attitudes of the professors [at Howard University] and the school general climate of acceptance fostered a sense of ownership among the individuals . . . interviewed" (2003, 94).

With appropriate mentoring, several HBCUs have demonstrated that students with a wide range of preparation in secondary education can be brought up to par. According to Ellis Cose, "Xavier's secret of success lies in its techniques and its philosophy" (1997, 53). Xavier and Howard are used as prototypes of other HBCUs and as examples of what any college or university can and ought to do to facilitate formal education in a diversified student body. Mentoring as an academic technique is discussed in detail in the following paragraph.

Several years ago, John Monro, a faculty member of Miles College (an HBCU), experimented with teaching methods and techniques that are similar to those used at Xavier. He identified four principles of effective teaching:

1. "A close professional scrutiny of what [skills, information and attitudes] each student brings to college."
2. "A program of teaching and learning that deals directly and efficiently with the needs of students in a firm and supportive way . . . [realizing that] students need much *individual help* and much practice in gaining fundamental skills" (emphasis added).
3. "A competent, dedicated faculty who are interested in teaching

students, rather than just teaching a subject. . . . [In other words,] faculty is what matters"

4. "A management that keeps close tabs on . . . how students and teachers are doing, what works well and what doesn't, and what new developments in learning theory can help" (Monro 1978, 236).

At the end of this list, Monro asserted that "any college can do this [HBCUs as well as TWIs]. The problem is awareness and concern." Finally, he concludes that colleges that show "concern and undertake this kind of program . . . will be richly rewarded" (1978, 236–237).

For reasons discussed in this essay, we bring attention to the art of mentoring and remediation with which HBCUs have experimented over the years with good outcomes. It should be obvious that some students in all kinds of schools need mentoring from time to time because of or despite their high school preparation or racial identity. Thus, the experience of HBCUs could be of help to TWIs if there is awareness, concern, and the belief that many students can learn and should have the privilege of learning in institutions of higher education.

References

Bennett, Lerone, Jr. 1977. "The last of the great school masters." *Ebony*, 32 (December): 74–79.

Carter, Lawrence Edward, Sr., ed. 1996. *Walking integrity, Benjamin Elijah Mays: Mentor to generations*. Atlanta, GA: Scholar's Press on behalf of Morehouse College.

Cook, Samuel DuBois. 1971. Introduction, *Born to rebel*, by Benjamin E. Mays. New York: Charles Scribner's Sons.

Cose, Ellis. 1997. *Color-blind*. New York: Harper Collins.

King, Martin L., Jr. 1958. *Stride toward freedom*. New York: Harper and Row.

Lawrence-Lightfoot, Sarah. 2000. *Respect*. Cambridge, MA: Perseus Books.

Lofton, Fred C. 2002. *Posthumous reflections: A letter to my mentor, Dr. Benjamin Elijah Mays*. Jackson, MS: Four-G Publishers.

Mays, Benjamin E. 1971. *Born to rebel*. New York: Charles Scribner's Sons.

Monro, John W. 1978. Teaching and learning English. In *Black Colleges in America*, ed. Charles V. Willie and Ronald R. Edmonds. New York: Teachers College Press.

Teel, Leonard Ray. 1982. Benjamin Mays—Teaching by example, leading through will. *Change*, 14 (7): 14–22.

Treisman, Uri. 1992. Studying students studying calculus: A look at the lives of minority mathematics students in college. *College Mathematics Journal*, 23 (5): 314–316, 318, 320, 322.

Willie, Charles V. 1983. The education of Benjamin Elijah Mays: An example of effective teaching. *Teachers College Record*, 84 (4): 955–962.

———. 1986. *Five black scholars*. Lanham, MD: University Press of America and ABT Books.

———. 2000. Confidence, trust, and respect. *The Journal of Negro Education*, 69 (4): pp. 255–262.

Willie, Charles V., Michael Grady, and Richard O. Hope. 1997. *African Americans and the doctoral experience*. New York: Teachers College Press.

Willie, Sarah Susannah. 2003. *Acting black, college, identity and the performance of race*. New York: Routledge.

Talbert O. Shaw

Dr. Talbert O. Shaw, former president of Shaw University, was officially designated president emeritus during the university's commencement ceremony, May 10, 2003. Dr. Shaw was named president of Shaw University in 1987 and served in that capacity for more than fifteen years.

Dr. Shaw has served for more than thirty years in higher education, creating, advocating, and directing innovative programs to prepare future leaders to value commitment to individual and social responsibility. He came to Shaw during a critical time, when the school was on the verge of closing its doors, and he led the university on a steady uphill climb. During Dr. Shaw's tenure, the university's endowment grew from nearly zero to $12 million, and student enrollment nearly doubled to more than twenty-five hundred. Dr. Shaw provided leadership that inspired a renaissance in the university's life and its impact on the larger community.

A number of significant programs were implemented at Shaw during his service as president. Most noteworthy was the establishment of an ethics and values program. In 1993, the university made courses in ethics and values central to the general education of all its students to emphasize the university's commitment to high personal standards and citizenship in its graduates. Dr. Shaw's commitment to ethics was recognized in the 2000 edition of *The Templeton Guide: Colleges that Encourage Character Development*. The guidebook, which was released nationwide, is designed for students, parents, and educators who believe that character matters. President Shaw was cited in the presidential leadership category for exercising leadership in character development.

In 1995, Shaw University dedicated the Talbert O. Shaw Living Learning Center on its northeast campus. Completion of this facility marked the first major building initiative to occur at Shaw University in ten years and the largest single construction project in the university's history.

Dr. Shaw earned his A.B. at Andrews College in Michigan and his M.A. and Ph.D. from the University of Chicago. His dissertation developed an integrative theory of social responsibility using descriptive and normative principles in the social sciences, philosophy, and theology. Dr. Shaw spent his years as a professor and administrator at Howard University, Catholic University of America, and Federal City College, all in Washington, D.C.; Bowie State College and Morgan State University, Maryland; and Princeton University, New Jersey, before going to Shaw in November 1987.

7

CHARACTER EDUCATION

The Raison d'Être of Historically Black Colleges and Universities

On May 17, 1954, the Supreme Court ruled in *Brown v. Board of Education* that segregation in all publicly supported academic institutions must be terminated. Embracing this historic opportunity, most Black college students, perhaps as many as 80 percent, now attend majority institutions. These data have spawned ongoing questions regarding the need for historically Black colleges and universities (HBCUs). The continuance of these institutions, some analysts claim, creates a two-tiered system of education.

That concern forms the backdrop of this essay regarding the founding and documented need to preserve Black colleges. Black Americans were legally and systematically excluded from educational opportunities before the Civil War. Covering a period of 110 years, beginning with the founding of what is now called Cheney State University in 1837 and Texas Southern University in 1947, the number of HBCUs grew at a steady pace. Begun first by religious bodies and later funded by the second Morrill Act in 1890, HBCUs appeared mostly in Southern states. The act established land-grant academic institutions to serve African Americans, primarily, but these institutions were public.[1]

Of the 109 Black schools that now operate on American soil, thirty-eight are private institutions, mostly religion-related, beginning with the founding of Wilberforce University, Wilberforce, Ohio, in 1856, followed by Shaw University in Raleigh, North Carolina, in 1865. These thirty-eight private Black institutions constitute the United Negro College Fund, Inc., the central purpose of which is to provide funding for scholarships and operating expenses for its member institutions.[2]

Deeply rooted in the rise and success of Black colleges—addressed later in this essay, along with the need for their preservation and support—is the very raison d'être for their existence. The mind is, indeed, "the measure of the man," a fact greatly compromised by physical and psychological constraints. The barbaric shackles of slavery effected, among other burdens, psychological and physical castration of the enslaved. Legally excluded from educational opportunities, Black Americans, both bond and "free," faced a dismal future. The separate but equal system did nothing to improve their academic plight, for institutions designated for Blacks only were never adequately funded or staffed, which essentially perpetuated Black exclusion from an excellent American education.

Into this yawning void stepped religious bodies with a worldview and a mission dedicated to liberating both body and soul. In the wake of this initiative by religious groups, private HBCUs grew steadily. Shaw University in Raleigh, North Carolina, is the oldest private Black university in the Southern states. The American Baptists, headquartered at Valley Forge, Pennsylvania, started this college for the newly "freed" slaves, a visionary and bold venture in those days, in the heart of Dixie.[3]

Shaw's philosophy of education is trumpeted by its founding motto, "That education and religion go hand in hand." Shaw's current mission statement, which declares that it is possible and desirable to be liberally educated for the world of work, concludes,

> Ultimately, the mission of Shaw University is the graduation of students with demonstrated competencies including a basic knowledge of the liberal arts and sciences, analytical, cognitive and communicating skills, an understanding of self, knowledge of planet earth, awareness of and commitment to values, and possession of specialized technical skills necessary for economic and professional success in their fields of choice."[4]

These components of Shaw's mission are critical constituents of liberal arts education.

The Carnegie Challenge, published by the Carnegie Corporation of New York, expands on these ingredients of liberal education by identifying intellectual vitality, integration of learning, multicultural and global perspective, accessibility, affordability, and a vision that can be shared. Value-laden themes characterize the Carnegie "Challenge." They further legitimize curricular offerings at HBCUs, whereas graduate research institutions have largely abandoned the classical tradition of liberal education in favor of specialization. HBCUs preserve the humanistic flavor that promotes integrative learning and civic responsibility.[5]

It is not accidental that HBCU graduates are among the most outstanding and effective Black leaders in the federal, state, and local arenas. One reason is the comprehensive exposure to the liberal arts that prepares Black students for the dual role of personal development and civic responsibility, a critical role for the Black intellectual. It is conceivable that W.E.B. DuBois's "Talented Tenth" and Booker T. Washington's economic focus have effected a marriage on Black campuses where political leadership, preparation for economic well-being, and general preparation for the world of work take place.

Graduation rates provide an accurate barometer for the vitality and indispensability of HBCUs. Also, their alumni excel in political leadership, public policy making, in the arts, athletics, entertainment, economics, and social change. Although little noticed, but very significant, most presidents of HBCUs earned their baccalaureate degrees at HBCUs.[6]

Graduation rates at these institutions provide convincing evidence of their viability. Although approximately only 17 percent of all Black students in American colleges enroll at Black colleges, these institutions are responsible for approximately 54 percent of those earning baccalaureate degrees. The following data prove the academic excellence of these institutions. HBCUs graduate 79 percent of those Blacks who later earn Ph.D.s; 46 percent of Black business executives; 50 percent of Black engineers; 80 percent of Black federal judges; 85 percent of Black physicians; 50 percent of Black attorneys; and 75 percent of Black military officers.

Most persuasive is the persistence of Black graduate students who earned undergraduate degrees at Black colleges. Studies show that they are more persistent in their pursuit of graduate studies in majority institutions than are White students. Further, according to these same studies, Black students who earn baccalaureate degrees in White institutions do not fare as well in graduate studies as those who graduate from Black colleges.[7]

The significant role of Black academic institutions has been established convincingly. Julian B. Roebuck and Komanduri S. Murty's *Historically Black Colleges and Universities: Their Place in American Higher Education* presents a cogent argument for the need to preserve and support these academic organizations adequately.[8]

The milieu-defining characteristic on Black campuses is what I choose to call a culture of ethnic consciousness, which runs the gamut from admissions to graduation. It includes campus orientation, residential experience, student support services, pedagogy, expectations, territorial integrity, and campus leadership, all reinforced by values that engage the student in a dialogue between morality and history. In this light John Dewey states, "Education is not a preparation for life. Education is life itself."

Accessibility to a Black college predisposes the student to hit the ground running. At such institutions, students feel a sense of territorial integrity, a right to be there, a feeling of ethnic pride. And although some come more academically prepared for college life than others, the common ground is a sense of authentic selfhood, an experience Black students rarely have on White campuses. Orientation to campus is routinized. At Shaw University, where I served as president for over fifteen years, orientation extends through freshman year. Its written code of conduct requires students to agree to:

1. hold in trust the traditions, practices, and laws that govern this university;
2. respect all properties that belong to others;
3. respect self while upholding the values, morals, discipline and cultural matrix upon which Shaw University was founded;
4. be always accountable for my personal, social, and professional conduct;
5. celebrate diversity, recognizing and affirming the dignity and worth of those who live, work, and study in this academic community;
6. discourage any behavior within self or among peers that would jeopardize the integrity and reputation of this university; and
7. foster an open and caring environment.[9]

In addition to the value-laden themes in this campus code, the residential experience on most Black campuses provides a laboratory where these commitments are given an environment that fosters growth and maturation. In this context, community sensibilities and cooperation, prerequisites to civic consciousness, take root. Here, discovery, learning in adjustment, and engagement in mutually rewarding enterprises, as well as social maturation, receive university-wide reinforcement. Together, all of these factors help reduce attrition and promote learning.

Student support services play a critical role on Black campuses. Special tutorials for the less academically prepared and specialized counseling sessions move students from marginal performance to dean's list at Shaw University. Also, affordable tuition and generous scholarships provide the only option for most Black students, whose annual median family incomes often fall below $25,000.

Sensitive pedagogy that demands high performance in an environment of expectancy and empathy stimulates learning. A teaching methodology that is both academically challenging and informed by different styles of student learning produces impressive results. Competent Black faculty of high caliber who choose to teach on Black campuses, despite lucrative offers from majority institutions, are driven by a sense of mission. They are accessible to students and committed to establishing a teaching/learning environment predicated on the proposition that most students can learn. Such a confidence-building approach, fueled by the catalyst of expectancy, fosters high retention and graduation rates.[10]

Similar ethnicity of faculty and students sharing a common history and destiny generates a pedagogy and curriculum dedicated to preparing students to develop a worldview more inclusive in scope and humanistic in character. Self-improvement and civic responsibility are inseparable twins in this grand academic enterprise. Whether tacit or expressed, the African American graduate is expected to be a freedom leader for his or her race. Speaking against the "system" that makes HBCUs necessary in the first place is often expected.

A consequence of this way of thinking is the likelihood of unshackling one's mind while leaving one physically and politically unfree. In this sense, "stone walls do . . . a prison make." Accordingly, civic consciousness and the inevitable drive for comprehensive freedom are natural results of liberated minds. It is not accidental that the Student Nonviolent Coordinating Committee (SNCC) was founded at Shaw University and that Martin Luther King, Jr., visited Shaw's campus when SNCC was organized in 1959. Nor must it be forgotten that four students from North Carolina A&T College initiated "sit-ins" at Woolworth's segregated lunch counters in Greensboro, North Carolina, in 1969, an act that spread throughout the South. It is not excessive to state that the socioeconomic-political landscape in America has radically changed as a direct result of Black leadership produced by HBCUs. Remember, Dr. Martin Luther King, Jr., was a graduate of Morehouse College.

So far, I have briefly described the rise and continued vitality of HBCUs. Their phenomenal success in terms of graduation rates, training of African American leaders, and developing the middle class has been cited, particularly by Williams and Ashley, who brilliantly summarize the argument in this essay:

> The accomplishments of Black colleges have been essential to the social, moral, humanitarian, and economic development of our country. Tradi-

tionally, revered institutions of higher learning were created in the seat of wealth and literary enlightenment. HBCU's, however, built themselves up from the muck and mire of poverty, illiteracy, opposition, and the vestiges of war. It is perhaps the honorable spirit of that struggle that continues to guide HBCU's and keeps them on track toward their mission to give young African Americans access to higher education when they otherwise might not have an opportunity. It is nearly impossible to overstate the educational, political and social contributions of historically Black colleges. With continued and increased support of alumni, foundations, corporations, and individual donors it is equally impossible to overstate the possibilities for HBCU's and their students.[11]

The final section of this essay addresses the fundamental question, Why do Black colleges perform so brilliantly? One word summarizes a multifaceted response—values. Every other collateral contributor to the rise, growth, and vitality of these institutions revolves around their unflinching commitment to the total development of the student, including the mental, physical, and spiritual dimensions of each student. Indeed, character education is the raison d'être of HBCUs. Of course, access, orientation to college, support services, service learning, affordability, and a congenial environment also play major roles in the education of African Americans.

But if these are critical contributors to this culture of learning, they are predicated on the mission of these institutions that views ethics, morality, and values as preconditions, as indeed, the foundations of learning.

Most of the thirty-eight Black colleges and universities constituting the United Negro College Fund, Inc. (UNCF) were founded by religious bodies and still maintain affiliations with their founders. They are liberal arts institutions, thus perpetuating the classical education tradition of humanistic studies that includes concerns with and commitment to civic responsibilities. According to Roebuck and Murty, "Liberal Arts education remained the domain of the Black private college."[12] It is the infusion of humanistic studies into these curriculums that prepares the Black student for his or her dual role of personal development and civic service.

Majority research universities have largely shorn their curriculums of the liberal arts by emphasizing specialization in the sciences and professional studies. Moving away from the classics by mimicking the German model, higher education focuses primarily on the cerebral at the expense of the attitudinal, producing highly trained technocrats devoid of humanistic values and altruistic concerns. This academic model represents a significant shift from earlier American education when religious values formed critical components of curricular offerings.

Such prestigious universities as Harvard, Yale, Princeton, and the University of Chicago gestated in the womb of religious values; although schools of divinity still exist on their campuses, except for divinity students, they are often considered empty gestures to the past. Universities have largely become technology-driven, commercial enterprises.

Commenting on the status of American higher education, Steven Muller, president emeritus of John Hopkins University, states, "We are now good at training a new generation not only to function with what we have discovered but to become discoverers themselves. The bad news is that the university has become godless. We must confront so many value issues, from euthanasia to genetic engineering, to weapons that can destroy the world, and we no longer have the strong religious point that we had in the nineteenth century. We have developed a new value system."[13]

Muller precisely describes the moral dilemma in American higher education. Warren Bryan Martin expands on this moral drift in our educational system: "Whereas, earlier, the chapel and the library symbolized the essential axis on which the university turns—the transcendental and the humanistic, the spiritual and the intellectual—now on most campuses the chapel seems to be more like a burnt-out volcano. It may have been at the center, full of light and heat, if not fire and smoke. But no longer. It may still be the focal point of campus architecture, but certainly not of campus life."[14]

Such indictment of American higher education does not apply to HBCUs, especially the private institutions. Chapels are much more than vestiges of the past. Weekly services challenge students to wrestle with life's most critical problems encountered at the intersection of the vertical (the spiritual) and the horizontal (the social dimensions of life). Here, theory and practice meet. It is this philosophy of education contained in Shaw University's founding motto: "That religion and learning go hand in hand," and, more recently rephrased, it is possible and necessary to be liberally educated for the world of work.

Shaw University is now known for its emphasis on character education. In 1993, after persuading the Board of Trustees that the university's curriculum should be more representative of its value orientation, I directed the faculty to infuse the curriculum with courses in ethics and values. Accordingly, all students enrolled at Shaw, regardless of their majors, must take nine credits in ethics, beginning in their sophomore year. To ensure academic integrity in teaching these courses, only faculty with terminal degrees in theology, philosophy, and ethics teach them. Ethics integrates methodologies from the normative and descriptive sciences in its effort to demonstrate the confluence of theory and practice. Thus, its practical emphasis makes it the science of conduct.

Courses in ethics and values engage students in grappling with such timely issues as euthanasia, genetic engineering, business ethics, journalistic ethics, ethical issues spawned by technology, and general professional ethics. Parents applauded when these courses were introduced, and alumni, who did not have an opportunity to take these courses during their years at Shaw, have asked why this program was not introduced sooner.

Preparing board and faculty for this radical restructuring of Shaw's curriculum, I proposed the following constructive statement: Free, functioning, and orderly societies are usually held together by values designed to promote the common good. In such societies, value-laden themes such as justice, self-discipline, honesty, courage, truth, responsibility, and the pursuit of excellence prevail.

When its traditional value system breaks down, a society slips into chaos, unable to function optimally. This chaotic state creates a numbness of social consciousness, resulting in loss of personal integrity and the critical societal bond of altruistic tendencies. Numerous patterns of antisocial behavior emerge, accompanied with the loss of moral leadership by such value-forming institutions as family, church, and the academy. When these institutions abandon or shed their traditional ideals, moral decline seems inevitable.

Such conditions create a crisis of belief precipitating social anomie and rebellion against usually accepted structures of justice and the common good. Widely recognized breakdowns of private and public morality in America—whether of corporate greed (Wall Street), family disintegration, the drug culture, youthful rebellion against authority, or lack of respect for life and limb, to name just a few of our social pathologies—testify to this crisis of belief regarding what is right, good, or appropriate. Absent from public policies, practices, and social programs are any agreement regarding the necessary ingredients to promote the common good. As selfishness and rugged individualism reign, despair of the dispossessed abounds as America continues it slippery slope and moral drift.

In keeping with the thrust of this essay, I argue that academic institutions significantly contribute to this moral confusion, for they offer no guiding vision, no moral ideal beyond self-interest. Curricular modifications in academe over the past century have replaced value studies and humanities courses with those that are largely vocational and professional. Accordingly, studies in moral philosophy have substantially disappeared or are restricted to departments of religious studies.

Thus, a steady stream of graduates departs our universities technically sophisticated, scientifically superior, cerebrally excellent, but devoid of any real concern for traditional values, altruism, fiscal integrity, tolerance, and mutual respect. Such notions as the common good and shared values are alien.

Into this moral void stepped Shaw University, with it liberal arts orientation, its value agenda committed to the total development of each student. Its curriculum encompasses the arts, social and natural sciences, humanities, business, computer science, education, religious studies, and ethics. Its moral thrust requires all students to earn credits in ethics and values; thus, the pre-med students learn about medical ethics, business students are exposed to business ethics, and all students understand the ethical dimensions of their major fields of study. Shaw's curriculum aims at quantitative and qualitative education with a focus on holistic development of each student. It is an educational program predicated on the philosophy of an inspired author who declares that true education is the "right development of the physical, intellectual, and moral powers" of students.[15]

Reinforcing this ethically infused curriculum are pragmatic engagements of students in service-learning situations, since one tends to become what one does. In this regard, Shaw University mimics Aristotelian philosophy that describes the ideal citizen as that political animal habituated by action, by doing. Shaw is in consonance with other HBCUs' requiring students to engage in service-learning assignments. In fact, most of these institutions now require service learning for graduation. An ethnically congenial population on Black campuses facilitates student involvement in a variety of campus and off-campus activities.

Shaw University's strong emphasis on character education received national recognition in the 2000 edition of *The Templeton Guide Regarding Colleges that Encourage Character Development*, which named Shaw's president among the fifty presidents who encourage character development on their campuses.

In conclusion, I propose that salient reasons for the rise, need, viability, and incontrovertible success of HBCUs reside in their accessibility, orientation, affordability, congenial/supporting environment, pedagogical sensitivities, and commitment to the total development of their students. This comprehensive pedagogy is driven by an anthropology that sees each person as a whole, and moral development as the catalyst. The goal of authentic education is the development of character.

Endnotes

1. Gloria Scott, "A Historically Black College Perspective," in *Civic Responsibility and Higher Education*, ed. Thomas Ehrlich (Phoenix, AZ: Onyx Press, 2000), 262–264.

2. Private HBCUs, now numbering thirty-eight, constitute the United Negro Fund, Inc. (UNCF).

3. The author of this essay served as president of Shaw University in Raleigh, North Carolina, from 1987 to 2002. The similarity of the president's and the university's names is purely coincidental

4. Explicitly stated or implied, mission statements of all HBCUs, especially private Black colleges, focus on holistic student development.

5. Carol M. Brooks, *Liberal Arts for a Global Society* (New York: Carnegie Corporation of New York, 1999).

6. Julian B. Roebuck and Komanduri S. Murty, *Historically Black Colleges and Universities: Their Place in American Higher Education* (Westport, CT: Praeger, 1993), 201–204.

7. Harold Wenglinsky, *Students at Historically Black Colleges: Their Aspirations and Accomplishment* (Princeton, NJ: Policy Information, Educational Testing Service, 1997), 16–17.

8. Roebuck and Murty, 203.

9. Quincy Scott, Jr., et al., *A Guide for a Successful Freshman Year Experience at Shaw University* (Littlejohn, MA: Tapestry Press, Ltd., 2002).

10. All HBCUs constituting the United Negro College Fund are federally accredited.

11. Juan Williams and Dwayne Ashley, *I'll Find a Way or Make One: A Tribute to Historically Black Colleges and Universities* (New York: Harper Collins, Publishers Inc., 2004), 305.

12. Roebuck and Murty, 27.

13. Steven Muller, "At 350, the US University Is Vast but Unfocused," *New York Times*, September 7, 1986, 14

14. Warren Bryan Martin, "History, Morality and the Modern University" in *Higher Education and the Modern University*, ed. Dennis L. Thompson (New York: Brigham Young University Press, 1991), 111–124.

15. Ellen G. White, *Fundamentals of Christian Education* (Nashville, TN: Southern Publishing Association, 1923), 57.

Quiester Craig

Quiester Craig, who received his B.A. in business from Morehouse College, his M.B.A. from Atlanta University, and his Ph.D. in accounting from the University of Missouri (in 1971), is a certified public accountant in Missouri and North Carolina.

Dr. Craig taught accounting at South Carolina State University, Lincoln University, and Florida A&M University before being appointed professor of accounting and dean of the School of Business and Economics at North Carolina A&T State University, Greensboro, North Carolina, in 1972. He also served as acting vice chancellor for fiscal affairs from May 1980 to June 1981. During his tenure, the undergraduate business programs at A&T received a unanimous vote for Association to Advance Collegiate Schools of Business (AACSB) accreditation in 1979, and the accounting program was the first program at a historically Black college or university to receive AACSB accreditation, in 1986.

He received the Distinguished Service Award of the National Association of Black Accountants in June 1985 and the Administrator of the Year Award from North Carolina A&T State University at the university's May 5, 1986, commencement. In March 1991, he was honored with the North Carolina Association of Certified Public Accountants' "Outstanding Educator Award," and in August 1994, he was recognized as the Beta Alpha Psi Accountant of the Year (Education) at its annual meeting.

Dr. Craig has served on committees of many professional organizations, including the Minority Recruitment Committee, the Standards Committee, and the Project Service Management Committee of the AACSB, among others. He also completed a four-year term on the AACSB Executive Committee and Board of Directors. In 1991, Dr. Craig was elected vice president/president-elect of the AACSB and assumed the position of AACSB president for 1992–93. In 1992, he became the first African American to assume the AACSB presidency in the organization's seventy-five-year history.

Dr. Craig serves on the Strategic Development Board of the College of Business and Public Administration at the University of Columbia-Missouri and on the boards of the Management Education Alliance, the Salvation Army, and the Greensboro Workforce Development Commission. He is also active in the United Way and other civic organizations.

8

FACTORS THAT INFLUENCE SUCCESS FOR AFRICAN AMERICAN STUDENTS

Institutions of Higher Education

The media, publications, and other materials are replete with examples highlighting or confirming the virtues, productivity, and quality of programs and activities of institutions of higher education (colleges and universities). To be certain, many of these institutions have a long history of outstanding achievements in teaching, research, and service.

The African American community and society in general should be proud of the presence and achievements of an increasing number of highly successful African Americans. For most, their achievements have been enhanced by the educational foundation of and experiences at a college or university.

Success in colleges and universities, as in life, frequently reflects individual choices and the relevance and significance of responses to the environment and other circumstances. African American students can choose to enroll at historically Black colleges and universities (HBCUs) and other institutions of higher education. Profiles are available for a number of successful African Americans who attended research or majority institutions. Just as important, if not more impressive, is the significant number and proportion of highly successful African Americans who attended HBCUs.

Colleges and universities are communities for learning, and the African American student must be aware of, prepared for, and committed to the requirements and expectations for success in that community. Awareness and preparation must begin early. Based on the heritage, mission, attitudes, resources, and environment, institutions and programs may differ, and the success of the enrolled African American student depends on many factors—some are common, but others are particularly associated with the particular institution. However, primary and often deciding factors are the student's confidence and pride in success and the recognition that education can be pivotal in a knowledge-based economy that is characterized by globalization, changing technology, and a diverse workforce.

Factors for Success

African American students succeed or fail in colleges and universities for different reasons. Some are successful because they have always been successful. Success breeds success with these students; it is in their minds, their culture, and their expectations. Success is the embodiment of their opportunities, background, and experiences before enrollment and can be evidenced as a driving characteristic during matriculation. These students probably will be successful regardless of the college or university they choose. Conversely, the limitations or absence of the opportunities, experiences, and characteristics noted above contribute to the relevance and significance of other determining factors for success for a larger number of African American students.

Many factors influence success, but the following seem to assume greater importance for many African American students:

1. Impact of parents and family
2. Prior academic preparation
3. Motivation to excel
4. Role models and mentors
5. College or university environment

Economic and Social Exposure

African American students come from a variety of economic and social backgrounds. The economic, professional, and social status of students' parents or family affect the opportunities for exposure and involvement with a diverse group of people or circumstances. Exposure is often associated with lifestyles, and students with highly successful economic or social family circumstances are more likely to be impressed or convinced of the role and significance of educational success to these circumstances. The nature of the exposure can influence students' maturity, stability, and knowledge of the world and the processes of the university community.

Prior Academic Preparation

The quality of academic and learning experiences at high schools or secondary schools provides meaningful support for further academic development. Attendance at selective private schools or public schools with a college-prep curriculum, quality administrative and educational processes, measurable objectives, and continuous assessment contribute to preparing students for success at the next level. The availability of a qualified and conscientious faculty, instructional technology and other resources, and definitive standards and expectations for learning also positively affect academic preparation. High schools and secondary schools should provide early opportunities for students to establish priorities and develop a persevering work ethic. Activities and involvements that develop leadership, communication, problem-solving, and other core skills provide premium benefits. Relationship building, including learning and interaction with students from other backgrounds and cultures, provides breadth and support for the transition to colleges and universities.

Motivation to Excel

Dreams, family, life experiences, competitiveness, and a desire for recognition and respect may be factors behind the motivation to excel. Others could include pride; peer influences; lifestyle aspired to, and expectations of parents, family and interested or influential teacher, counselor, or role model. However, since motivation is considered to come from within, African American students should develop or experience the desire to excel and firmly establish the importance of a successful record in an institution of higher education in the pursuit of excellence.

Role Models and Mentors

Based on economic, neighborhood, and other conditions, role models and mentors often provide invaluable support for African American students' academic and other success. In addition to fostering pride, inspiration, and encouragement, effective role models and mentors expand hope and confidence by students' association with achievers. Role models and mentors may be family members or other individuals in high schools, college/university campuses, business and industry, and the community. The resulting incentive and potential for academic success are enhanced if the role model or mentor has a similar background, and a college or university education was a factor for his or her success.

College or University Environment

One should never underestimate the role and importance of the college or university environment for the success of African American students. College and university students come from a variety of backgrounds and have different levels of preparation, experiences, motivations, and needs. The university is home away from home for at least four years, and students should recognize some sense of purpose, belonging, and direction. Successful students must also understand and commit to the expectations, work ethic, and other requirements for success.

Conversely, the university of enrollment must recognize the diverse range of students' backgrounds and needs. The university should also recognize that as its students and graduates succeed, the university succeeds. This is certainly true for African American students and graduates. Therefore, the university must be committed to the success of its students, and its environment must be characterized by attitudes, programs, services, and other attributes to maximally respond to that commitment.

Important considerations include the following:

- **Community**. The vision, mission, goals, objectives, and strategies, resources, and activities for achievement define the university. To foster student success, the university must be a community of learners with appropriate and responsive interactions among faculty, students, alumni, and other internal and external constituents.

    For African American students, the quality, experience, and commitment of the faculty are also primary factors for academic success. In addition to facilitators of learning and advancement of knowledge, the faculty can support the success of the student with their interest, patience, encouragement, and concern. Many students respond positively to the knowledge that the faculty really care about and depend on them to contribute to their success.

- **Enrollment**. The background, motivation, adaptability, and other characteristics of the enrollment can contribute to the learning environment and success of African American students. Since students are often influenced (good or bad) by their peers, develop allies, or become a part of a group, their academic success can be affected by the direction and activities of their chosen associations. Other students recognize the value of relationships but possess the motivation and individual initiative to foster success. Talented and motivated African American students may contribute to the learning environment, not only by the quality of their performances but also by other students' competitive reaction to their performance.

Experience and observation suggest that answers to the following questions can be relevant success indicators or predictors for the African American student:

1. Did the student seek enrollment because everyone in his or her high school class, group, or community planned to attend a college or university?
2. Did the student seek enrollment because of the mandate and/or expectations of parents and family?
3. Did the student seek enrollment because a quality and successful academic record is considered to be consistent and necessary to realize personal and professional goals, aspirations, and achievements?
4. Did the student seek enrollment at a particular institution because of the assessed capability of the institution to provide a competitive and quality learning experience or because of the not-so-lofty perception and expectations of the institution's standards?

The combination of these factors, as well as the other students enrolled, comprises the learning environment. Among other things, African American students' motivation and response to the circumstances and characteristics of the student body provide support for academic success.

Extracurricular Activities

Extracurricular activities and involvements are important extensions of the classroom and learning. What students learn from engagement and successful participation in activities outside the classroom promotes or sustains the tendency for success. Extracurricular activities contribute to the breadth and total development of the student and provide additional opportunities to enhance leadership, communication, team, and other core skills necessary for success. Students have also determined that associations and involvements create friends and initiatives for study, relaxation, and enjoyment that are beneficial for success and the quality of continued learning.

Advisement

A well-staffed and -defined advisement program is an essential element for the success of many African American students. Advisement plays an important role before and during enrollment and should provide information about and understanding and clarification of programs, activities, expectations, requirements, and strategies for success. Effective advisement should include a monitoring process by qualified and concerned professionals who demonstrate their caring about the success of the students. Many students appreciate and respond positively to this support system and to the belief that others are dedicated and committed to their success.

Financial Support and Services

Tuition increases and other educational expenses create barriers and challenges to the success of many African American students. The institution of enrollment, financial or economic status of the student, significance of advance planning, and level of commitment and sacrifice are relevant factors for consideration and concern.

In addition to family planning and support, it is imperative that students are aware of the existence of and eligibility and procedures for applying for academic scholarships and for federal, corporate, foundation, community, and other sources of educational funds. Students receive outstanding benefits from high school counselors who have access to this information and seek and encourage students to respond on a timely basis.

The existence and quality of financial support and services at the college or university can have varying effects on the academic success of African American students. A knowledgeable, patient, and understanding staff; information services; accessibility; and the institution's commitment to maximum financial resource development and allocation benefit eligible students. Academic success should be strengthened by the availability of financial support and services to reduce the concern of students and their families about needed funds for the current and next term and minimize the need for excessive outside employment.

Choices for Success

Post-civil rights African American students recruited by colleges and universities do not have personal knowledge of the time when the choice of college or university was severely limited. Fortunately, choices now are more numerous, but the decision of where to attend can be a primary factor in students' academic success.

Majority Institutions

Continuous social and legal efforts to dismantle the vestiges of segregation, requirements for federal funding, demands of alumni for successful athletic programs, and selected societal changes have all contributed to racial and ethnic diversity in many colleges and universities. As a result, a number of majority institutions now aggressively recruit talented African American students. These institutions offer scholarships and state-of-the-art facilities, emphasize research and other contributions of selected faculty, and highlight the benefits associated with name recognition and the success of noted alumni. An increasing number of African Americans choose to enroll in these institutions, and many possess the background, experiences, and other attributes referred to earlier to be successful.

Historically Black Colleges and Universities

Most HBCUs were born out of necessity, because America did not sufficiently recognize or accept qualified African American students' right to and need for equal choice of institutions of higher education. With very limited resources and those students only they wanted, HBCUs were not supposed to survive. However, HBCUs did not know this, and not only have they survived, but they have been bastions of accessibility, opportunity, and achievement. Indeed, this writer is a proud HBCU graduate.

It has been emphasized that the community of parents, family, faculty, counselors, role models, churches, and other organizations influences student success. HBCUs are a part of the educational and social fabric of these communities and have come to represent significant symbols of hope, pride, and perseverance. The century-old legacy of HBCUs and the multitude of their successful alumni provide compelling evidence of the intrinsic and other capacity of these institutions to encourage, support, inspire, and provide environments that foster confidence, technical competence, leadership opportunities, core skills development, and experience to support high academic achievement.

However, success is not automatic for African American students who enroll in an HBCU. Successful African American students must be conscious of the requirements and expectations for success and maintain their focus on and determination to attain excellence.

Conclusion

Because of the history, attitudes, and characteristics of society, the economy, and colleges and universities, it is obvious that the playing field is not always level. A quality performance in higher education can change at least the slant of that field. Regardless of the higher education institution they choose,

African American students must develop a thirst for learning. This thirst must be highlighted and sustained by establishing priorities, the feature of "learning to learn," and the grit and determination to be successful in the face of obstacles and distractions. One of my students who is focused on success recently quoted to me, "If it is to be, it is up to me."

James G. Wingate

James G. Wingate, president of Lemoyne-Owen College in Memphis, Tennessee, is a 1966 graduate of Allen University, Columbia, South Carolina, where he earned a bachelor of science in chemistry and mathematics. He also earned a master of science and a certificate of advanced study (CAS) in secondary education and educational administration from the State University of New York and went on to obtain his Ph.D. from Syracuse University, with emphases in higher education administration and supervision, quantitative methods, and systems analysis.

Dr. Wingate's educational career spans three decades, and his job titles have ranged from teacher to vice president at the community college campus and system levels, executive assistant to the chancellor at Winston-Salem State University, and, currently, the tenth president of LeMoyne-Owen College.

In addition to his doctoral dissertation, Dr. Wingate has ten publications of note and has presented many occasional papers on education, management, quantitative methods, teacher appraisals, and team building. He also frequently contributes editorials to several newspapers.

9

THE ROLE OF BLACK COLLEGES IN PROMOTING SELF-CONCEPT AND STUDENT CENTEREDNESS AMONG STUDENTS

Historically Black colleges and universities (HBCUs) are undoubtedly American treasures because of their unique contributions and their longevity. They have transcended mission and purpose while producing the Black middle class. A former president of the United Negro College Fund (UNCF) probably said it best: if HBCUs did not exist, we would need to invent them. The primary question that remains is, What contributions have they made and continue to make?

According to Drewry and Doermann (2001) HBCUs provide a "brief refuge from a tense and difficult world," the first bright opening to that world, a place of convocation and memory, a pipeline to graduate and professional schools. Students are said to enroll because of proximity to home, family tradition, affordability, and the presence of a significant number of Black faculty and staff who serve as surrogate parents, mentors, and supporters. Moreover, say Drewry and Doermann, these significant others typically have a track record of and reputation for working with students who exhibit a wide range of intellectual abilities and precollege levels of preparation.

What do these colleges and universities really do? The case can be made that they enhance the self-concept of African American students particularly, and, in so doing, they affect behavior positively. To make the case, one first needs to define terms and operationalize them accordingly. Let us begin with self-concept. Self-concept is a group of feelings and cognitive processes that are inferred from observed or manifest behavior . . . the person's total appraisal of his or her appearance, background and origins, abilities and resources, attitudes, and feelings that culminates as a directing force in the person's behavior (LaBenne and Greene 1969). Purkey (1970) states that once we have acquired an idea about ourselves, it serves to edit all incoming information and influences our future performance.

Wingate (1979) concludes that self-concept is not inalterably fixed among adult students and is related to academic achievement. Moreover, he found that significant others (friend, spouse, parents, teacher, counselor, minister)—those who are in a position to dole out rewards and punishment—contribute significantly to the development of self-concept. He demonstrated, using a group of financially disadvantaged students, that when one controls for self-concept, the relationships between achievement and other demographic and academic variables become insignificant. In other words, students who are encouraged, nurtured, coached, corrected, directed, and taught by caring and empathetic individuals generally go on to achieve academically and in life.

HBCUs have long been developers of minds, purveyors of dreams, and the pipeline to opportunity and success. They have helped students to overcome the ambivalence of youthful aspirations and focus on career goals and objectives. One needs only to examine how they do it. If one looks closely, one can discern their process, method, and even madness. A scenario will help to elucidate this claim. HBCUs work hard to ensure that potential students and their parents are aware of the benefits that can accrue to those who matriculate at an HBCU. This information is disseminated via brochures, college fairs, public service announcements, and paid advertisements.

Potential students typically are told about HBCUs by teachers, counselors, parents, or other relatives. They learn even more from college fairs, campus visits, and friends who attend these institutions. Currently attending students inform potential attendees that college life on an HBCU campus is a positive experience that offers opportunities to engage in various activities. If potential attendees are lucky, or their parents insist, they will have an opportunity to spend a weekend on campus and sample campus life before making a final decision.

On a weekend visit, these potential students meet student ambassadors and ask lots of questions. They sample the cafeteria food, attend an athletic event, watch a step show sponsored by the Greek letter sororities and fraternities, and meet faculty, staff, and the president. Based on their experiences and the promise of scholarships and financial aid, they decide to attend the specific college.

Their decision and subsequent notification are countered with a barrage of information and forms to be completed in a timely fashion. Depending on the specific HBCU, they may receive a telephone call from the president of the college, the purpose of which is to ensure that the new admits are reassured that they made the right choice. From that point on, the enrollment management staff works hard to ensure that these incoming students are properly advised.

Questions pertaining to financing the college-going experience are pervasive, so a number of financial aid counselors are deployed to assist these acceptees and their parents. Completing the registration process can be an awesome task for the neophyte; however, caring and nurturing staff members help to mitigate the process and circumstances. Thus the rite of passage is consummated.

Many African American students observe African American professionals functioning in decision-making capacities for the first time, with the possible exception of what they may have observed in church. For example, the chief financial officer (CFO) may devise a payment plan for a student, or the dean or provost may devise a course of study to address a specific need. One can expect these behaviors to be part of the norm at HBCUs.

During orientation sessions, these new students meet some of their professors. For the first time, students may come face to face with an African American linguist, mathematician, or chemist. They may see in person the actor or performer in a certain production. They can expect to see the band director of the famous marching 120 that has appeared on television during football halftime shows. Needless to say, these experiences build pride, excitement, college spirit, and a sense of belonging that these students may have not experienced to date. Students feel within their element, and, as a result, their ambitions are heightened and their self-concept is elevated.

Students begin classes with some trepidation, but they quickly determine that they are in for a new educational experience characterized by rigorous debate, fluid discussions, and collaborative learning. From their syllabi, they determine that they will read diverse authors, including a significant number of African American authors; they will write papers in which they will analyze, argue, and explicate; and they will encounter and solve dilemmas associated with identity. Summarily, they will learn about themselves and their culture quickly.

As they read their program paradigms and related materials, they note that there will be career fairs, service learning projects, internships, field studies, international experiences, and capstone projects. Life on the campus of an HBCU will truly constitute a sea change for these students. Several weeks pass with a flurry of activity that is punctuated by a hands-on lesson in time management. In a short time, these students take several exams, participate in student government, attend meetings with the housing council and security, and attend no less than four college functions. One could conclude that the intervention of a number of variables that build on one another and the comfort level of the student have greatly facilitated the students' adjustment to college.

Since many of the individuals whom they met on their initial visit have come to know them and have tended to nurture, support, and keep them engaged and focused, most of these students will return for a second semester. What has happened with these students is indicative of what most colleges attempt, but what HBCUs tend to do better. The following three examples illustrate this success.

John Smith (all individual and college names are fictitious) represents the third generation of his family that has attended Brooks College. John's parents and grandparents met at this college. John grew up hearing his parents' stories of the glory days of Brooks and was convinced from an early age that Brooks was the best place for him. In view of this, he only took a cursory look at other HBCUs.

He feels a bit of pressure to succeed because he feels obligated to uphold the family tradition. On the other hand, he feels good about the fact that some Brooks faculty and staff still remember his parents. The extended family concept is alive and well. Because of relationships of this type, John is compelled to make contact with the career services director, the director of international programs, and the head of the summer school. In addition, members of his father's fraternity have been cultivating him since his arrival on campus, and he has observed since his first day on campus that female students outnumber male students three to one. Given the nature of his engagement, there is little doubt that he will persist.

Donnell Thompson's situation is a bit different. His mother passed away during his senior year in high school, and his father abandoned him shortly after his mother's death. Thanks to his high school principal and a counselor, he received support and a scholarship to attend Brooks College. When he enrolled in Brooks, the dean of students and the freshmen class advisor befriended him. The college became his home, and during holidays, he divided his time between the dean and advisor. He was mature beyond his chronological years, and, due to his ingenuity, he soon acquired a part-time job and a used automobile. He had succeeded in obtaining what college students call "walking-around money." Given his confidence, ingenuity, and aggressiveness, there is no doubt that he will succeed in the nurturing and supportive environment of which he is a part.

Some stories at HBCUs differ significantly from these two. Take, for example, the case of Mary Theron, who is living away from home for the first time and is grossly abusing her newfound freedom. May was caught smoking pot and using alcohol. Subsequently, she was suspended from campus housing and told to seek counseling.

The case of Tarey from Chicago is more tragic. On several occasions he was observed boasting about his former life as a gang banger. On campus, he had attempted to intimidate some students and extort from others. He was summoned to appear before the school's Judicial Council and suspended for a semester. He pleaded and cried, saying he could not go back to Chicago because he would be lost to the streets. He just could not return home.

He appealed his case to the dean of students, who overturned the suspension. She required him to have weekly meetings with the college's chaplain, assigned a mentor to him, and directed him to attend chapel services and the church of his choice. He agreed to the sanctions, and the dean is taking the situation one day at a time with respect to Tarey's rehabilitation.

The cases cited here are true stories that demonstrate the commitment of some of the individuals who work at HBCUs. These individuals realize that sometimes it takes going beyond the call of duty to get a student to persist to graduation. Administration and staff frequently confirm that the village concept has been expanded to the academy, and colleges that embrace the concept tend to have better retention and graduation rates.

The role of HBCUs is changing due to changes in the educational landscape in general. HBCUs have truly done so much for so many; they are now compelled to reinvent themselves and do even more without any significant increase in resources. John Dewey (1963) theorized that experience constituted the means and goal of education: "Education in order to accomplish its ends both for the individual learner and for society must be based upon experience which is always the actual life experience of some individual." HBCUs fulfill their various missions by keeping the students at the center of their operation. Epitomizing student centeredness is what separates HBCUs from other colleges. Taking time to assess and learn the needs of their customers and serving these needs accordingly are the operating principles that continue to validate their purpose and continued popularity. Some supporters of HBCUs describe this phenomenon as making bricks from straw or polishing rocks into diamonds.

In summary, HBCUs constitute 3 percent of U.S. institutions of higher education; enroll 16 percent of the Black students who attend college; and produce 27 percent of the African American graduates with bachelor's degrees in science and engineering annually. Approximately 35 percent of the African Americans who earn doctorate degrees obtained their baccalaureate degree from HBCUs (Wagener and Nettles 1998). This success can be accounted for by the following: a team effort by the faculty, staff, students, and administration; fostering continuous improvement in academic achievement and graduation rates on the part of faculty; fostering strong faculty/student relationships; cultivating a sense of history; and perpetuating an ethos of academic achievement that is spiritually and culturally and historically based (Wagener and Nettles 1998). Black students at HBCUs generally are more confident, more engaged, and interact more with their peers, faculty members, and staff. As a result, these students are more successful.

Since these colleges are so dependent on tuition for operation and survival, there is a definite need for better public policy pertaining to financial aid. Without attention to details associated with financial aid, they will be unable to assist many students. Grants, scholarships, and loans are a way of life for the majority of students attending HBCUs. In recent years, loans have increased significantly, resulting in mounting debt for graduates. Many HBCU presidents attest to the fact that their work is truly a calling, and they must not be dissuaded from it by zealous naysayers parading as do-gooders who would limit or terminate their existence by defining, advancing, and supporting nonviable futures. To continue the work and missions of these great institutions, more supportive individuals are needed who understand, appreciate, and respect the African American experience. Needless to say, in the words of Drewry and Doermann (2001), these colleges only need to stand and prosper.

References

Dewey, John. 1970. *Experience & education.* New York: Collier Books.

Drewry, Henry N., and Humphrey Doermann. 2001. *Stand and prosper.* Princeton, NJ: Princeton University Press.

LaBenne, Wallace D., and Bert I. Greene. 1969. *Educational implications of self concept theory.* Los Angeles: Goodyear Publishing Company, Inc.

Purkey, William Watson. 1970. *Self-concept and school achievement.* Saddle River, NJ: Prentice-Hall, Inc.

Wagener, Ursula, and Michael T. Nettles. 1998. *It takes a community to educate students.* New York: Heldref Publications.

Wingate, James G. 1979. Self-concept, selected demographic and academic variables, student expectations, and student experiences as they relate to attrition in a compensatory education program for adults. PhD diss., Syracuse University.

Henry Ponder

Henry Ponder was appointed eighteenth president of Talladega College by the Talladega College Board of Trustees and assumed leadership of the 134-year-old historically Black institution in May 2002.

A distinguished educator and noted economist, Dr. Ponder formerly served as president and CEO of the National Association for Equal Opportunity in Higher Education (NAFEO), a nonprofit, voluntary, membership organization of 188 historically and predominately Black colleges and universities.

Dr. Ponder received a bachelor's degree from Langston University, a master's degree from Oklahoma State University, and a doctorate from Ohio State University.

An economist of national and international stature, Dr. Ponder has served as a consultant for the Federal Reserve Bank of New York, Philadelphia National Bank, Chase Manhattan Bank, the Irving Trust Company, and Omaha National Bank. He also served for six years on the Board of Directors of the Federal Reserve Bank of Richmond, Virginia (Charlotte branch), the last two years as chairman. Additionally, he served on the Board of Directors of the J.P. Stevens & Co., Inc.; Suntrust Bank of Nashville, Tennessee; SCANA Corporation of South Carolina; and Community College of the Air Force. He currently serves on the board of the ETV Endowment of South Carolina.

Dr. Ponder has a long, distinguished career in higher education. He served as president of Fisk University in Nashville, Tennessee, for twelve years; president of Benedict College in Columbia, South Carolina, for eleven years; and vice president of academic affairs at Alabama A&M University.

Previously, he served as dean of the college at Alabama A&M University in Normal, Alabama; chairman of the Department of Business and Economics of Fort Valley State College, Fort Valley, Georgia; and chairman and assistant professor of the Department of Agri-Business at Virginia State College in Petersburg, Virginia.

Dr. Ponder has received numerous accolades and awards, including "Distinguished Alumnus Awards" from Langston, Oklahoma State, and Ohio State universities. He was the recipient of the Henry G. Bennett Distinguished Service Award from Oklahoma State University and was inducted into the Oklahoma State University Alumni Hall of Fame.

In 1986, Dr. Ponder was selected as one of the "One Hundred Most Effective College Presidents in the United States," and in May 2000, he was selected as one of the "100 Most Influential Black Organization Leaders" by *Ebony* magazine.

WHAT MAKES AFRICAN AMERICAN STUDENTS SUCCESSFUL AT HISTORICALLY BLACK COLLEGES AND UNIVERSITIES

The First-Year Program

Introduction

Historically Black colleges and universities (HBCUs) have a proven history of service and achievement. It bears remembering that, before the War Between the States, it was illegal to teach African Americans to read and write in the South. Most of the HBCUs are located in the South; therefore, they have had less than one hundred fifty years of educational history. When one considers the hostile environment of the South, the achievements of these colleges and universities are even more outstanding.

Most of the earlier HBCUs initially taught students to read; they were the equivalent of elementary schools. These graduates went out into the hinterlands and taught the masses of African Americans to read and write.

Next, these colleges and universities advanced to teaching through the junior high school level. These graduates went out and taught the African American masses.

The next level of instruction for these colleges and universities was high school. After high school, they moved to the junior college level. It was a few more years before HBCUs began teaching at the four-year college level.

Mission

Most of the HBCUs were founded to provide education for the formerly enslaved. Many of these institutions' charters reflect sensitivity to equality and learning. They have inclusive language to admit *all* citizens regardless of race or creed. Each charter states this differently; however, the inclusive language is in all of them.

The printed mission statements of HBCUs may differ in phraseology, but all have common themes:

1. fostering leadership;
2. education of the whole person;
3. communication—oral and written;
4. value of liberal education;
5. knowledge and appreciation of different cultures;
6. service to community; and
7. moral and spiritual values.

Open Admissions

It is important to state that not all HBCUs have an "open admissions" policy. Some, in fact, are very selective in their admissions policies. That said, the majority of HBCUs do have "open admission" policies, and they are *proud* of those policies. They boast that they are accepting the reality of high school graduates' educational level.

Many college educators lament that the secondary education system in the United States does not prepare its graduates for college adequately. These HBCUs take the position that they are addressing the problem rather than complaining about it.

Open admissions as practiced by HBCUs means having admission policies that are "inclusive" rather than "exclusive." The belief is that any high school graduate is entitled, by birthright, to an opportunity to seek a baccalaureate degree. However, success is determined by effort.

Open admission fosters a cooperative, team effort and a helping attitude among all enrolled students—high and moderate achievers. Students imitate this caring attitude and help each other succeed.

Faculty Commitment

The faculty at HBCUs has bought into the notion of accepting students where they are and preparing them to where they ought to be at graduation.

Faculty members have regular office hours, approximately fifteen per week, primarily for one-on-one meetings with students. Should the student have a classroom problem, the teacher can aid the student in getting to the real cause and solution. Teachers do this willingly and without complaint; they see it as part of their teaching responsibility.

Faculty members also take a few minutes after each class to respond to students. Sometimes, when these impromptu sessions interfere with the next class scheduled for that room, the teacher continues the session in the hall. Students appreciate this attention and are motivated to be successful.

Some teachers have "after hours" study sessions for their students, which often occur after 5:00 PM on weekdays and on Saturday mornings. To encourage attendance at the sessions, the teacher usually provides refreshments. The students interpret this as a caring attitude for their success.

At HBCUs *teaching* generally takes precedence over *research*. Again, I must emphasize that research is important at HBCUs. Some are doing cutting-edge research; for example, one HBCU discovered a heretofore *unknown* planet.

The point here is that teaching is considered to be very important at HBCUs. Class time spent on research is student-oriented: the student selects a research project, and the teacher guides the student through it. Research takes place, but teaching is the most important element.

The teacher and student are engaged in many hours of one-on-one contact, which reinforces the message—"My teacher is concerned for me as a person and wants me to succeed." And, incidentally, some quality research is conducted.

The First-Year Program at HBCUs

The preceding sections discussed the general climate for students at HBCUs. Students are exposed to these relationships from orientation to graduation, all of which help students to conclude that the college or university is interested in them and cares about their success. These relationships are reinforced as students progress toward graduation. All students are enriched, enhanced, and encouraged to succeed in this caring atmosphere, through completion of the baccalaureate degree.

The first-year program at HBCUs is a formal one, designed to help ensure success in the pursuit of a baccalaureate degree. It ranges in duration from one week to a full year.

All colleges and universities do not have the same program; however, many share these common elements:

1. early contact with students, via letters;
2. early registration;
3. orientation week;
4. academic advising;
5. counseling;
6. early academic warnings;
7. mid-term grades;
8. assembly program;
9. orientation seminar; and
10. probation counseling.

Early Letters

Once potential students are accepted by the college or university, they begin to receive letters from the institution. The first letter notifies them that they have been accepted to the institution. This letter congratulates them on their acceptance and states how fortunate the institution is to have been chosen by them. This letter is from the admissions office.

The next letter is from the dean of the school of their major. The dean states how fortunate he or she is to have the student as a major. The letter also lists outstanding graduates of the school and generally closes by saying, "We anxiously anticipate your enrollment."

Prospective students also receive a letter from the chair of the department of their major expressing how "Glad we are to have you. You are an ideal student, and we will all be proud to teach you."

The vice president for academic affairs also writes to the prospective student to inform the student about some of the recent achievements of the faculty and students, including national and international honors. One example would be a recent Rhodes Scholar.

The president of the institution will write the prospect as well, perhaps furnishing the names, addresses, and telephone numbers of alumni in the area. The prospect is asked to contact these alumni and begin to build a relationship.

Letters from the president of the student government association contain information on student activities and invite the prospect to become active in student government. Any outstanding organizational achievements are noted.

Most HBCUs have a Miss and Mr. "College/University"; the prospective student receives a letter from each of these indicating some of the social events available to students and inviting the prospect to come prepared to participate.

All of these letters are meant to encourage students to succeed. The subliminal message is that this college or university is adequately equipped and wants to help these students achieve their goals.

Early Registration

Many HBCUs invite accepted students to come to campus, along with their parents, for one or two days in June or July. A small fee is charged, which includes room and board for the one or two days.

There are sessions with the parents to clear up any issues or questions they have concerning college life. College or university administrators are present to help relieve parents' anxieties and to reassure them that their children will be taken care of.

Various administrators meet with the students they will come in contact with. The financial aid administrator explains the nuances of the financial aid process and makes it clear that rules and guidelines must be followed if financial aid application is to be offered.

The business office administrator explains the college or university costs, taking time to explain all costs so they are understood, for example, how the bill is to be paid, penalties for late payments, deferred payments, and payment plans.

The housing administrator provides information about when housing is available, when the residence halls are closed, and the rules governing the residence halls.

The vice president for academic affairs discusses fall class registration and advising, class loads, and class attendance requirements.

All of the administrators stress the importance of doing one's best. The faculty and staff of the college or university will do all they can to make the college experience successful.

Orientation Week

Generally, first-year HBCU students report to the campus a week before upperclass students are scheduled to arrive. This provides time to orient first-time students to campus life without the confusion and misdirection of returning students.

First-year students receive their class schedules and take campus tours, which are usually conducted by a select group of upperclass leaders. These leaders identify all of the buildings and highlight campus landmarks.

The library is one of the main stops on the campus tour. The librarian explains how to use the library and what services it offers, and tour leaders stress the importance of time spent in the library and discuss the use of the library study rooms.

Tours also include the surrounding areas—shopping areas, churches, and other social places. The idea is to orient the first-year students to their surroundings.

Perhaps the most important part of orientation week occurs the last night, when there is a formal, serious, and solemn induction ritual. On this night, first-year students come to the campus chapel in formal dress for a program presenting the institution's illustrious graduates. The students repeat the oath of induction into the student body of the college or university, and the speaker admonishes the students to live up to the school's expectations. After the ceremony, the audience congratulates and greets the students. The object is for first-year students to strive to become what other graduates have become. They leave the ceremony believing they can and must become successful citizens.

Academic Advising

All students are assigned a faculty advisor who helps students with their academic needs, including selecting the appropriate courses and the right number of courses to take. These advisors are available to the students throughout the students' college experience.[1]

Counseling

Students are introduced to counseling center personnel early on and are encouraged to seek counseling for all difficulties. Counseling center staff are on call at all times to help solve any student problem, be it academic, social, or personal.

Early Academic Warnings

Faculty members know which of their students are in their first year. These faculty send grade reports to the first-year program staff after two to four weeks of school, who then contact and counsel students with difficulties and

---

[1] Claflin University, 2003–2006 Catalog, 75.

provide them with tutors, extra class sessions, and help at the computer lab. These extra sessions are conducted by upperclass students.

Mid-Term Grades

In addition to sending mid-term grades to first-year program staff, as mentioned above, teachers at HBCUs give mid-term grades to students to let them know where they stand halfway through the semester.

Assembly Program

The first-year assembly program is designed to inform first-year students. While concerned with the academic development of students, the college or university, through this program, also provides access to social, cultural, personal, career, historic, and civic information designed to pique students' interest to lead to further examination of these and other topics.

The assembly generally meets for one hour each week; students are usually required to attend each session, and they receive academic credit for doing so.

The assembly program offers students a consistent model of the basics of a formal program. After attending for a year, they are able to organize a program for any event.

Upperclass students and first-year program staff initially demonstrate the format of the assembly, which is then continued by students from the current first-year class. This intentional demonstration-to-action component permits students to see themselves and their peers as *doers*, not merely recipients, of the program. Their participation seeks to continue the peer-to-peer structure begun during orientation week.

The assembly format intentionally includes career/personal/social design, so that students begin to *present* a construction of a template for *future* use in their personal, professional, and social lives.

Students are required to wear business attire to the assembly programs to begin accustoming them to the requirements of career and adulthood.

Orientation Seminar

The orientation seminar is a credit course, lasting for one term or an entire school year, taught by the finest and most sensitive faculty, staff, and administrators, The seminar is specifically meant to assist first-year students with their transition to college. The orientation peer leader, orientation teacher, and first-year student form a team, thus providing a source for first-year students to get accurate information and create timely meetings to deal with issues of relevance to them. Many first-year students form mentor relationships with both teachers and other students throughout their college experience.

Probation Counseling

At the beginning of the second term, all first-year students' grades are sent to the first-year program staff, and all students with grade point averages (GPAs) below the college or university's acceptable standard are called in for conferences. These students are counseled and put on a schedule of tutoring and special seminars to help them get back on track.

Summary

HBCUs check into the backgrounds of their students; they want to know as much about these individuals as possible, including their cultural, spiritual, and family background. This information enables the institution to know more about the needs of their students. With this information in hand, the college or university is more capable of making its students' college experience more challenging, meaningful, and successful.

Today colleges and universities are expected to do more for their students. HBCUs accept this challenge willingly; they accept students at their own "reality level." They accept students where they are academically and proceed to educate them to the level where they ought to be at graduation. These institutions feel this responsibility to their students, their parents, their alumni, the community, the nation, and the world. They are committed to making potential tax-burden citizens into tax-paying citizens.

If HBCUs are to accomplish this, their first-year programs take on added significance. All of the activities of these programs are designed to motivate first-year students to succeed. To ensure student success, the first-year program attempts to inculcate in all students the desire to:

1. be the best students they can be;
2. be the best people they can be;
3. be competitive in society;
4. earn a comfortable living;
5. have a successful career;
6. live morally and spiritually upright lives;
7. think logically and clearly; and
8. read and interpret information.

This is not an exhaustive list, but it is an example of what the first-year program is designed to accomplish. Each college or university first-year program is different; however, their objectives are basically the same—to encourage students to succeed.

Embodied within the mission of HBCUs is the historical desire to provide an opportunity for students to earn a baccalaureate degree. Thus, they aim, through the first-year program, to:

1. provide first-year students with intensive educational experiences that will help them to understand and appreciate their roles as university students;
2. introduce first-year students to the tools necessary for academic and personal success at the institution;
3. provide first-year students with the necessary motivation to maximize their efforts and take responsibility for their own learning;
4. prepare and offer the diagnostic mechanisms that will result in proper placement of first-year students and provide them with accommodating program and services; and
5. monitor the progress of first-year students and provide enhancement activities tailored to their specific needs throughout the year.[2]

If a college/university graduate can perform as described above, to paraphrase Rudyard Kipling, "Yours is the Earth and everything that's in it, and—which is more—you'll be a woman/man, my daughter/son."

[2] Ibid., 76.

Orlando L. Taylor

Orlando L. Taylor, a national leader in graduate education and within his discipline, is vice provost for research, dean of the Graduate School, and professor of communications at Howard University. Dr. Taylor has served as chair of the Board of Directors of the Council of Graduate Schools and as president of the Northeastern Association of Graduate Schools, the National Communication Association, and the Consortium of Social Science Associations. He is a national leader and spokesperson for preparing the next generation of college and university faculty members and for enhancing access and equity in higher education. During his career at Howard, Dr. Taylor has raised millions of dollars in research, training, and program development grants from federal and private sources and has published numerous journal articles, monographs, book chapters, and books on communication disorders, sociolinguistics, educational linguistics, intercultural communication, and graduate education.

Dr. Taylor received his bachelor's degree from Hampton University and his Ph.D. from the University of Michigan.

Terrolyn P. Carter

Terrolyn P. Carter is coordinator of Howard University Graduate School's Preparing Future Faculty Program and an administrator in the university's Alliance for Graduate Education and the Professoriate, a project of the National Science Foundation designed to increase the number of underrepresented minority Ph.D. recipients and faculty members in science, engineering, technology, and mathematics. She also serves as a coordinator for an innovative project funded by the U.S. Department of Education to develop faculty Learning Communities at four historically Black colleges and universities (HBCUs), including Howard, Jackson State, Talladega, and Xavier University of Louisiana.

Dr. Carter received her undergraduate degree from Xavier University of Louisiana and her Ph.D. in rural sociology from the University of Missouri. She has held teaching appointments at both Missouri and Howard, principally in sociology and education and human development, and she has published on topics pertaining to doctoral education and faculty preparation. Dr. Carter represents the Howard University Graduate School on the Research University Consortium on the Scholarship of Teaching and Learning.

II

FUTURE FACULTY FOR THE NATION'S HISTORICALLY BLACK COLLEGES AND UNIVERSITIES

Challenges and a Model for Intervention

In many ways, the faculty is the core of any institution of higher learning. Students come and go, as do many administrators, but, it is the faculty, especially the tenured faculty, that gives substance to an institution and provides its intellectual ethos and character.

Also, faculties are the stewards of their respective disciplines within institutions. Through their teaching and facilitation of learning, they prepare the next generation of leaders and professionals. Through their research and creative activities, they are the creators of new knowledge. And, through their engagement with communities, they provide service designed to enhance the quality of life for humankind.

The nation's historically Black colleges and universities (HBCUs) are no different. They depend on their faculties to do these same things; however, they also provide another dimension. By virtue of the fact that many of their faculty members are African Americans, HCBUs provide a cultural umbrella under which their largely African American student bodies experience a "safe haven" for their academic and research pursuits, without having to deal with the burdens of marginalization, dismissal, and, sometimes, the discrimination often reported at predominantly White institutions (PWIs).

Today, the 105 HBCUs enroll approximately 14 percent of all African American students in higher education, although they constitute only 3 percent of the almost forty-one hundred institutions of higher education in the United States. In 2000, these institutions accounted for approximately 24 percent of all African American students enrolled in four-year colleges. They awarded 24 percent of all baccalaureate degrees to African Americans (25,508 of 107,891); 13 percent of all master's degrees (4,722 of 35,625) and 14 percent of all doctoral degrees (225 of 1,656).

Faculty at HBCUs

In 2002, the Frederick Patterson Institute of the United Negro College Fund (UNCF), the organization that raises funds on behalf of thirty-four private HBCUs, reported that African Americans comprised a little more than 60 percent of the faculties of HBCUs, with African American males accounting for 33 percent and African American females accounting for 29 percent (see table 1).

Further examination of this rather surprising finding reveals that African Americans are a minority on some HBCU campuses. For example, at Xavier University of Louisiana, only sixty-eight "Blacks" are listed among the 226 faculty members (30 percent). At Tougaloo College (Mississippi), only eleven "Blacks" (17 percent) are reported in its sixty-four-member faculty.

Many might be surprised to learn the level of diversity in HBCU faculties. However, racial/ethnic diversity has been a significant—and celebrated—aspect of the HBCU culture almost since the inception of HBCUs. Indeed, HBCUs should be recognized as having perhaps the most diverse faculties in the United States. A strong argument can be made—and these authors make one—to support the notion that it is a good thing for a largely African American student body to have access to faculty members of different races, ethnicities, and nationalities. In the HBCU environment, a significant number of America's African American college students are privileged to have professors who bring diverse perspectives. The data on faculty diversity at HBCUs suggest that faculty of any race can facilitate academic success of African American students if they have high expectations and if they commit themselves to mentoring and enhancing student learning.

At the same time, it might be argued that in institutions with a targeted population focus—African Americans or women, for example—the faculties of such institutions should have a critical mass of faculty from that targeted group. Those making such an argument might claim that faculty from the targeted group can serve as role models for the targeted students and, therefore, are likely to better understand the issues students might face as they pursue their education. This argument has merit, although we hasten to add that it is fallacious to believe that only African American faculty members can serve as role models or mentors to African American students.

Nonetheless, those who hold the latter view, as do we, are particularly concerned about the declining presence of African American faculty members on HBCU campuses; these institutions are losing a critical attribute that has attracted many African American undergraduate students and their families. Specifically, that attribute is the presence of a critical mass of African American faculty role models to mentor their predominantly African American students and to provide the nurturing and support systems that address the unique challenges many of these students face in attending college (for example, low self-esteem and expectations, inadequate academic preparation, and limited social and cultural capital). Indeed, the case could be made that without a critical mass of African American faculty, HBCUs would eventually lose their institutional ethos and become challenged to remain viable as educational institutions. After all, one would find it hard to imagine Smith College (Massachusetts) with few to no female faculty, Notre Dame with no Catholic faculty, or Brandeis with no Jewish faculty! Would these institutions lose their institutional ethos? Would they, therefore, lose their attractiveness to their traditional constituencies? These are questions that HBCUs must ponder—and address—in the years ahead.

The decline of African American faculty at HBCUs is one of the unintended consequences of racial integration in the United States. During the period of forced racial segregation in the Southern states and de facto segregation and discrimination at Northern colleges and universities, African American doctoral recipients and those aspiring to the college/university professoriate once found HBCUs to be "the only game in town." However, as desegregation has occurred—and the pipeline of new African American Ph.D. recipients has remained shockingly low—demand far exceeds supply. As late as 2003, African Americans still earned barely over 4 percent of the forty thousand Ph.D.s awarded annually in the United States, and almost half of these degrees were in education and the social sciences. In some biological science, physical science, engineering, technology, and mathematics fields, these percentages dip to 1 percent—or less!

In any case, new African American Ph.D. recipients and professorial aspirants today find themselves with far more choices than ever. The approximately four thousand traditionally White institutions (TWIs) are often willing and able to make more attractive offers than can HBCUs to hire a

TABLE 1
Racial/Gender Composition of Full-Time Faculty, Fall 2002

Institution	Black			Non-Black			Grand Total
	Male	Female	Total	Male	Female	Total	
Barber-Scotia College	12	5	17	8	1	9	26
Benedict College	41	46	87	25	10	35	122
Bennett College	12	19	31	10	11	21	52
Bethune-Cookman College	33	37	70	38	28	66	136
Claflin University	30	15	45	21	14	35	80
Clark Atlanta University	121	93	214	69	21	90	304
Dillard University	39	54	93	19	19	38	131
Edward Waters College	16	12	28	7	6	13	41
Fisk University	17	18	35	13	7	20	55
Florida Memorial College	31	31	65	28	14	42	107
Huston-Tillotson College	6	11	17	10	9	19	36
Interdenom. Theological Ctr	5	8	13	6	0	6	19
Jarvis Christian College	7	5	12	11	2	13	25
Johnson C. Smith University	20	29	49	26	8	34	83
Lane College	14	5	19	17	7	24	43
Lemoyne-Owen College	18	18	36	14	4	18	64
Livingstone College	13	20	33	8	4	12	45
Miles College	30	27	57	24	6	30	87
Morehouse College	126	35	161	0	0	0	161
Morris College	10	20	30	12	6	18	48
Oakwood College	27	43	70	21	12	33	103
Paine College	21	25	46	21	5	26	72
Paul Quinn College	14	10	24	8	5	13	37
Philander Smith College	14	11	25	9	10	19	44
Rust College	17	9	26	12	5	17	43
St. Augustine's College	39	21	60	9	7	16	76
St. Paul's College	15	6	21	6	5	11	32
Shaw University	41	20	61	19	5	24	85
Spelman College	30	75	105	21	29	50	155
Stillman College	22	18	40	20	13	33	73
Talladega College	8	14	22	16	7	21	45
Texas College	7	8	15	8	4	12	27
Tougaloo College	10	1	11	18	36	53	64
Tuskegee University	74	48	122	77	19	96	218
Virginia Union University	23	25	48	25	11	36	84
Voorhees College	22	13	35	6	2	8	43
Wilberforce University	15	15	30	11	9	20	60
Wiley College	12	11	23	24	3	27	50
Xavier University of LA	34	34	68	97	61	158	226
Total	1,046	915	1,964	794	424	1,216	3,182
% of Grand Total	33%	29%	62%	25%	13%	38%	100%

Source: Frederick Patterson Institute of UNCF.

handful of African American faculty as they seek to meet their "diversity goals." In this environment, HBCUs are increasingly challenged in their efforts to recruit and retain a critical mass of African Americans with Ph.D.s to replace aging faculty and launch new programs.

Howard University's Leadership Role in Preparing Future Faculty

Recognizing the need to increase African American Ph.D. productivity and the need to prepare the next generation of faculty of all races to meet new challenges in faculty roles and responsibilities (for example, a focus on learning—not teaching—the uses of technology, the importance of outcomes assessment, and the scholarship of teaching and learning), Howard University has launched a significant effort to address the shortage of African American faculty, generally, and at HBCUs in particular. Howard is the nation's largest on-campus producer of African American Ph.D. recipients and a pioneer in the national Preparing Future Faculty movement.

In recent years, Howard has convened two major national symposia on this topic, one in collaboration with the U.S. Department of Education and the other in collaboration with the Lilly Endowment/UNCF HBCU Initiative. It has also launched a component of its nationally acclaimed Preparing Future Faculty (PFF) Project, a special HBCU initiative designed to prepare a cohort of Ph.D. candidates with the tools needed to be effective faculty members at HBCUs.

The Howard PFF model also recognizes that in the last decade or so, achieving faculty diversity has been at the forefront of many major higher education issues. Yet, it is still one of the least successful elements of institutional efforts (Smith 1996). Faculty diversity in higher education is important not only to achieve national social justice goals, but also to meet future workforce needs of an aging and nearly homogeneous professoriate. More important, Howard and the nation's other research universities must produce a cadre of individuals who are prepared to teach and conduct research from culturally diverse perspectives. Although we know and perhaps understand the significance of having a diverse faculty, institutions of higher education still lag behind the ethnic, cultural, and demographic changes of today's society.

The number of underrepresented minorities in faculty positions in PWIs in the last twenty years appears to show that there has been a significant increase. Despite this increase in the number of full-time faculty of color, however, the percentage of such faculty has remained virtually unchanged (Harvey 2003). Specifically, approximately 8 percent of full-time faculty members in higher education are underrepresented minorities, of which only 5.1 percent are African American, and close to half of these are thought to serve on HBCU faculties! Hispanics comprise 2.5 percent of the American professoriate and Native Americans only 4 percent. These percentages suggest two things. First, disparities still exist, thus furthering the need to continue producing faculty of color and to prepare them for the roles and responsibilities of faculty at colleges and universities. Second, the small pool of African American Ph.D. recipients and the even smaller number pursuing professorial careers means that HBCUs face a significant challenge in replacing their aging African American faculty members with new African American hires, that is, unless there is some type of systematic intervention, which we propose below.

For most doctoral students of any race, preparation for a faculty career has consisted of gaining expertise in a particular field of study through course work, conducting research, and writing a dissertation in an area of specialization (Gaff, Pruitt-Logan, and Weibl 2000). In the past, there has been little if any preparation for doctoral students to develop the capabilities to teach and assume the other responsibilities of a faculty member (for example, mentoring and evaluating students, etc.). Jules LaPidus, president emeritus of the Council of Graduate Schools, and other leaders in graduate education have recognized a need for doctoral students to be formally trained for the professoriate. It was evident that the job market was changing, and a mismatch existed between the needs of colleges and universities and the preparation of their future faculty. Still, universities were not changing the socialization process for doctoral students entering academia. Thus, a national initiative was developed that sought to train graduate students beyond the traditional preparation they received during their graduate education.

The Birth of the Preparing Future Faculty Project

In 1993, the Association of American Colleges and Universities (AACU) in conjunction with the Council of Graduate Schools (CGS) worked to develop the national Preparing Future Faculty (PFF) Project. Supported by The Pew Charitable Trusts, PFF was created to prepare graduate students in participating institutions across the country for the full range of faculty roles and responsibilities. Howard University was among the first research universities in the nation to join the PFF movement and has intensified development of these programs over the ensuing years.

A discussion of Howard as a model for preparing the next generation of faculty of color, especially for HBCUs, is significant for two major reasons. First, and perhaps foremost, is the fact that the university is the nation's largest on-campus producer of African American Ph.D.s (approximately sixty out of nearly one hundred students per year), and these recipients come from each of the university's approximately thirty Ph.D. programs. In some fields, Howard produces upwards of 50 percent of all African Americans in the nation receiving doctoral degrees in a given year (for example, communication and mathematics). It is also the nation's leading producer of African Americans with Ph.D.s in the social, behavioral, and economic sciences. Simply stated, Howard has the greatest capacity of any university in the United States to produce African American faculty in future years. Indeed, one cannot have a serious conversation about producing more African American faculty for our nation's colleges and universities without including Howard University.

Second, Howard was and remains among the national leaders in the Preparing Future Faculty movement. Indeed, the leaders of the national PFF efforts report that this movement would have had very little African American presence were it not for Howard and its students (Gaff, Logan, and Weibl 2000). Equally important, Howard is the only university in the United States to have participated in all four phases* of the original PFF enterprise, and PFF is now completely institutionalized at the university. Approximately two hundred students from throughout the university's vast array of doctoral programs have participated in some phase of the Howard PFF program over the past decade. Moreover, some have enrolled in the

---

*Phase I (1993–1997): Developed alternative models of faculty preparation (institutions tailored programs to local needs and circumstances).

Phase II (1997–2000): Institutionalized models and spread program—move from developing a pilot model to institutionalizing (for example, began with five departments at Howard and became campuswide).

Phase III (1998–2001): Developed PFF in sciences and mathematics with support from the National Science Foundation (partnerships with Association of Physics Teachers, American Chemical Society, American Mathematical Society, etc.).

Phase IV (1999–2002): Developed PFF in social sciences and humanities—involved societies in six humanities and social science disciplines, including American Historical Association, American Political Science Association, American Psychological Association, American Sociological Association, National Council of Teachers of English, and National Communication Association (Gaff, Pruitt-Logan, and Weibl 2000).

university's recently established and innovative Graduate Certificate Program in College and University Faculty Preparation.

Needless to say, preparation of future faculty is a major priority of the Howard University Graduate School. In addition to having participated in the four phases of PFF, the university recognizes its historic legacy of providing faculty for the nation's HBCUs as well as for TWIs. Indeed, Howard sees its connectivity to HBCUs and other minority-serving institutions (MSIs) as a special part of its mission and responsibility. At the same time, the university, through its graduate school, believes that it also must produce faculty for the nation's TWIs, which often have no African American faculty in many departments, not to mention their schools/colleges. In particular, many science, technology, engineering, and mathematics (STEM) departments appear to suffer even more from the lack of diversity within their faculty.

To support these efforts, the Howard Graduate School has raised several million extramural dollars to support PFF and PFF-like efforts on the Howard campus over the past several years. Among these successful efforts are the following:

1. *Alliance for Graduate Education and the Professoriate (AGEP) Program*: Originally funded by the National Science Foundation (NSF) in 1998 and joined by the University of Texas at El Paso (UTEP) in 2003, Howard University has formed a unique partnership with UTEP and other HBCU partners to increase the number of underrepresented minority Ph.D. recipients and the preparation of these recipients for faculty careers in the STEM disciplines. With $5 million from NSF to date, this unique partnership represents an important endeavor in graduate education for both a research-extensive historically Black university and a research-intensive university to address the severe underrepresentation of African Americans and Hispanics earning doctoral degrees and entering the professoriate. The Preparing Future Faculty Program is a major component of the alliance, in which doctoral students are prepared for challenges and issues pertinent to faculty in the STEM fields.

2. *Frederick Douglass Doctoral Scholars Program*: Initially supported by Howard University's president, H. Patrick Swygert, in 1999 and by a $1 million grant from the HBCU United Negro College Fund/Lilly Endowment Initiative, the Douglass Doctoral Scholars Program seeks to attract the nation's most talented students, particularly African

Americans, to pursue doctoral studies at Howard University and then to enter the professoriate, particularly at an HBCU. All Frederick Douglass Doctoral Scholars participate in Howard University's PFF program, with an emphasis on faculty life at HBCUs. Each year, scholars have the opportunity to visit up to two HBCU campuses. Most of the Douglass Doctoral Scholars have come from the social science and humanities disciplines.

3. *The GAANN Fellowship (Graduate Assistance in Areas of National Need) Program in Chemistry, Mathematics, and Physiology*: With funds from the U.S. Department of Education, these programs have provided underrepresented minority graduate students of superior ability with demonstrated financial need to pursue doctoral degrees in areas of national need in the aforementioned disciplines. Recipients in this program receive supervised research and teaching experiences designed to prepare them for a faculty career in several different types of postsecondary institutions, including HBCUs. GAANN fellows participate in the PFF program and teacher training workshops sponsored by the Graduate School and its departments.

The Howard PFF program requires a two-year commitment from doctoral students to be exercised simultaneously with the pursuit of the Ph.D. within their disciplines. Students are required to take a course in faculty roles and responsibilities, participate in two-day teaching assistant workshops each fall, participate in a minimum of four professional development workshops each year on a variety of topics, visit a minimum of two campuses outside of Howard University each year to gain an understanding of faculty life at diverse institutions, and engage in a supervised teaching experience within their home departments. Students also have the option of enrolling in the aforementioned twelve-credit-hour Graduate Certificate in College and University Faculty Preparation; those enrolled could be selected for a year-long prefaculty internship at any one of approximately twelve colleges and universities around the country to get an "up close and personal" glimpse of faculty life at an institution different from Howard University.

A National Strategy for Increasing the African American Faculty at HBCUs

If one accepts the notion that HBCUs *must* have a critical mass of African American faculty to maintain their institutional character, then it is imperative for these institutions to develop a national strategy to address this need. Rather than competing with one another for the relatively small number of available African American Ph.D. recipients, we believe that they must pool their resources and seek an integrated approach. The problems they face are likely to worsen as the current crop of African American faculty age and retire in the coming decade and replacements become necessary.

Thus, a comprehensive, national strategy to address this issue should include, at the least, the following elements:

1. **Enhance existing Ph.D. programs at HBCUs such that the number of doctoral recipients are increased significantly.** Despite the small number of HBCUs that offer doctoral degrees (fewer than twenty), they already produce about 11 percent of all Ph.D.s awarded to African Americans. These impressive statistics suggest that HBCUs can successfully recruit and graduate African Americans with doctoral degrees. The problem is that there are too few such doctoral programs in too few fields (mainly in the social sciences and education) at HBCUs. However, with increased enrichment of the existing programs through more financial and other kinds of support, quality can be assured and enrollment capacities increased. As a result, the number of African American doctorates produced by these institutions could increase.

2. **Create more Ph.D. programs at HBCUs.** Because the number of HBCUs that offer doctoral degrees is reasonably small and the disciplinary range of such programs is reasonably narrow, these institutions could become even greater producers of African American Ph.D. degree recipients if more programs were created. While the cost of doctoral education is expensive, HBCUs with reasonably strong existing infrastructures, faculty, and other resources might consider launching new doctoral programs or, if they do not offer doctoral degrees currently, consider launching doctoral education. Again, such programs should not be initiated without sufficient resources.

3. **Develop a national HBCU mentoring program and campaign to encourage academically talented HBCU undergraduates to pursue doctoral study and to consider a future faculty career at an HBCU.** African American undergraduate students receive a disproportionately small amount of mentoring for graduate education in relationship to job enticements. Moreover, many are victims of an

intimidating mystique with respect to their perceptions of doctoral education, so they opt out from pursuing such studies—even if they have the credentials to do so. On the other end of the spectrum, those receiving doctorates also generally have stereotypical ideas about faculty careers at HBCUs. Clearly, HBCUs as a group need to do a better job of mentoring their undergraduates to pursue doctoral degrees and faculty opportunities at their institutions.

4. **Encourage academically talented HBCU undergraduates to consider an HBCU for graduate study.** Many HBCU undergraduates have inadequate information about the availability and range of doctoral programs at HBCUs. At a very minimum, HBCUs should consider launching a national initiative to inform their undergraduates about these doctoral programs and offer them the available data on retention and graduation rates. HBCU doctoral programs might consider developing linkages and agreements with HBCU undergraduate institutions that guarantee admission and, possibly, financial support for academically talented students.

5. **Construct a Web site and print media describing graduate and doctoral degree opportunities at HBCUs.** Information in these formats would supplement and enhance local recruitment efforts of HBCU institutions. For example, construction of a Web site focusing on graduate education at HBCUs would serve as a "virtual kiosk" for aspiring African American graduate students across the nation, providing easy access to every HBCU in the United States.

6. **Organize an annual collection and dissemination program of academically capable HBCU rising seniors.** The list of such names (with contact information) might be disaggregated by discipline for distribution to all HBCU graduate schools for recruitment purposes. This proposed initiative could be patterned after the National Name Exchange Consortium based at the University of Washington Graduate School.

7. **Encourage greater HBCU participation in national future faculty movements.** The Preparing Future Faculty Project and the Compact for Faculty Diversity are two programs explicitly designed to prepare graduate students to acquire competencies in the roles and responsibilities of faculty members, especially teaching.

8. **Establish prefaculty internships at HBCUs for African American doctoral students in their last year of study.** Such internships would provide opportunities for doctoral students to experience faculty life

at HBCUs (for example, teaching a course, attending faculty meetings, engaging in research) at an HBCU before completing their Ph.D. Howard University has had great success with such an initiative at several TWIs. A similar effort involving HBCUs could go a long way toward eliminating stereotypes and correcting misinformation that many doctoral students have concerning faculty life at HBCUs.

9. **Develop an ongoing database or national job bank of African American doctoral candidates.** This information should be prepared for annual distribution to HBCU hiring officials. Such an effort would provide HBCU officials and search committees with information for an early start on matching upcoming doctoral recipients with expected faculty openings at HBCUs.

10. **Develop a strategy for HBCU leaders to periodically hear the voices of current African American doctoral students about faculty careers.** This effort would provide a forum for HBCU leaders to stay in touch with student needs, aspirations, and perceptions about HBCUs with respect to research support, teaching loads, governance participation, salary expectations, resource requirements, systematic faculty mentoring, etc. Such information also would provide HBCU leaders with critical facts for making faculty careers at their institutions more attractive to newly minted Ph.D. recipients.

Conclusions

The faculties at HBCUs play a vital role in the academic, social, and personal development of African American students. As many current African American faculty members at these institutions are approaching retirement age, HBCUs must be innovative in their efforts to recruit new African American faculty members to maintain the critical mass of individuals required to sustain their legacies and institutional character. In today's faculty hiring environment, African American Ph.D. recipients, unlike those in previous generations, have far more institutional choices than ever before, particularly at traditionally White institutions. To be competitive, HBCUs must become more creative and assertive in preparing future African American faculty members and in creating attractive packages for recruiting and hiring new African American faculty members to their institutions. In this chapter, we have made an effort to begin that process.

References

Gaff, J. G., A. S. Pruitt-Logan, and R. A. Weibl. 2000. *Building the faculty we need: Colleges and universities working together.* Washington, DC: Association of American Colleges and Universities.

Harvey, W. B. 2003. *Minorities in higher education: Annual status report.* Washington, DC: American Council on Education.

Smith, D. G., with L. E. Wolf and B. E. Busenberg. 1996. *Achieving faculty diversity: Debunking the myths.* Washington, DC: Association of American Colleges and Universities.

Delbert W. Baker

Delbert W. Baker earned his bachelor's degree from Oakwood College in 1975, his master of divinity from Andrews University in 1978, and his Ph.D. in organizational communication from Howard University in 1992. He has written numerous scholarly articles and seven books—most notably *Millennium Lesson Book*, *Telling the Story*, *Make Us One*, *From Exile to Prime Minister*, *The Unknown Prophet*, and seven volumes in the continuing *QuoteBook* series, which are presented annually to Oakwood graduates.

Dr. Baker has served as president of Oakwood College since 1996. Under his aegis, the college has increased enrollment to its approximately eighteen hundred students. More than $25 million has been raised through donations and grants. Also during Dr. Baker's tenure, the campus has received awards for academics, campus beauty, and community service. For the last five years, Oakwood College has been listed in *US News and World Report* as among the best colleges in the southern region.

Dr. Baker's professional experience includes ten years of pastoral leadership in Ohio and Virginia (1975–1985), seven years as editor of *Message Magazine* (1985–1992), and four years as special assistant to the president and professor at Loma Linda University and Loma Linda University Medical Center (1992–1996).

Susan M. Baker

Susan M. Baker, who earned her bachelor of science in physical therapy, master of physical therapy science, and doctor of physical therapy science degrees from Loma Linda University, is a board-certified geriatric specialist. As a physical therapist, Dr. Baker has had an independent practice, worked in administration and management of rehabilitation facilities, and taught at Loma Linda University and Oakwood College. She currently works as an educator and clinical physical therapist, has conducted research, and is published in professional journals. She is married to Delbert Baker, president of Oakwood College, Huntsville, Alabama.

12

PATHWAYS TO SUCCESS

Recruitment and Retention Methods
at Oakwood College

Stories. Every historically Black college and university (HBCU) has them: stories of students obtaining an education and reaching their personal goals, even when the odds are against them. Students who have been affected by exposure to racism, sexism, and social programs gone awry. Some are the first in their family to matriculate in college, others come from homes where the level of formal education is high: young people who break the ceiling of academic achievement, others who are average students used to getting by, and still others with low academic performance who are casualties of inept or unconcerned educational systems. Students come to college on scholarships and cash, financial aid, loans, and prayer.

Students with these and countless other stories come to HBCUs in search of an educational milieu that provides them the safety and support to flourish, not fail. Statistics say that HBCUs face enormous challenges, but despite that they are, in many ways, the singular institutions that have realized consistent success in educating Black young people. Yet, even in the face of success, some statistics cause concerns that educators must address.

According to statistics, 21 percent of Blacks do not attend school long enough to get a high school diploma, compared to 11 percent of Whites.[1] Only 30 percent of Blacks eighteen to twenty-four years old attend an institution of higher learning,[2] and, of those, only 17 percent earn a four-year degree.[3] These statistics are particularly meaningful when considered in the context of the advantages that having a college education bestows: college graduates can expect to earn approximately 70 percent more in lifetime income than the typical high school graduate without a college education[4]; less than 1 percent of incarcerated persons are college graduates[5]; persons with college degrees consistently report that they have better health,[6] smoke less as a group,[7] and participate in volunteer activities more often than do their less educated peers.[8]

Two Students, Two Perspectives

Brenda (not her real name), according to the statistics, never should have made it. She had been abandoned by a drug-addicted mother and was homeless in a large metropolitan city. Her chances of remaining within the cycle of poverty and living as a marginalized person in the land of opportunity were overwhelming. However, two women determined that she could defy the negative statistics and, through Herculean efforts, Brenda found herself enrolling at Oakwood College. It was a huge undertaking. There were sleepless nights; some spent studying, others spent wondering where next semester's tuition would come from. Still, within six years, Brenda graduated with a bachelor's degree. She got a job in her high-demand profession and joined the ranks of other HBCU graduates who give credit to the institutions that nurtured them.

Travis (not his real name) has a different story from Brenda's but is also representative of many students at HBCUs. Travis's parents were college graduates; from the time he was a toddler, he knew he would go to college. Academics came fairly natural for him, and he enjoyed an environment that supported academic achievement. Travis graduated from high school at the top of his class and was a National Merit Scholar with a full ride to the college of his choice.

Even though he had other impressive choices, he chose Oakwood College, primarily because he recognized that it provided a culturally rich academic environment where he could thrive. During his years at Oakwood, Travis continued to excel academically. He also developed leadership skills in student government and engaged in meaningful community service, which formed the basis for his career choice of political science. Travis graduated in four years, again at the top of his class, and was accepted into a prestigious graduate school.

A Rich Tradition

The stories of Brenda and Travis occur, to a greater or lesser degree, regularly at Oakwood College and other HBCUs across the nation. These successes are not accidental but require purpose-driven, institution-wide planning and implementation.

Oakwood College has a rich tradition as a provider of higher education. Established in 1896 by the Seventh-Day Adventist Church, Oakwood started its educational endeavor with sixteen students, the majority of whom were descendants of slaves. The property purchased in Huntsville, Alabama, for the establishment of the institution was a former slave plantation with a history. As the Job Key plantation in the early 1800s, the grounds were home to Dred Scott, the famous slave who sued for his freedom. Visitors to the campus today can view the historical Slave Cemetery, believed to hold the remains of Scott's first wife.

In pure irony, Oakwood College's administrative offices stand on the location of the central plantation house, where disadvantage and inaccessibility were daily realities for Blacks on the land. Now Black students traverse the same ground with far different daily realities and access to privileges and opportunities that their ancestors could scarcely imagine.

Oakwood College Today

Oakwood College is a four-year liberal arts institution that offers approximately sixty bachelor's and associate degree programs in sixteen academic departments. There are 110 full-time teaching faculty, approximately 60 percent of whom hold terminal degrees. Staff employees—considered "non-classroom educators" because of the role they are encouraged to take in campus-wide holistic learning—number 230. In the 2003–2004 academic year, 1,787 students from almost every state and more than forty countries enrolled at Oakwood College. Female students were in the majority (60 percent), and Blacks comprised 88 percent of the student body; however, every ethnic group was represented at Oakwood College.

Oakwood programs emphasize holistic education, as articulated in the school's mission statement: "Oakwood College, a historically Black Seventh-Day Adventist institution of higher learning, provides quality Christian education that emphasizes academic excellence; promotes harmonious development of mind, body, and spirit; and prepares leaders in service for God and humanity."

To fulfill this mission, Oakwood has instituted a variety of policies and practices aimed at recruitment and retention. Many of these strategies are effective, as aggregate data from the annual survey of graduates suggest. In response to the italicized survey statement, graduates (2004–2005) responded positively with agree/strongly agree in the following percentages:

- *As I leave Oakwood College, I know I am a better person*: 92 percent
- *I have grown spiritually while at Oakwood College*: 88 percent
- *I received an excellent education at Oakwood College*: 86 percent
- *The instructors at Oakwood College really care about students*: 85 percent
- *The education I received at Oakwood College has prepared me for my profession*: 82 percent
- *The education I received at Oakwood College was worth the money it cost*: 73 percent

The impact of Oakwood College's mission to develop leaders can be seen as well in the lives of alumni who are affecting society at every level. Take, for example, Mayor John Street of Philadelphia, Pennsylvania, whose health initiatives have turned around obesity rates in his populous city. There is Rear Admiral Barry Black, chaplain of the U.S. Senate, the first African American to hold that position and minister to the political leaders of our country. Angela Brown, operatic diva, has thrilled critics with her voice and presence in *Aïda* at the Metropolitan Opera. Wintley Phipps, recording artist, has not only made significant contributions to the music industry but, as founder of the U.S. Dream Academy, he provides specialized educational programs for children of incarcerated parents. These individuals are representative of the many other Oakwood College graduates who are making a difference in society.

Meeting Challenges

Oprah Winfrey once quipped: "When I look into the future, it is so bright it hurts my eyes." To continue to ensure a bright future for minority students, HBCUs must face and surmount many challenges, such as academic underpreparation, decreased retention after the second collegiate year, financial hardship on students who are already economically disadvantaged, and adverse cultural messages regarding educational achievement. Additionally, the twenty-first century demands a different educational paradigm that emphasizes incisive analytical/critical thinking skills and ignites a commitment to lifelong learning.

Oakwood College is committed to meeting these challenges and providing quality educational services. To do this effectively, faculty and staff are motivated and programs are designed to facilitate strategies and interventions that enhance recruitment and retention. These strategies and interventions, which result in student success, can be categorized into the following four areas.

Academic Support and Enhancement

Oakwood College endeavors to create an educational environment that provides support and builds relationships with students for learning to take place naturally. The institution has an open enrollment policy that includes recruitment of students who are at different points within the academic continuum. Meeting the responsibility of challenging the gifted student and bringing the underprepared student to acceptable levels of performance, while at the same time motivating average students to reach their potential, is the academic test. It requires balancing high expectation, recognition of effort levels, and academic support.

At the beginning of academic support is advisement. Educational research has validated the importance of good academic advisement that mentors students and propels them toward graduation. Further, student satisfaction and retention can be correlated positively to effective advisement practices. Therefore, Oakwood College has focused on enrichment of the advisor-student interaction. With this strategic approach, students are more informed and are able to be focused and self-directed.

Oakwood has an intensive advisement program that (1) provides ongoing faculty training in best practices using workshops, seminars, and one-to-one coaching by experienced, effective advisors within the institution, and (2) uses advisors who are specifically trained to meet the needs of freshmen students as they adjust to college life.

The freshman advising program works in close coordination with the Center for Academic Success and offers a week of freshman orientation, which occurs before returning students arrive on campus. The college also offers a one-hour academic credit course, *Orientation Seminar: OC101*, which is like other college orientation courses in that it examines aspects of collegiate life and offers ingredients for college success. However, *OC101* also includes a module that teaches students the history, mission, values, and raison d'être of Oakwood College in particular and HBCUs in general.

Oakwood recently began a pilot program implementing the *College Student Inventory (Form B)*, which is part of the Retention Management System.[9] The objective of this program is to increase retention through the enhancement of advisement. The *College Student Inventory* gives faculty advisors valuable insights into their advisees' academic motivation, general coping skills, and receptivity to support services. With this instrument, the faculty advisor has tools that were previously unavailable to enhance advisement based on specific individual student characteristics.

Another strategy for academic success can be found in the establishment of satellite support services around the campus. Some examples include:

1. *The Center for Academic Success (CAS).* CAS provides a wide range of services whose objective is to reach students where they are and provide a bridge to where they want or need to be academically. CAS offers free peer tutoring in most academic areas. It also conducts laboratories in mathematics, reading, and writing; monitors the academic progress of at-risk students; orients freshman; provides services in accordance with the Rehabilitation Act (1973) for students with physical or learning disabilities; and conducts reviews for exit examinations, such as English proficiency. Students particularly appreciate that the center is open on Sundays and evenings until 11:00 PM.

2. *Residential Hall Living/Learning Centers.* These centers feature on-site tutorial assistance, mentoring by upper-division students, Internet/computer stations, "quiet zones" for study, and separate areas for socialization. The active involvement of residential deans and assistants in these centers increases a sense of support and high academic expectation.

3. *Department-based research and academic support programs.* Programs of various types can be found in every academic area, but are prominent in chemistry, biology, mathematics, and education. These programs allow students to gain skills, experience, and national/international exposure within their disciplines, as evidenced by collaborations with NASA, NSF, NIH, and other recognized entities. Oakwood College students were privileged to have one of their scientific projects included in the experiments aboard the space shuttle *Columbia.*

Financial Recruitment Incentives

Most minority students could only dream of college attendance if they had to depend on family wealth to finance their education. Even with grants and federal loans, students still struggle financially to achieve their educational goals. Indeed, lack of financial resources is a primary reason for student attrition at Oakwood College. The institution, which is private and tuition-driven, diligently seeks to keep tuition affordable while providing necessary academic and support services.

To assist students in financing their education, Oakwood sets aside approximately $3.4 million annually for scholarships and underwrites 34 percent of each student's actual annual costs for tuition, room, and board. Recently the institution implemented additional financial strategies to increase recruitment and retention. Examples of these strategies include:

1. Restructuring the Oakwood College scholarship program so that it supports the college's inclusive admission policy. Students with demonstrated academic achievement (grade point average [GPA]: 3.0–4.0) continue to receive the largest scholarship award amounts. However, with the restructured program, students with average GPAs (2.0–2.9) can also receive scholarship assistance. All scholarship programs are contingent on the student maintaining or improving his or her admission GPA. Students can renew their scholarships for four years as long as they meet the guidelines.

2. Equipping faculty advisors with financial aid information so that they can function as extensions of the Office of Financial Aid. With *College Student Inventory* information, faculty advisors know how important finances are to their students. While they are not expected to replace the financial aid counselors who work with the individual student, advisors can play a role in alleviating financial stressors by sharing their knowledge about financial aid.

Life Skills Development

Oakwood College has a history of values-based education that is part of its Christian perspective: students are encouraged to maintain high ethical and moral principles. The campus atmosphere and activities are intentionally designed to facilitate development of individual responsibility, personal integrity and ethics, spiritual receptivity, community service, and a sense of ecological and environmental conscientiousness.

Several years ago, Oakwood College students participated in a campus-wide *Health Risk Behavior Survey* that was modeled after the National College Health Behavior Risk Survey. Data were collected that identified drug use and abuse, suicide ideation, violence and weapons, sexual behaviors and practices, and nutrition and exercise as priority areas. These areas have formed a foundation for focused programs to reduce the incidence of risky health behaviors among students and promote physical, social, and character education. These programs include:

1. Having a *10,000 Steps-a-Day Plan*, a campus-wide fitness emphasis program, through which students and employees are provided with a pedometer and instruction in beginning and maintaining an exercise walking and nutritional fitness program.

2. Hosting a community AIDS Awareness Day, along with programs that promote sexual abstinence and provide sex education at the collegiate level.

3. Offering anger management, personal negotiation skills, and emotional intelligence programs to educate students away from the use of violence and toward self-management through self-awareness. Oakwood also has a zero tolerance policy for fighting and carrying weapons.

4. Recognizing the role of depression in suicide ideation/attempt and encouraging more discussion regarding the signs of depression so that students, faculty, and staff can make appropriate use of and referrals to the professional counseling services available on campus. In addition, suicide hotline resources are advertised in the residential halls and other prominent places on the campus.

5. Enforcing the zero tolerance policy for drug trafficking and implementation of educational/counseling programs about drug use. Although the campus has a one-strike rule for drug use, students who seek help for drug problems can receive services without any disciplinary action being taken.

6. Offering eclectic programs that promote character education, such as *Womanhood/Manhood Week*, *Romance Week*, *Binding the Wounds Workshop*, *Back to School Revival*, and others.

Community service and leadership development are *caught and taught* in a variety of ways. The National Association for the Prevention of Starvation (NAPS), an internationally recognized humanitarian organization with wide campus-based student support, that has given aid to families in Africa, Haiti, Jamaica, and the United States. NAPS joined concerned citizens in Los Angeles to help end gang violence in South Central; it was featured in the *New York Times* for its role in bolstering the spirits of rescue workers, grieving families, and the people of New York following the tragedy of 9/11; and it conducted an aid mission to Sri Lanka and India to help tsunami victims rebuild their lives and communities.

Also, each year students join the Oakwood-operated Global Mission Service program. In this program students spend a year or more in a foreign country working with indigenous development projects. Most students who spend time in Global Mission Service describe it as a pivotal experience that adds depth and breadth to their education. This program enlarges personal perspectives and appreciation of diverse peoples, cultures, and geographies. Through the work of these outreach programs, the lives of students are transformed into what, for many, will be lifelong participation in humanitarian service.

The President's Ambassadors (PA) is an organization that seeks to provide leadership training. Each year approximately twenty-four students join the PAs and represent Oakwood College at official functions and campus events. Through monthly seminars and mentoring, PA members have the opportunity to develop and hone characteristics that contribute to personal and professional success.

At the end of summer, just before the start of the new academic year, a Leadership Retreat is held to prepare new campus leaders for their responsibilities. Attending the retreat are students who will be employed as residential hall assistants, chaplain's assistants, and student government officers. During the retreat, students learn the policies of the college but, more important, they learn how to relate effectively to peers when in a leadership position. Workshops highlight a variety of topics. A recent retreat workshop featured "Emotional Intelligence," which has been called one of the most important skills for leaders in the twenty-first century. Students were taught the basic skills necessary to increase their ability to control their emotions and help to understand the emotions of others.

Seven years ago Oakwood College established a partnership with a historically White college to provide a novel program designed to increase ethnic sensitivity on both campuses. The Diversity Educational Exchange Program (DEEP) enabled White and Black students from each campus to attend the other institution for one semester. During the semester they received diversity training in formalized settings that facilitated cross-cultural friendships and increased diversity understanding. After several years of successful student exchanges, faculty, staff, and student leadership retreats were incorporated into the program.

Proactive Strategies

The adage, "An ounce of prevention is worth a pound of cure," can be applied to educational programs, and it is the philosophy underlying many of the proactive strategies at Oakwood College, such as:

1. The Early Alert/First Alert Program for students who are exhibiting academically risky behavior in the classroom facilitates faculty in making a referral to Counseling and Testing Services, residential hall deans, CAS, or the academic advisor if there are problems because of absenteeism, poor examination performance, or consistent neglect turning in assignments. Some ask, "Do college students need such monitoring?" Some do, and such services are especially effective as they show concern and care and are directed toward achieving academic success.

2. Academic safety nets such as minimal GPA requirements for participation in intramural sports; CAS phone/mail and individualized services for students on academic probation because of low GPA; and specialized services to academic high achievers who forfeit scholarships because of unsatisfactory progress.

3. A process for any student seeking terminal withdrawal that necessitates obtaining the signature of course professors, the academic advisor, the financial aid/student accounts officer, and the vice president for academic affairs. Each person in this chain has the opportunity to assist the student in creative thinking and problem solving before making a final decision to withdraw from the academic process. Of course, this intervention is collaborative and sensitive to the student's reasons for withdrawal.

4. Employment of a retention director who oversees the retention program and related quality services that may affect it. Additionally, the director assesses trends or factors that may affect retention across the institution and in particular student groups. The director also examines retention and attrition data to help facilitate initiatives to increase academic success.

5. Parent Partner Program (PPP) brings together parents of freshmen and Oakwood College administrators to receive feedback regarding their students' experiences at the institution during the first year. Parents may volunteer for the program, which involves participating in a conference call with the administration once each semester. The agenda for the call includes a brief campus update by the administrators and then opens the discussion for parents to voice any concerns, make observations, ask questions, make commendations, or receive clarification about any aspect of the institution. Following the conference call, a feedback list of issues, questions, criticisms, and compliments is generated and presented to the administrative council. Each

administrator then takes feedback items appropriate to his or her area, takes appropriate action depending on the nature of the comment, and provides the president with a response. PPP participants receive a written response from the president outlining the action taken or recommended or other strategies appropriate to the original feedback. Support for the PPP has been enthusiastic from both groups— parents appreciate the open, responsive forum, and administrators appreciate interacting with parents in a collaborative manner.

Conclusion

Integral to the success that Oakwood College has had in educating Black students is its aim: *Education. Excellence. Eternity.* These words synthesize the educational objectives of the institution. *Education* refers to the preparation and training students receive so that they can enter a career, job, or graduate or professional school with the academic skills necessary to be a success. *Excellence* is an attitude and expectation that students will excel in their academic endeavors, and that the college will provide a solid foundation for the development of mental, physical, social, and spiritual skills. *Eternity* highlights the importance placed on values and spiritual development.

Oakwood College recognizes that the process of education is not just a four-year undertaking but, if done well, has eternal implications for the individual and for society.

Endnotes

1. U.S. Census Bureau, *Educational Attainment in the United States: March 2002* (Washington, DC: Author, 2003).

2. National Center for Education Statistics, *Digest of Education Statistics* (Washington, DC: U.S. Department of Education, 2002).

3. U.S. Census Bureau.

4. G. C. Day and E. C. Newburger, "The Big Payoff: Educational Attainment and Synthetic Estimates of Work-Life Earnings," *Current Population Reports* (2002): 23–210.

5. C. W. Harlow, *Education and Correctional Populations*, Bureau of Justice Statistics, NCJ195670 (Washington, DC: U.S. Department of Justice, 2003).

6. National Center for Education Statistics, *The Condition of Education* (Washington, DC: Author, 2004).

7. D. DeWalque, "Education, Information, and Smoking Decisions: Evidence

from Smoking Histories, 1940–2000," Policy Research Working Paper 3362 (Washington, DC: World Bank, 2004).

8. Bureau of Labor Statistics, *Volunteering in the United States, 2003* (Washington, DC: Author, 2003).

9. Noel-Levitz, Inc., *Retention Management System* (Iowa City, IA: Author, 2004).

M. Rick Turner

M. Rick Turner has served as the dean of the University of Virginia's Office of African-American Affairs since August 1988. Since his arrival, the university has boosted its African American graduation rate to 87 percent, among the highest of any public institution in the nation. Before coming to UVA, Dr. Turner served in various student affairs positions of leadership at institutions across the nation, including the University of Connecticut, University of California-Irvine, and Stanford University.

In addition to his role as dean, Dr. Turner serves as adjunct faculty member of the University of Virginia's Department of Sociology. He has served as a consultant/speaker for numerous education foundations, higher education institutions, public and private schools, community organizations, and municipal and federal agencies. He has also spoken and written extensively about African American academic achievement; affirmative action; and the recruitment, retention, admission, and graduation of African American students, other students of color, and student athletes. Dr. Turner founded the Saturday Academy, an educational enrichment program for families, and he is active in community affairs, working closely with parents and children.

For his work, Dr. Turner has received numerous awards, including the Crispus Attucks Award for Higher Education Leadership, the Ron Brown Award for successfully educating African American youth and other students of color, the Parents Advisory Association Warrior Award for his student advocacy, NAACP Award for his commitment to the needs of the community, and Outstanding Black Faculty/Staff award for his devotion to his students. During the university's spring 2001 convocation exercises, Dr. Turner received the prestigious Algernon Sydney Sullivan Award in recognition of excellence of character and service to humanity.

A native of Hartford, Connecticut, Dr. Turner earned a bachelor of arts from Linfield College, master of social work from the University of Connecticut, and doctor of philosophy in higher education administration/policy analysis from Stanford University. His dissertation, "The Academic Achievement and Retention of Black Students in White Institutions," is the foundation of his life's work.

In addition to his lifelong dedication to African American student success, Dr. Turner also served his country in the U.S. Army and completed a tour of duty in Vietnam.

13

RECREATING THE EXTENDED FAMILY FOR AFRICAN AMERICAN UNIVERSITY STUDENTS

A Formula for Success

It was clear to me from our first encounter that Dean Turner's leadership as a father figure is the reason why OAAA feels like a "home away from home." Dean Turner is highly respected and admired by African-American students at the University of Virginia. The Black student community looks to Dean Turner as a father figure; a man who is caring, yet stern; has high expectations, yet is supportive.

He serves as a protector who doesn't hesitate to offer his support to students when they have been wronged. When students feel that their professor is racist, or that they have been spotlighted; or if someone is offended by a racial slur, charged with an honor offense or harassed by the police, there is a sense of, "Ooh, I'm going to tell my daddy," Dean Turner, that is.

Dean Turner's role requires him to listen to a variety of concerns, but that does not mean he will always side with students. Yet, rest assured that Dean Turner will always be fair and offer his advice, encouragement, and unwavering support to African-American students, whom he affectionately refers to as "our children."

Black students know they can't half step around Dean Turner; he expects nothing but the best. He has no problem telling students to get serious and shape up. He always offers to treat students to lunch, a benevolent gesture for struggling college students. He encourages students to hold their head high, be proud of who they are and where they come from, be confident and walk tall.

Dean Turner is insistent about establishing a relationship with African-American parents. He understands that parental involvement is essential to students' success, whether in second grade or in the second year of college. The fact that many students can say, "Dean Turner knows my mother and has talked with my daddy," makes him unique and much more significant than any other administrator at the University.

His leadership assures parents that their children have a support system, that they have an advocate, and most importantly, they have a home away from home.

LaTaSha Levy, UVA Class of 2001,
Interim Assistant Dean, OAAA

As dean of the Office of African-American Affairs, I accept the role as a father figure for African American students. It is important for me and the university to recognize and understand that in this role I must be a strong advocate for African American students and their parents. It is also important to point out that the University of Virginia's Office of African-American Affairs (OAAA) serves two major purposes: internally, we serve as a home away from home for students; externally, we serve as advocates for the Black students on campus. As dean of the OAAA, I sometimes see myself as a "pinch hitter" for parents. I see it as my duty to encourage students to take full advantage of the rich resources at the university and to inspire them to fulfill their greatest ambitions.

To help bridge the gap between students' literal home and their figurative home, the OAAA created the Parents Advisory Association (PAA). When I assumed leadership of the University of Virginia's Office of African-American Affairs, the PAA was already in place. After studying the model that was in place, I reformatted it a bit and began to reactivate this innovative component of our extended family. The association's mission is to work with the OAAA in improving the academic, cultural, and social life of Black students at the University of Virginia. The association was born out of a need to assist the OAAA in fulfilling its mission of providing academic support services to Black students. The organization is based on the premise that the parent-child bond represents the most powerful of all human attachments.

The Parents Advisory Association grew, in large part, out of conflicts with academic affairs offices regarding the management and operation of academic support programs for incoming Black students. The OAAA's *Summer Transition Program* was of particular concern as the university threatened to discontinue this program. Though parents were never directly involved in this conflict, they were kept abreast of events through the Office of African-American Affairs. In the midst of this situation, parents did eventually meet with the interim dean of African-American Affairs and the vice president for Student Affairs. They wanted to emphasize their concerns that academic support was essential to their children's survival at the university and they did not want anything to impede it. Stemming from this significant relationship between the OAAA and concerned parents, the Parents Advisory Association was revived in 1989.

The goals/objectives of the PAA are as follows:

- to provide creative opportunities to share our cultural heritage with students;
- to establish strategies for fund-raising to support scholarships, emergency loans, and special services provided by the OAAA;
- to work with the staff of the OAAA and the University of Virginia on the effectiveness of its programs and services for Black students;
- to establish working relationships with University of Virginia student organizations and Black alumni; and
- to provide outlets for parents to exchange information and ideas.

The overwhelming reason for the OAAA's Parents Advisory Association is simply that it makes good sense, and had there not been one in place when I arrived at the University of Virginia, I would have created one. Black parents whose children attend predominately White institutions need to be visibly involved in these institutions. The Black parents involved with the OAAA recognize that their involvement makes a difference in their children's overall university experience. Pat Broussard, mother of two sons (now distinguished alumni) and former president of the PAA, puts it this way:

> Many people, including parents, believe that direct parental involvement in a college-bound child's education should cease once she has been dropped at the gates of some institution. I differ in this belief, and have been fortunate to [find] comrades who not only share, but practice the philosophy of continued parental involvement for college-age students. Our children don't stop needing us and craving our involvement simply because they reach college age.
>
> Many unenlightened folks still measure our children by a different yardstick, and we must be vigilant to guarantee that they receive the opportunities for which they have worked . . . . I don't see how African-American parents can expect others to do for our children that which we are not willing to do ourselves. We must affirm and support our college-age children, and we must reinforce their value not only to their biological family, but to the world family through [our] involvement.

Retention studies reveal that students are more likely to thrive in college if they are in a supportive and caring environment. I contend that one of the primary reasons why the University of Virginia has achieved the highest

Black student retention and graduation rates (87 percent) at any public institution in the nation is because of the active involvement of Black parents.

Over the years, we have been able to establish two chapters of the PAA—one in the Washington, D.C., metropolitan area, where families of the majority of the University of Virginia's Black students' families live, and the other in the Richmond/Tidewater area of Virginia, where the second-largest number of Black students' families live.

My role has always been to encourage parents to interact with the OAAA and their children as well as with the larger university community. In supporting the OAAA, parents support their children. In turn, the OAAA supports parents as well. For example, I make a point of calling at least one family a week to let them know that I am here for them. It's important that parents know that. Our job is to "run interference for them" whenever necessary. I have made it my life's work to practice what my mentor, Samuel Proctor, asserted about black administrators on predominantly White campuses, "The most meaningful and useful function for African-American administrators on a white campus is to become advocates for African-American students."

As for the structure of the parents' organization—Parents Advisory Association chapters meet quarterly throughout the year to organize various activities held both in students' home areas and at the university. For example, the PAA organizes a picnic each year for new students and parents in their respective areas. This event gives incoming parents and students an opportunity to meet for the first time to get acquainted with each other and with the OAAA staff before classes start. Meeting parents at this early date gives us an opportunity to provide a mini-orientation and to address incoming families' questions. Parents and students also meet current Black students and alumni at these picnics. Current students who attend the picnics include Office of African-American Affairs' peer advisors. So, even before they arrive "on grounds" to start classes, new students have the opportunity to become acquainted with other university students, faculty, and staff. This activity sponsored by the PAA also gives the association an opportunity to recruit new members.

Family Weekend in October offers another opportunity to meet with parents. We have an early morning breakfast, and I provide parents with an update on the "state of African American affairs" at the university and in the Black community as it affects their children. We also take this opportunity to recognize outstanding achievements of Black students. And, finally, the PAA uses this occasion to interact with parents and to recruit them to become active members in the association.

Through the PAA, parents have also organized various activities to raise funds that they have contributed to the OAAA to support cultural programming and to establish an emergency loan fund for students. Fund-raising activities have included raffles, parties, dinner dances, tennis tournaments, and art auctions.

Perhaps one of the most important activities of the PAA is an annual meeting with the president of the university, John T. Casteen. In the spring of 1991, President Casteen began to invite parents from both chapters to an annual luncheon. President Casteen recognizes the importance of the PAA and makes a genuine effort to remain connected to this group. This annual meeting is an excellent opportunity for parents to discuss their concerns regarding how the University as a whole is interacting with the OAAA and with their children. Specific issues of concern—for example, the University's position on affirmative action, racial profiling, OAAA budget, and space allocations—are also discussed.

I have repeatedly introduced the PAA model to colleagues across the country at conferences and in other settings. The PAA model will work at other universities if a cadre of faculty, staff, students, and administrators is committed to it. Unfortunately, Black faculty and staff on many predominately White campuses are often not very strong advocates for Black students; hence, they don't recognize that parents can play a viable role in their advocacy for Black students. No doubt, some feel they have enough to do to meet the needs of students and may not see how cultivating the interest of Black parents could possibly assist them in their endeavors.

At the University of Virginia, we have been successful with our model, largely because, as an Office of African-American Affairs, we are primarily responsible for meeting the needs of Black students. We are a "stand-alone" office, whereas, many institutions today have offices of multicultural affairs, which often means that they serve various cultural groups with many different issues. Our commitment, first and foremost, is to Black students. This makes a huge difference in how we are able to plan, develop, and operate our programs. When Black administrators, parents, and students feel that parental involvement in the life of the university is essential, then a PAA can succeed in other settings.

My goal for the PAA is to encourage more parents from other areas to become actively involved and to help them understand that the more they connect with the university, with Black alumni and with the Office of African-American Affairs—whose job it is to take care of their children—the greater the success their children will enjoy in this institution.

James E. Hunter

James E. Hunter is vice provost at Virginia State University (VSU). He has been at VSU for thirty years, fifteen in the office of the provost/vice president for academic and student affairs. He has worked in different capacities as an instructor and administrator: as chair of the Department of Health, Physical Education and Recreation, as chair of the Department of Curriculum and Instruction, and as interim dean of the School of Education. As dean, he provided leadership for the reaccreditation of the School of Education with the Commonwealth of Virginia's Department of Education, State Council of Higher Education in Virginia, and with the National Council for Accreditation of Teacher Education (NCATE). He also served as cochair of the Self-Study Committee for the reaccreditation of Virginia State University by the Southern Association of Colleges and Schools (SACS).

Dr. Hunter obtained his bachelor of arts from Shaw University and his master of science and doctor of philosophy from the University of Illinois, Champaign-Urbana. All his degrees in higher education were in physical education, with a concentration in education administration.

W. Eric Thomas

W. Eric Thomas, provost/vice president for academic and student affairs at Virginia State University since 2003, has twenty-four years of experience in higher education. During that time he has demonstrated his expertise as an educator, researcher, and administrator, writing papers, chapters, and abstracts that have appeared in nearly eighty publications. In addition, Dr. Thomas has developed twenty research projects that were funded by the federal government and private companies totaling more than $900,000.

In 1998, he left administration to return to teaching and research at Mississippi Valley State University as a research professor. After serving in that capacity for one year, he became an associate vice president for undergraduate studies and professor of biological sciences at Illinois State University, Normal. In that position, he had oversight responsibility for the admissions office, financial aid, registrar, general education program, University College, and the Honors Program.

Dr. Thomas received a bachelor and a master of science degrees in biology from Tennessee State University in 1973 and a doctorate in biochemistry from Meharry Medical School in 1980.

14

PERSONAL REFLECTIONS OF FACULTY MEMBERS AT VIRGINIA STATE UNIVERSITY

Introduction

Virginia State University (VSU) was founded on March 6, 1882, by Delegate Alfred W. Harris, a lawyer from Dinwiddie County, Virginia, who sponsored a bill in the General Assembly of Virginia to create the Virginia Normal and Collegiate Institute. This event occurred seventeen years after the Civil War ended. Delegate Harris had a vision for developing an institution of higher education for Black people where they could come "to drink from the fountain of knowledge until their ambition is satiated . . ." (Toppin 1992, 15). Since the university opened in 1883, many students have traversed these hallowed grounds seeking an education that would permit them to become self-sufficient, law-abiding citizens. Many VSU students have achieved significantly and been recognized nationally and internationally for their outstanding contributions to society. VSU has produced students who have become medical doctors, lawyers, engineers, generals, educators, scientists, psychologist, psychiatrists, social workers, sociologists, mathematicians, computer programmers, politicians, educational administrators, accountants, entrepreneurs, and judges.

Virginia State University has played a significant role in assisting students in becoming leaders in their respective communities. The question that needs to be asked is: "How did Virginia State University help thousands of students who graduated over the past 123 years to be successful in the various disciplines and/or professions?" The authors chose to do a qualitative study to find the answer. Four current faculty members who are alumni were asked to submit personal tributes to their experiences at VSU, and faculty members received e-mails asking them to identify successful strategies they were using to help students succeed in the classroom. Several faculty members responded to the e-mail and identified effective retention strategies. It is hoped that readers will better understand what VSU is doing to facilitate African American students' success in their pursuit of academic excellence.

Personal Tributes from Alumni of Virginia State University

Several alumni, who are also VSU faculty members, were asked to share their opinions about "What makes African American students succeed at Virginia State University?" Their personal stories were very revealing.

Why African Americans Succeed at Historically Black Colleges and Universities
Dr. Christine Smith, Assistant Professor

The primary reason for the success of African Americans at historically Black colleges and universities (HBCUs) is "identification." This means that these students feel a sense of belonging in an environment surrounded by others with a shared cultural ethnic background. Traditionally, HBCUs have provided African American students the opportunity to pursue higher education not afforded to them by other universities. These schools have understood that the traditional assessment tools (for example, SAT or ACT tests) should not be the sole indicators in predicting academic success.

African Americans generally have shared a collectivist worldview. That is, as a people they have been concerned about the success of "us." Whenever one African American does well, that individual's success has not been viewed only as an accomplishment for that person but for the group as a whole. Therefore, HBCUs were established so that we could educate our own. Traditionally, these schools have employed talented faculty who mentor, expect excellence, and provide hands-on teaching. These faculty members understand the students because they understand the culture. They have been caring, dedicated, and loyal teachers of African American students. Further, HBCUs have demonstrated success in doing so. A plethora of students have matriculated through Virginia State University (VSU) with great success.

In the 1970s many public secondary school systems were still segregated. Such was the case of the high school that I attended. However, in the high school setting, I identified easily with school and was a good student. Even with few resources, my teachers were dedicated and expected the best from us. On graduation from high school, the choice of where I would attend college was almost automatic. Because Virginia State College (later changed to university) was nearest to home, my choice was easy. I did not want to be far because of very close family ties. Further, other members of my family had attended VSU and were successful in their academic pursuits.

From day one, I felt the family-like atmosphere of this college campus. There was a sense of belonging. I could identify with the president, faculty, staff, and other students because we shared a similar cultural background. Nurturing was provided to "individual" students, classes were smaller than in some other institutions of higher learning, and teachers knew you by name. The perception that "I am somebody" and the teachers want me to be the "best" was paramount in my success at VSU.

The ideology of collectivism is so much a part of who I am because now I see myself in the position of role model, teacher, and mentor to my students. I, like those who helped to shape my generation, have the responsibility of helping this generation of learners. I take this charge seriously. I believe that my students see me and much of the faculty just as I viewed those before me. They are able to identify with VSU because it is a comfortable, nonthreatening academic environment for students who share a cultural background embedded in understanding the importance of education for success.

I always tell students that VSU is home for me. I have had experiences at other (predominantly White) institutions. I did what was expected and required of me with success. The perception was that of "salience"—associated with feelings of uneasiness and tension. I never felt at those schools the sense of belongingness I experienced at VSU.

Attributing My Success

Dr. Linda Person, Assistant Professor

Had anyone told me thirty years ago that I would be a college professor at Virginia State University (VSU), I would have said, "You must be kidding." Never would I have imagined that I would be guiding students at a university into the teaching profession. The experience really has been gratifying. In the following paragraphs , I share the beliefs and feelings that have contributed to my success over the past thirty years.

A large majority of the students attending VSU during the seventies were first-generation college students. Parents and guardians warned, in very few words, that the door of opportunity was open and we needed to take advantage of it. In those days, very few students attended White institutions on a regular basis, and I knew when I graduated from high school that I had to attend an HBCU. Relatives and friends at home informed me that the HBCU experience would be fun and nurturing at the same time.

In many ways, I feel that those of us who attended VSU were more grounded and demonstrated a higher level of confidence and self-esteem than many of the students matriculating in higher education today. I was provided more opportunities to make decisions before entering VSU, and these experiences afforded me the opportunity to "spread my wings." I quickly learned from right or wrong choices and moved forward. Students today face so many different kinds of challenges than some of the challenges in the past. Students today also have fewer responsibilities (particularly at home); therefore, they appear to be more indecisive, particularly when confronted with opportunities to make crucial decisions. I attribute this behavior to parents who may not have allowed their children to make decisions for themselves; hence, students appear not to be armed with the critical thinking skills necessary to assist them in making appropriate choices.

I also felt a sense of community with other students from the local communities and townships as well as other states, and I developed great friendships and strong alliances with my college acquaintances. There were few students with cars, and this general lack of transportation provided many chances to interact with friends and bond on a daily basis. This quickly provided the impetus for lasting friendships. It also allowed us to get to know a large percentage of the students who attended VSU. Alumni over the years have indicated that friendships created at VSU were stronger than those created in grade school, high school, or their formative years. This sense of community permeated the VSU community.

As a VSU student, I participated in many extracurricular activities (basketball, swimming, the marching band, and student organizations). I was not an avid reader, nor was I very fond of studying after classes were over, but I had an insatiable desire to please people. Through compassion, strong leadership, support, and commitment to service from my professors and peers, I managed to graduate cum laude.

The instructors in the Health and Physical Education Department were a very close-knit crew who recognized the need to cultivate relationships with students at first contact. Many times what appeared to be brief encounters turned into short stories before the communication ended. These short stories were usually situations involving previous students or a direct order about how students should govern themselves on and off campus.

Other professors all over campus had stories to share. They often made comments about a recent graduate, particularly someone who was well known for his or her accomplishments. Professors would welcome certain discussions involving a relative and would compare us to them in the classroom. This alone provided fuel to ignite discussions. We either felt great (sometimes embarrassed) or we felt that we had a lot of growing up to do. Smiles and laughter would fill the room. Students demonstrated great respect for their professors because they had been taught strong values at home. The need to challenge authority might have crossed the minds of many students, but rarely did a student demonstrate such actions.

I had so many angels (faculty, administrators, staff, etc.) who cared about my total well-being. There was obvious commitment and passion in the hearts and minds of many faculty members at VSU, which was reflected in the thirty years or more they spent at this great institution. During my experience at VSU, there was always a sense of family. I believe coming from a strong African American family assisted in my transition from home to college. Those of us who attended VSU thirty years ago were informed early that this was our one chance to do something with our lives. We knew when we left home to attend college that we had to take advantage of such an opportunity, and we were reminded and assured of the support system awaiting our arrival. The structure in place (dormitories, cafeteria, library, faculty, staff, and administration) sat on a firm foundation. Structure and a sense of family allowed VSU students to develop a caring attitude and a desire to learn. Faculty and peers demonstrated a deep sense of caring, and this is what made the support system at VSU so strong. This was tradition, and the VSU family demonstrated a lot of pride and passion in guiding and preparing us for the toils of life.

My Experience at Virginia State University

Aishia Bailey, Assistant Professor

When it was time to make my decision about what college to attend, I was torn in the beginning. Having spent my first two years of high school in a rural, predominately White environment and the last two years in a suburban, predominately White environment, I had not been encouraged to attend a college that was meant to enrich my cultural awareness or instill in me a sense of racial pride. Instead, at the first rural high school, I, like most of the other Black students—despite test scores, demonstrated academic abilities, or personal inclinations—was encouraged to attend a community college, become a beautician, or join the army. At the second, suburban high school, I was grouped together with all of the college-bound students and groomed to attend one of the state's more traditional schools. Whenever I, or the few other Black students in my graduating class, so much as mentioned HBCUs, our teachers openly scoffed at us and did their best to turn us away from such ideas. I watched several of my classmates fall into the mind-set that HBCUs must inherently be substandard or bad schools simply because they were traditionally for Blacks. These sentiments were not only perpetuated by the teachers, but they were also reinforced by the guidance counselors. I never learned about Spelman College, Howard University, Virginia Union University, Hampton University, Virginia State University, Norfolk State University, and others from any high school guidance counselor—my parents and older sister told me about them. Because I was not yet ready to go too far away from home, I ultimately chose to attend Virginia State University (VSU), and it remains one of the best decisions I have ever made.

Although I am the daughter and granddaughter of college professors, I did not encounter many other Black professionals in my daily life while I was growing up. This was why attending VSU, an HBCU, was so special and important to me. While attending college there, I was fortunate enough to see scholars and community leaders regularly who looked like me! I had Black, White, and international professors, of course, but the faculty at VSU was predominately Black, a completely new experience for me and many of my peers. We were used to the politics and dynamics of always being in the minority in the learning environment, and most of us suffered from the inherent damage this does to one's psyche. It was very gratifying and inspiring to see Black scholars teaching and leading the next generation of Blacks to success in their chosen fields of study. This instilled in me a sense of pride and responsibility to give back to my community that lives in me to this very day. I even chose to teach at an HBCU as a result of my experience.

Accordingly, as a student, I had deep respect for all of my professors and the administrators; I admired them and was proud to see in them what life could be like if I worked hard and did my best at everything. I received this message from most educators, but it meant so much more to me coming from my Black professors and administrators, like President Eddie N. Moore

Jr., Ms. Linda Fitzgerald, Dr. Robert Turner, and Dr. Claude Flythe, who took time out of their busy schedules to encourage and mentor me. I felt a sense of nurturing that I had never known in an educational environment until I experienced it at VSU. My professors were deeply invested in me and in my peers. They cared about whether we learned what they were teaching; they believed in our abilities; they saw more in us than we saw in ourselves; and they would not accept less than the best. They truly celebrated our successes with us; opened their arms when we experienced failure, losses, or defeat; and said what needed to be said *when* it needed to be said every time we did not live up to their high standards or expectations. In essence, they gave us what we needed. I strive every day to become the kind of professor I had as an undergraduate at VSU.

Attending college at an HBCU was like combining the community feeling of a church family with the structured atmosphere of an educational environment. We were fortified in culture, character, knowledge, and survival skills in a way that would not have been the same anywhere else. One of my favorite classes was called University Success/Freshman General Assembly. It was a class that every first-year student took, and in it, besides other practical types of knowledge, we were taught the history of the university, the school songs, the names of all of the presidents and their wives, and the history behind every building on the campus. This class helped me to understand that I was walking on soil rich in history, and it kept me aware of the struggles of my ancestors. This really helped me to stay focused on living out the dreams that my forefathers and foremothers had and on making sure that I never forgot to reach back and give to my community when I finally achieved my own goals.

Finally, many of my professors, whenever they had the opportunity, would incorporate cultural connections into the curriculum. Whether they were having me and my classmates trace our family histories, encouraging us to perform annually in culturally based activities, or sitting with us and listening to highly decorated black poets, authors, scholars, and leaders of the Civil Rights Movement deliver inspirational speeches—my professors played a major role in my life as a student at VSU. My college experience was full of memorable moments that have solidified my sense of importance in society, my sense of racial awareness, and my personal sense of pride. Ultimately, attending an HBCU, specifically VSU, was educationally, culturally, spiritually, and intellectually enlightening. I know that I am a stronger, more grounded individual because of this priceless and unique experience.

Acts of Kindness Received: I Owe So Much to Virginia State University

Dr. Leon Bey, Associate Professor

Gratitude is a very prominent word that comes to mind when I think of my collective experiences at Virginia State University (VSU). In as much as VSU has been the conduit through which I have been afforded a number of rewarding professional and personal experiences, my debt to this great institution is incalculably great.

I love VSU and feel peculiarly favored to have been graduated from this extraordinary institution. Since my undergraduate days, I have benefited from many special "acts of kindness" from a wide variety of individuals. For example, I received much appreciated *personal* advice from my professors/advisors and coaches such as Dr. Cora Salzberg, who literally "made the call" that resulted in my receiving a graduate assistantship to attend Indiana University (IU), and Coach Harold Deane, the former men's basketball coach, with whom I've subsequently worked in a number of different capacities. The former is in large measure why I earned magna cum laude laurels, the Health and Physical Education Department's "1975 Male Student of the Year" award, a master's degree from IU, and a doctorate from Temple University. The latter speaks to the great concern that my coaches had for my well-being, even though I was, at best (and I'm not being modest here), a marginal athlete. These tremendous, nurturing role models will probably never know how much they have meant to me.

When I left VSU, I was armed with the homegrown (I am a product of an immeasurably supportive two-parent household) and VSU-inspired self-confidence that gave me the wherewithal to compete with some of the best. After having been graduated from IU, I became the head men's basketball coach and a member of the health, physical education, and recreation (HPER) faculty at Penn State-Behrend College (PSBC), a four-year institution in Erie, Pennsylvania.

After two years at PSBC, I was brought back to my alma mater as a member of its HPER Department's faculty, where the author of this chapter, Dr. James Hunter, was serving as department chair. Now, Dr. Hunter (who has since ascended to his erstwhile role of dean of the School of Education and his present vice provost position) is my man, but at one time he wasn't at the top of my list. You see, I was happy teaching and coaching with my master's degree but he kept encouraging . . . well, let's call it what it was . . .

"bugging me" about "going back to school" to earn my doctoral degree. Simply put, I did not want to go, but the man was relentless. He kept on "bugging me," until eventually I acquiesced, and now I'm so glad that I did. Incidentally, I try to thank him as much as I can now, especially since he has finally stopped "bugging me." In fact, I have since returned the favor. I now "bug him" about all types of professional and personal advice.

Another great mentor to whom I owe an enormous debt of gratitude is Dr. Claud Flythe, who served principally as HPER professor, baseball coach, and athletic director while I was a student and during the early stages of my professional career. He also served VSU as its (and my) HPER Department chair, vice president for student affairs, and chief of staff. For parts of four decades, I've watched this man reach great heights in the aforementioned and other capacities. During all of these years, he has continued to make time for me . . . no matter the hour . . . no matter the situation. On numerous occasions, I've sought counsel in his office, during athletic and other events, and even at his home. Speaking of his home, my wife and I were frequent visitors at his residence (particularly during my coaching career), and my children, who are all grown now, still speak fondly of their childhood days in his swimming pool. Even now, well over thirty years since we first met, I still call on him for advice. At one point, however, I wasn't all that excited about accepting it.

You see, after I left "State" as an undergraduate, I let (then athletic director) Dr. Flythe know of my strong desire to return to my alma mater as a member of its basketball coaching staff and HPER Department. He told me that I had to get more experience before he could help me. I really, really wanted to return . . . very quickly, mind you, but I knew that I had better follow his advice if I expected his support. Well, true to his word, he did help me, but only after I had gotten the requisite experience. I trusted Dr. Flythe, and he didn't let me down . . . nor did Dr. Hunter. To this day, I still trust them and admire their integrity, sacrificial service, and great humility.

When working with students, I try to give them the type of support that Drs. Hunter and Flythe (and many others) provided me. For example, it is customary for students to meet with me in the office during scheduled sessions or, when possible, when they drop by unexpectedly. I also spend time with them during athletic, cultural, and other events, or when I see them at the mall. They also call me at home and e-mail me regularly. I try to be as accessible as possible to our former and present students and their family members and friends. In addition, I write letters of recommendation for a variety of reasons and network with those whom I think can help students accomplish their goals. I use a variety of teaching styles to enhance the instructional delivery process and teach them life lessons on a regular basis. I love our students and try to demonstrate that affection through my words and deeds.

I also love Virginia State University and am happy to have served it in a number of capacities (for example, teacher, coach, athletic director, HPER chair, dean of the School of Liberal Arts and Education, and acting director of the Academy for Faculty Development). For these and other great opportunities, I am grateful. Oh, I am also grateful because my wife and I met during our first year at VSU. Incidentally, our middle child (son) is also a graduate of VSU, and the other two children are products of two other sister institutions.

My wife and I celebrated our thirtieth class reunion in May 2005. Just think, had it not been for VSU, we might never have met.

Faculty Retention Strategies

Faculty members have played a major role in retaining students at this institution. The retention rate for students after spending their first two years at the university is 71 percent. This two-year time span is when colleges and universities usually suffer the greatest loss of students. Currently, the university has an overall retention rate of 50 percent for students who graduate within four years (Ridley 2004).

Departmental faculty uses different strategies in retaining and motivating students; these strategies vary by department. Rosezelia Roy (2005), director of the Students with Disabilities Program, reports that she uses the following retention strategies with her students:

- Focus on each individual in a holistic manner (academically, socially, and wellness of each individual).
- Have open communication with and a welcoming environment for students. Meet students where they are and then proceed. Offer support when needed. Present a nonjudgmental environment.
- Make students aware of services provided at VSU.
- Help them to practice sound decision making.
- Build communication skills, verbal as well as written.
- Encourage students to be aware of self—to know their strengths and weaknesses and build on the strengths to help counteract the weaknesses.

- Encourage independence.
- Promote career exploration, internships, and employment opportunities.
- Strongly encourage visiting Career Placement Services.
- Use time management techniques.

Lera Johnson (2005), Department of Psychology chair, indicates that faculty in her department practice the following retention strategies:

- Students who have not preregistered for the upcoming semester receive a personal phone call.
- Students who have been placed on warning or probation due to low grade point averages (GPAs) receive a reduced course load (twelve semester hours), advisement designed to raise their GPA, and referral to tutoring service (Academic Support Center), counseling, and/or mentoring program.
- Every psychology major is assigned to an advisor who remains the student's advisor from freshman through junior year. As students go on to their senior year (ninety credit hours), they become the advisees of the chair, who works with them to make sure they have completed their requirements for graduation.
- Faculty members academically advise students and do not permit them to take courses out of sequence of their curriculum.
- Academic advisors review students' mid-term grades and refer those students who are struggling to the Academic Support Center after conferencing with them.
- The Psychology Department maintains a psychology graduate student in the Psychology Experimental lab for twenty hours a week who is available to tutor in any psychology course.
- Members of Psi Chi, the National Honor Society in psychology, and the Psychology Club also offer their tutoring services.
- Students who earn a 3.0 or higher GPA are invited to join Psi Chi, the National Honor Society in Psychology.

Wesley Hogan (2005), a faculty member in the Department of History, reports that the faculty in his department practice the following retention strategies:

- Enforce a very strict attendance policy (and more than two unexcused absences results in a grade no higher than D).

- Use multimedia (photography, video, role-plays, and smart board technology) in classroom lectures.
- Encourage students to visit their instructors during office hours for remediation and one-on-one help.
- Know students by name (even in big classes, by using name plates) and making oneself available before and after class for individual attention.
- Assign a lot of writing assignments and give detailed feedback.
- Assign independent research projects and enforce rigorous standards of evidence and presentation.
- Give warm, encouraging individual attention to fix skill areas that are weak, apprising students of volunteer and paid internship opportunities as well as scholarships.

Delores Greene (2005), associate dean and director for the Teacher Education Program, identified the following strategies to work effectively with students who are seeking an endorsement in teacher education:

- Have open dialogue sessions within classes.
- Have individual conferences to meet student needs.
- Schedule individual and group tutoring sessions.
- Prepare study guides and learning modules to address academic gaps in learning.
- Establish performance criteria.
- Articulate high expectations for academic performance and dispositions.
- Provide opportunities for participation in leadership initiatives.

Summary

Since Virginia State University opened its doors to students, the university has always had a cadre of dedicated faculty to teach its students. The single theme restated in the personal tributes of alumni was the caring faculty who assisted them in becoming the people they are today. The writers also mentioned the family-like atmosphere on campus and the nurturing they received from administrators, faculty, and staff. African American faculty members understand the culture that African American students come from; in many cases, the environments these students come from are the same environments African American faculty experienced when they were younger.

Therefore, these professors can relate to these students because of their common experiences. They enjoy helping "their own" overcome their shortcomings and preparing them to take their rightful places in society.

In conclusion, the reason why African American students have been able to succeed at Virginia State University is the commitment of its faculty to teaching and mentoring them as well as creating a nurturing environment that allows students to grow without being penalized. I sincerely believe that commitment plays a major role in the success of African American students at all HBCUs.

References

Bailey, Aishia. 2005. *My experience at Virginia State University.* Petersburg, VA: Virginia State University.

Bey, Leon. 2005. *Acts of kindness received: I owe so much to Virginia State University.* Petersburg, VA: Virginia State University.

Person, Linda. 2005. *Attribution to my success.* Petersburg, VA: Virginia State University.

Bibliography

Greene, Delores. *Retention Activities to Support Students in Teacher Education.* (Petersburg, VA: Virginia State University, 2005).

Hogan, Wesley. *Retention Activities in the Department of History.* (Petersburg, VA: Virginia State University, 2005).

Johnson, Lera J. *Retention Activities in the Department of Psychology.* (Petersburg, VA: Virginia State University, 2005).

Ridley, Emmett. *Retention Data.* Office of Institutional Planning and Assessment. (Petersburg, VA: Virginia State University, 2004).

Roy, Rosezelia W. *Retention Strategies for Students with Disabilities.* (Petersburg, VA: Virginia State University, 2005).

Smith, Christine. *Why African Americans Succeed at Historically Black Colleges and Universities.* (Petersburg, VA: Virginia State University, 2005).

Toppin, Edgar. *Loyal Sons and Daughters: Virginia State University 1882 to 1992.* (Petersburg, VA: Virginia State University Foundation, 1992), 15.

T. J. Bryan

Even though Dr. T. J. Bryan's parents never finished high school, they always stressed the importance of education, believing that success in life takes hard work. Dr. Bryan took those words of wisdom to heart. On July 1, 2003, she was named chancellor of Fayetteville State University, the second-oldest public university in the Old North State.

Dr. Bryan attended graduate school at Morgan State, where she earned a master's degree in English. As a Ford Foundation National Fellow, she enrolled at the University of Maryland at College Park, where she earned a doctoral degree in English language and literature. Dr. Bryan joined the English faculty at Baltimore's Coppin State College in 1982. There, among her accomplishments, she established one of the nation's fourteen original Ronald McNair Post-Baccalaureate Achievement programs. At Coppin she was progressively promoted to department chair, dean of the Honors Division, and dean of arts and sciences at Coppin State, where she worked through 1998.

In 1998, she was selected by the thirteen-campus University System of Maryland to become its associate vice chancellor for academic affairs. In this role, she focused on faculty affairs, academic policy, and educational equity issues. She is the primary author of *Miles to Go: Maryland* and *The Road Taken*, two works that led to legislation in 2000 and 2001, creating a governor's task force and passing legislation in 2002 that provided a college intervention program and guaranteed financial assistance to low-income students.

In 2002, The Pennsylvania State System of Higher Education recruited her to the position of vice chancellor for academic and student affairs. She also served as chief academic officer and chief student affairs officer for the system. In 2003 she was appointed chancellor of the Commonwealth's fourteen state-owned universities. A year later, The University of North Carolina System appointed Dr. Bryan chancellor of Fayetteville State University.

Since Chancellor Bryan's arrival at FSU, enrollment has increased to approximately 5,500 students, and the student to faculty ratio has improved from 23:1 to 21:1. She has also made international education one of her priorities. Fund raising has increased in 2004–05—in large measure because of Investment 136, her initiative to call on alumni and friends to match the university's investment of $136 for land on which FSU's predecessor institution—the Howard School—was erected in 1867.

15

PATHWAYS TO STUDENT SUCCESS AT FAYETTEVILLE STATE UNIVERSITY

Introduction

The United States is home to more than thirty-five hundred colleges and universities—two- and four-year; public, private, tribal, and proprietary; research and doctoral; comprehensive and liberal arts; serving historically Black, traditionally White, and Hispanic populations. Within this wide assortment of institutional types, a variety of degree programs is available to the millions of students who enter college each year. These entering students are by and large optimistic about the future and about their chances for success. Of course, they do not all enter college classrooms with the same level of preparedness for success, nor do they enter with the same academic experiences or credentials across the board. But they generally expect that they will do well and that they will obtain the preparation they need for the next phase of their lives.

But while the United States is considered in important ways the "land of opportunity" academically, our institutions are failing many of our students. Those students who enroll in college expecting success often find that they have not been well prepared for the rigors of higher education. Many of them wind up losing whatever confidence and aspirations with which they began their higher education careers when they encounter their first real academic challenges. For others, the problem is not a lack of academic preparation or confidence in their abilities but, rather, a lack of financial resources and a dearth of knowledge about pursuing student-aid opportunities. For some, the problem is at least threefold: lack of preparation, dearth of financial resources, and hardships posed by difficult family circumstances. These burdens are particularly overwhelming for first-generation college students and students of color.

Data collected by the National Center for Education Statistics reveal the depth of the problem. In a study of first-time college students whose progress was followed from 1996 through 2001, only 29 percent of the students who began college in 1996 had earned bachelor's degrees by 2001. Ten percent had earned associate's degrees, and 12 percent had earned a certificate of some kind. Fourteen percent were still enrolled in college in 2001, but 35 percent of the students left without earning a degree.

If present trends continue, only sixty-eight of one hundred students who are currently in the ninth grade will graduate from high school on time. Only thirty-eight will go directly to college, and of those thirty-eight, only eighteen will end up graduating from college. For African American students, the numbers are even worse. Of one hundred ninth graders, just forty-nine will graduate from high school on time. Only twenty-seven will go directly to college, and of those twenty-seven, only nine will graduate.

Other studies—including the Joint Center for Political and Economic Studies' examination of the Black worker's plight in the twenty-first century—indicate that the unemployment rate among African Americans remains twice as high as the unemployment rate of White Americans. The center's report blames this disparity not only on discrimination but also on differences in education. Speaking more broadly, unemployment data for the country indicate that, in 2001, when the country's overall unemployment rate was 3.5 percent for people ages twenty-four to sixty-four, 2 percent of college graduates were unemployed; for those who had only graduated from high school, however, the rate was 4.2 percent.

As a nation, we know how important earning a college degree is—not just for the individual who earns the degree but also for the family, the community, and society at large. Many organizations, including the Institute for Higher Education, have linked attainment of a college degree to participation in civic life and community service. U.S. Census data underscore the connection between a bachelor's degree and economic prosperity: individuals with bachelor's degrees earn almost $1 million more during their working lives than do individuals with only a high-school education.

Sadly, as readily available as these data are, and in spite of the clear picture they paint of a nation divided, our country has often lacked the will to address the problems that lead to the disparities—the nagging issues of inadequate preparation, insufficient financial aid, and inadequate emotional support, all of which can make attaining a degree an unrealistic goal for millions of students.

An article in the fall 2004 issue of the *Journal of Blacks in Higher Education* notes that in a study of graduation rates at forty-four of the largest historically Black public and private institutions in the country, two-thirds or more of all entering African Americans at twenty-four of these campuses dropped out. Yet, as someone who has spent most of my life either studying or working at historically Black colleges and universities (HBCUs), I believe that HBCUs as a distinct and important subset of American campuses are uniquely equipped and positioned to deal with the challenge of graduating African American students.

The programs that many HBCUs have in place to enhance retention benefit not just African American students but also other groups of students as well, particularly students who are the first in their families to participate in higher education. I think it is important to keep this point in mind in any discussion of retention efforts because our society suffers when higher education systematically fails *any* group of students—whether they are African Americans, Appalachian Whites, Latinos, or Hmong refugees.

Not all of the news about African American education is disheartening; indeed, some of it is uplifting. U.S. Census data reveal that 17 percent of African American adults over age twenty-five held bachelor's degrees in 2002, compared to 11.3 percent in 2000 and 3.1 percent in 1960. Meanwhile, according to the National Opinion Research Center's "Doctorate Recipients from United States Universities: Summary Report 2003," 1,708 African Americans earned doctorates in 2003, an all-time high. African American doctoral recipients accounted for 6.5 percent of all doctoral-degree recipients in 2003, a 4 percent increase over 2002.

But the data are mixed, and, in any case, the numbers alone fail to convey the full story. There is an old saying that if you do not know where you are going, any road will take you there. For several decades, many of us in higher education have been wandering—always with good intentions but not necessarily with a clear destination in mind. We have often focused on data, that is, the numbers of students entering colleges, the numbers of students graduating, the length of time to degree, etc. Yet, we have too often been blind to what the data could potentially reveal to us because we do not always "connect the dots," and we have not always used the findings to make our institutions, whether they are HBCUs or traditionally White institutions, places of success for students. At this critical stage, however, our society seems to have reached a tipping point when policy makers and educators are united around one very simple idea: at a time when an increasing number of college and university students are students of color, and at a point at which our nation's economic future is so closely linked to the success of our educational systems, we simply cannot afford to fail to graduate most of the students who actually enter our campuses.

The Bronco Way

My own institution has engaged in a number of student-success strategies over the years. Fayetteville State University (FSU), a constituent institution of the University of North Carolina, was founded in 1867 initially as a normal school for the education of Black teachers. In fall 2004, FSU enrolled 5,441 students, of whom 4,085—or 75 percent—were African American. In 2003–04, more than half of our undergraduate students received aid in the form of grants and scholarships, and over 43 percent of our undergraduates had student loans.

Many freshmen who enter FSU possess characteristics that are linked to high dropout rates; they are low-income, first-generation students with SAT scores below 900. An annual study of the sixteen campuses within the University of North Carolina indicates that Fayetteville State has one of the highest percentages of freshmen with family incomes below $25,000.

We have attempted to ensure student success by establishing core values for everyone in the university community—students, faculty, administrators, and staff. Our sports mascot is the Bronco, and our mantra, "The Bronco Way," summarizes our beliefs about the university and our roles in it. Our mantra appears on pole banners throughout the campus. Faculty members are oriented to "The Bronco Way" and share it with their students. We all invoke it whenever we can—at commencements, class meetings, student orientations, alumni gatherings, and in all manner of contexts.

The attributes of "The Bronco Way" are positive energy, unity, high expectations for all (no exceptions), and accountability. Positive energy means that we believe in ourselves, we believe in each other, and, most of all, we believe in the enduring strength of our learning community, Fayetteville State University, and that we stand together as a family. It means that we commit to a purpose that is higher than ourselves, and that, in spite of occasional disagreements, we come together to lift each other up through encouragement and support. Our common focus and sense of purpose enable us to set high expectations, the third tenet of "The Bronco Way." Achievement is our highest priority. We set high expectations for each of our students while also recognizing that they come to us with different learning styles, multiple intelligences, and different needs. We also set the highest expectations for our faculty, administrators, and staff. The final tenet is accountability, which means that we do the things we promise to do. We take responsibility for both our achievements and our failures. Our students are accountable for their performance, but we are accountable to *them*, and we are also accountable to each other!

Our premise is that adhering to The Bronco Way and making it our philosophy strengthens us as a community, for through these shared values, all of us at the university are connected in ways that would not otherwise be possible.

Fayetteville State University Retention Programs, Including Outcomes Data

We have implemented a number of initiatives to improve our retention and graduation rates. Some have been in place for a number of years, others are in their first year or still in the planning stages. Descriptions of some of our programs and summaries of their efficacy follow.

Project Cheer

We work extensively with incoming freshmen through Project CHEER (Creating Higher Expectations for Educational Readiness), a four-week, summer-enrichment program. CHEER provides an opportunity for admitted students to earn six hours of university credit (Introduction to College Algebra and Grammar and Usage); improve study skills through workshops; and meet other students before the regular academic year begins. In addition, participants receive a university-funded scholarship that covers the full cost of tuition and books.

To be eligible for CHEER, students must be North Carolina residents and have the potential to contribute to and gain maximum benefit from the program. Each CHEER student must attend an orientation session with a parent or guardian; attend and arrive on time for all classes and workshops presented as part of the program; and complete all assignments associated with classes and workshops. Students who miss more than three days for reasons other than *documented* personal illness or family emergency are withdrawn from the program and are required to repay the scholarship.

As the fall 2004 semester ended, the sixty-three students who participated in CHEER were performing better than the freshman class as a whole, with an average grade point average (GPA) of 2.57, compared to 2.35 for the entire class. In addition, 69.4 percent of the students are on track to graduate in four years, based on earning at least fifteen credit hours in the fall, compared to 22.7 percent for the class as a whole. The CHEER students achieved these milestones despite having lower SAT scores and lower high-school GPAs than did the freshman class as a whole. Furthermore, of the twenty CHEER students who participated in the program in summer 2003, nineteen enrolled for the spring 2005 semester, a retention rate of 95 percent. Significantly, fourteen of the summer 2003 students are on track to graduate in four years.

University College

The University College implements a number of activities, beginning with summer orientation. Students receive information and are encouraged to take advantage of resources. They complete profile examinations and, based on the findings, are registered in specific courses. Students are placed in specific "Bronco Cohorts" and are likely to have three or four courses with other members of their cohorts. Students who need assistance are assigned to the Mathematics Laboratory and the Reading/Writing Center. They may be preselected for participation in the Student Support Services Program, which provides tutoring, academic counseling, and enrichment activities.

We implemented our Freshman-Year Initiative (FYI) in 1996, although individual components of the program had been in place before that time. Prior to full implementation of FYI, it had become increasingly clear that far more students were falling by the wayside than were graduating. FYI is based on several assumptions drawn from current research on the factors that lead to student success:

- Programs must address a variety of academic, personal, and social needs as they assist students in making the transition to college.
- Students must be both academically and socially integrated into an institution; they must feel as though they *belong*. This connection occurs as students discover congruence between their individual goals and the institution's mission and resources.
- Programs must incorporate intrusive advisement and early-alert systems during the freshman year, when students are most vulnerable to dropping out.
- Students must receive rapid, regular feedback from faculty members.

One simple step is to check attendance in classes and activities and to communicate to students that their presence and absence are noticed.

- To the extent possible, support resources should be coordinated by a single campus office; in our case, our first-year efforts are coordinated by the University College, the unit to which all freshmen are admitted. Primary components should be housed in a single building on campus.
- All components of the program should be assessed regularly, and the results should be used to make revisions when necessary.
- The campus chancellor or president and other high-level administrators must champion retention and graduation efforts.

Specific components of FYI include the following:

- *Freshman Seminar.* Students are enrolled in a two-semester sequence that covers a variety of topics designed to ease their transition to FSU: university history, policies, and procedures; study skills; health issues (particularly as they pertain to sexual matters); financial aid; and university services such as counseling and the library. The Freshman Seminar instructor meets with students weekly and advises all students in his or her seminar section. The importance of the seminar is that it provides a structure for monitoring student progress, intervening when necessary, and ensuring that students establish contacts with other university resources such as Career Services, the Library, Financial Aid, and alcohol- and drug-awareness programs.
- *Student Peers.* Freshmen Seminar is the context in which students are linked to student mentors. These Peer Academic Leaders, or PALs, are available to students to offer assistance and are often critical members of a student's support group.
- *Faculty/Administrator/Staff Mentors.* Following an application process, freshmen are paired with volunteer faculty/administrator/staff mentors for a semester. Each student and mentor pair signs a contract that outlines the parameters of the relationship. The expectation is that the parties will meet on at least three occasions during the semester—for a minimum of one hour each time. As often as possible, the meetings occur off campus. Mentors receive a mentoring manual and training/orientation to enable them to perform maximally. Evaluations are completed at different points during the semester. After the semester,

students and mentors may continue the formal mentoring relationship with each other or may discontinue the program.

- *Early-Alert System.* Students who are experiencing academic difficulty are identified through midterm grade reports. Because of their frequent interaction with the students, Freshman Seminar instructors are well positioned to assist students who have questions or are identified through the Early-Alert System.

- *Freshman Counselors.* Freshman counselors communicate with students who have particularly serious academic or personal problems. They help students to resolve problems and refer them, when necessary, to the Counseling Center or another appropriate resource.

- *Assistance with Choice of Major.* Students declare their majors at the end of the second semester and are transferred to the appropriate department. If they do not meet the requirements of the majors they want to pursue, they continue to be served by the University College.

- *Monitoring of Progress.* Members of the University College staff monitor students' progress to ensure that they complete core-curriculum requirements and enroll in the general-education courses required in their intended majors.

The results of our Freshman-Year Initiative have been gratifying. The cohort of students who entered Fayetteville State in 1996 had a graduation rate of 23 percent; the cohort of students who entered in 1995, a year before full implementation of FYI, had a four-year graduation rate of 14.8 percent.

Our success with FYI notwithstanding, we noticed that too many students who were being retained through the freshman year were dropping out in their sophomore or junior year as the attention and targeted resources they received diminished. In fall 2004, we rolled out the Sophomore-Year Initiative (SYI) to combat "sophomore slump," a period when the enthusiasm of the first year has waned and students may feel isolated and overwhelmed by the college experience.

SYI includes many of the components that define FYI: mentoring, intrusive advisement for those students who need it, tutoring, and supplemental instruction. Experience and research tell us that many low-income, underprepared students can excel in higher education, but they need very highly structured support systems to do so. We have a variety of such structures for first-year students; the goal is now to extend some of those resources to the second year. We are also working to create learning communities that will link students together and integrate them more fully into the academic and social environments.

Eleven items from the Noel-Levitz Student Satisfaction Inventory that are directly related to the University-College experience were reviewed. In general, the Student Satisfaction Inventory results indicate that the University College is achieving its goal of assisting students in their transition to the university and providing advisement and academic support.

In all eleven areas, for each of the past four years, the satisfaction level of our students has been higher than the satisfaction level of the national group, with only two exceptions. The 2002–2003 freshmen rated the advisors' knowledge about requirements at the same level as the national group. The 2002 freshman class rated the item on students' sense of belonging above the national group by a difference of just + 0.23, which was statistically insignificant. Differences in satisfaction between FSU students and the national group in the other nine areas are statistically significant (that is, they cannot be attributed to chance).

Bronco Men of Distinction Learning Community

Black males on college and university campuses are rapidly becoming an endangered species. Men of all races and ethnicities are now enrolled in higher education in lower numbers than are women. In our continuing effort to improve our retention and graduation efforts, we introduced the Bronco Men of Distinction learning community in fall 2004 to track selected male students from the freshman to the senior year.

Named in honor of the university's bronco sports mascot, the learning community is designed to serve first-generation males with at-risk characteristics such as low high-school GPAs and low SAT scores. We especially target for inclusion males who have participated in CHEER. The goals of the learning community are as follows:

- Awaken students to their personal strengths.
- Foster student achievement from a strengths-based perspective.
- Enhance student engagement through a strengths-based campus philosophy.
- Enable students to create actionable strategic plans that build on their strengths.

"Strengths Finder," at the core of the learning community, is used to train faculty and advising and residential staff. It is invoked to assess the strengths of all freshmen in the learning community, each of whom receives a copy. Bronco Men are all enrolled in course sections that are set aside specifically for them; course pedagogies include experiential learning and active learning. In addition, each semester, Bronco Men engage in at least three advising sessions. At the end of the freshman year, Bronco Men should have earned thirty-four credits.

In the sophomore year, they continue to enroll in sections of courses that are set aside for them; their activities include career-planning and strengths-development retreats as well as professional forums and career fairs. In year three, Bronco Men engage in service learning and cross-cultural courses, and in their senior year, they participate in internships tied to their strengths and engage in capstone experiences grounded in strengths-based reflection.

The Bronco Men are outperforming the other African American males in the freshman class (although somewhat below the class as a whole, which is 67 percent female). They earned a mean semester GPA of 2.21, compared to 2.11 for other African American freshman males. Of the Bronco Men, 18.9 percent were on track to graduate in four years, compared to 12.2 percent for other African American males in the class (and compared to 22.7 percent for the largely female class as a whole). The Bronco Men earned an average of 12.26 hours for the fall semester, compared to an average of 11.75 hours for the rest of the class.

The Pilot Gateway Program

The Gateway Program is a learning-living initiative designed to provide an opportunity for students to improve academic performance while living in an on-campus residential environment. Throughout the academic year, the students receive targeted academic support. Of the students in the pilot program, 73 percent have improved academically.

Experimental Programs at FSU

FSU recently implemented the following initiatives, which are promising, but for which we do not yet have outcomes data.

Bronco Parents and Family Association

Initiated in fall 2004 by the Academic Student Services Center, the Bronco Parents and Family Association (PFA) promotes and enhances opportunities for parents of our students to communicate, participate, and establish a sense of community with one another and with FSU faculty, staff, and administrators. Consisting of Fayetteville and area parents and families, the PFA's board seeks input from parents and families from across the country. Parents and other family members may volunteer for board membership at any time during their students' university careers. Once appointed by the associate vice chancellor for student academic services, board members serve terms of up to five years. The board meets twice annually to conduct the business of the association, once during the fall and once during the spring semester.

With input from the board, we plan to publish a handbook for parents that includes information about life at FSU. It will also include a campus map, a list of helpful telephone numbers, miscellaneous information about the campus and community, and the academic calendar.

Three hundred parents and family members attended the initial meeting, which was convened during summer orientation.

The FSU Graduation Project

The Graduation Project identifies students who left the university in good academic standing and were close to completing their bachelor's degrees. The purpose of the project is to encourage these students to return so that they can complete their degree requirements. Nonenrolled students with a minimum GPA of 2.00 and with ninety earned credit hours comprise the target population.

Sophomore Summer I

The most commonly stated reason for poor academic performance is an unbalanced division between work and school commitments. The primary function of Sophomore Summer I, which was implemented for the first time in summer 2005, is to provide students, at the end of the freshman year, with strategies that lead to their uninterrupted continuation in good academic standing at the university. The program is open to all second-year students who have not earned thirty hours or have below a 2.0 GPA. Program participants are housed in a residence hall and enroll in one or more Summer School Session I courses. Peer tutors provide academic support; the ratio of students to tutors is 5:1. Through a structured workshop on time management, students develop their own blocked schedules to include university courses and informational workshops; study time (such as individual study, study groups, peer tutoring, and computer-assisted learning); recreation opportunities; tours; enrichment activities; and employment. Assessment strategies include a pre- and postprogram student survey, and all workshops and activities are evaluated. In addition, advisement counselors continuously evaluate the program. Documentation of workshops and activities is provided through videotaping, publicity, sign-in sheets, and photographs.

Conclusion

As Hunter R. Boylan, director of the National Center for Developmental Education and a professor of education at Appalachian State University, has observed, successful retention efforts must focus on surrounding students with support, thereby making it difficult for them to "escape our grasp." My colleague at FSU, Jon Young, senior associate vice chancellor for enrollment management, keeps a quotation by John Dewey on his wall that serves as a good reminder that the conditions we create will often determine whether our students fail or succeed: "We never educate directly, but indirectly by means of the environment. Whether we permit chance environments to work, or whether we design environments for the purpose makes a great difference."

Students must not believe that they are at their own risk to sink or swim; rather, they must believe that the learning community will encourage and teach *all* students to swim. The conditions we have created at FSU encourage students to recognize and build on their strengths, and the environment provides structure that prepares students to take responsibility for the entire learning process—their temporary failures as well as their eventual successes.

Bibliography

Brown, M. Christopher. 2004. African-American student achievement in historically Black colleges and universities. *Association of American Colleges and Universities Diversity Digest*, 8 (1): 6, 7.

Conrad, C. 2004 *Building skills for Black workers: Preparing for the future labor market*. Washington, DC: The Joint Center for Political and Economic Studies.

National Center for Education Statistics. 2003. *Status and trends in the education of Blacks, 2003*. Washington, DC: Author.

National Opinion Research Center. 2003. *Doctorate recipients from United States universities: Summary report 2003*. Chicago: University of Chicago.

The persisting racial gap in college student graduation rates. 2004. *Journal of Blacks in Higher Education* (Fall): 13–14.

Tinto, Vincent. 2004. Student retention and graduation: Facing the truth, living with the consequences. Washington, DC: Pell Institute for the Study of Opportunity in Higher Education, Council for Opportunity in Higher Education, pp. 1–16.

The White House. 2004. Educating America: The president's initiatives for high school, higher education, and job training." Washington, DC: Author.

Anne S. Pruitt-Logan

Anne S. Pruitt-Logan became professor emerita of educational policy and leadership at Ohio State University in 1995. While at Ohio State, she also served as associate provost, associate dean of the Graduate School, and director of the Center for Teaching Excellence. Before joining Ohio State, she was a professor at Case Western Reserve University and held the positions of dean of students at both Fisk University and Albany State College in Georgia.

She served for eight years at the Council of Graduate Schools, where she codirected the Preparing Future Faculty (PFF) program, and she was principal investigator for combined grants totaling $3 million from the National Science Foundation and the Atlantic Philanthropies. A large part of Dr. Pruitt-Logan's career has been devoted to graduate education of underserved populations. At both Case and Ohio State, most of her grant support focused on graduate education for women and minorities in the sciences and engineering. Among her lengthy consultancies were the Southern Regional Education Board, the Southern Education Foundation, and the National Science Foundation.

In addition to journal articles and book chapters, Dr. Pruitt-Logan's publications include a collection of four books about the Preparing Future Faculty program, *In Pursuit of Equality in Higher Education* and *Student Services for the Changing Graduate Student Population*, which she coedited with Paul Isaac.

Howard University conferred her bachelor's degree cum laude in psychology, and Teachers College, Columbia University, her master's and doctorate. In addition to serving on the Central State University Board of Trustees, Dr. Pruitt-Logan served for fifteen years on the Board of Case Western Reserve University.

16

WHAT MAKES AFRICAN AMERICAN STUDENTS SUCCESSFUL IN OTHER UNIVERSITIES

Inclusiveness Rules of Engagement

The true teacher defends his pupils against his own personal influences.

Amos Alcott

My first thoughts in writing this chapter turned to the advice and guidance I offered to graduate students some years ago about how to be successful in graduate and professional school (Pruitt-Logan 2003). These thoughts arose from the fact that I know there are issues our students can control—ways they need to shape up—in the service of their own futures. Because I also know that a multitude of other factors can lead to success, I asked myself what one factor I could single out for policy makers. How can I turn our attention—for the moment—away from "fixing the students" to "fixing the institution"? Thus, I turned to inclusiveness.

Inclusiveness has come to be one of the watchwords for the colleges and universities where African American students succeed. The starting point for higher education in addressing the challenge of ensuring student success is an understanding of the many factors that make inclusiveness commonplace. One of those determinants is the cultural sensitivity of professors—current members of the faculty as well as those who aspire to join the professoriate.

It is impossible to speak with one voice about African American students because the group is heterogeneous. Students enter college with a variety of interests, motivations, talents, and backgrounds; yet, one aspect of their heritage is unmistakable—it is the history of discriminatory arrangements in the United States that lead to racism. Because our country has engaged in so many struggles to create and maintain a society that serves all individuals and groups, Americans of nearly every ilk are aware of this despicable history in such a way as to color our relations with one another. Today, as America faces a talent imperative, it is depending on its colleges and universities to transform themselves into models of equal opportunity. Many institutions, aware of this challenge, are turning to strategies for improving teaching and learning (Hurtado 1996).

Students' relationships with their teachers can promote success in college. It is not unusual for successful people—when asked to recount reasons for their achievements—to single out the positive relationships they had with teachers. In addition, some hasten to tell about dealings that were downright insulting. Thus, for many the relationship is satisfying, while for some others it can be off-putting. Regardless, teachers play a significant role in students' success.

I am writing from the vantage point of someone who has spent the major part of her career as a professor and administrator in predominantly White universities (PWIs). Not only are the students in these institutions predominantly White, so are the faculty members and administrators. Thus, although the learning environment ought to be comfortable and welcoming, there are times when race and culture get in the way. I have had occasion to talk with African American students about their relationships with faculty. One young man—talking about problems he was having with members of the faculty—said,

> A large part of the problem I've had with faculty has been subjects that I have identified which deal with Black people or minority-related issues. You'll get a glance, a look from them when you say, "This is what I want to do." And that look gives you the feeling that this [kind of research] isn't exactly what they really want you to pursue. (Ohio State University 1990)

Another student, nearing the end of doctoral study, said she was inviting me to serve on her dissertation committee because she wanted someone who understood what she was trying to do. Still another student recounts confronting her professor about how she resented holding up her hand to answer a question—for what seemed like an hour—and never being called on. These three situations involving race and culture—while anecdotal—reflect typical situations that occur between African American students and White faculty. The comments represent both a narrowness of scholarship and insensitive treatment of students. Where pedagogy is concerned, African American students—surely racial and cultural minorities in general—want to feel that they are not singled out to speak for the race. Indeed, they can share their perspective without providing the "African American perspective." They value praise for ordinary achievement—not for being stereotyped—not made to feel that they are achieving where people of their group are not expected to achieve. They feel respected if textbooks include minority subjects, issues, and photographs. If they are encouraged to speak out— participate in class—they want to believe their views are respected just as those of the dominant group are. Concerns like these, coming from African American students are not unusual.

More and more colleges and universities—as they attempt to understand and serve a student body that is welcoming to all students—are adopting what I call "rules of engagement" to deal with this issue by

- appointing African American faculty;
- recruiting and admitting African American graduate students;
- preparing graduate students to teach diverse students;
- developing cultural sensitivity among faculty; and
- administrative leadership, or taking charge.

Rule #1: The Presence of African American Faculty

After forty years of affirmative action, still only 5 percent of the professoriate is African American (Faculty in academe 1998). In my experience, the presence of African American faculty at PWIs often gives African American students feelings of security. Regardless of whether African American students have these faculty members for courses, comfort comes from the fact that they regard African American members of the faculty as approachable. They believe that they can share concerns—particularly those involving race— with someone who understands. Student issues can involve scholarly matters and even relationships. African American faculty members, by and large, have "been there," so to speak: they completed college and, certainly, graduate school where White faculty and students were in the majority, so they probably encountered similar problems. Thus, they can become mentors of a sort, often taking an interest in the students' personal and academic development.

Where African American students do have classes with African American professors, they frequently feel assured that the scholarship will be sensitive to issues pertinent to their heritage. These observations—regarding the presence of African American faculty—are not meant to suggest that faculty from other ethnic groups are incapable of developing positive relationships with African American students. Indeed, I have encountered scores of White faculty—although they are not in the majority—who model all of the characteristics I am suggesting. To that end, it is essential that the faculty of colleges and universities be inclusive in its makeup and that all members of the faculty be culturally sensitive. The Association of American Colleges and Universities (AAC&U) project, American Commitments: Diversity, Democracy and Liberal Learning, developed a manual for recruiting faculty of color in collaboration with the Preparing Future Faculty Program (http://www.diversityweb.org/) that is an excellent resource.

Rule #2: Recruiting and Admitting Graduate Students of Color

The number of African Americans on the faculties of colleges and universities is increasing (*Update* 1998). However, while their presence is growing, their proportion is unacceptably low. To help address this void, the Council of Graduate Schools adopted a statement in 1997 on inclusiveness, titled *Building an Inclusive Graduate Community: A Statement of Principles.* The graduate school is the source of the majority of college faculty members. A graduate school, in its recruitment and admission procedures, serves the best interests of higher education and the nation at large when it seeks talented students from groups underrepresented in graduate education and encourages them to pursue advanced degrees (see the Council of Graduate Schools' "Inclusiveness Series," http://www.cgsnet.org/PublicationsPolicyRes/index.htm). When they have needed assistance in locating African American students, many graduate schools have formed alliances with programs such as the Doctoral Scholars Program (http://www.sreb.org/programs/dsp/dsp-index.asp); the Ronald E. McNair Postbaccalaureate Achievement Program (http://www.ed.gov/programstriomcnair/index.html); the McKnight Doctoral Fellowship Program in Florida (http://www.fl-educfd.org/mdf.html); and the National Black Graduate Student Association (http:www.nbgsa.org/about.htm).

Rule #3: Preparing Graduate Students to Teach Diverse Students

Recruiting, admitting, and educating graduate students from underrepresented groups is necessary but not sufficient. Tomorrow's professors must learn to teach students from diverse ethnic and national backgrounds—African Americans included (Pruitt-Logan and Gaff 1999). An academic department that fails to include the teaching of a diverse student body in its preparation program is shortchanging these prospective professors. The Preparing Future Faculty (PFF) Program, an initiative of the Association of American Colleges and Universities and the Council of Graduate Schools started in 1993, includes preparation as a researcher, teacher, and academic professional. Over a twelve-year period, PFF programs became rooted in universities and colleges all over the United States. Several of these programs stand out. Seminars for graduate students—such as the ones conducted at Arizona State University—incorporate activities that focus on teaching diverse students. Additionally, North Carolina Central University—a historically African American institution—and Duke University have created programs to involve their aspiring faculty members with ethnically and racially distinct students in each other's institutions. Virginia State University—a historically African American institution—collaborates with PFF Program at Virginia Tech to help graduate students learn about approaches to teaching and learning with a predominantly African American student body. Howard University—another historically African American institution—takes its PFF students to Syracuse University to learn more about teaching in predominantly White classrooms. (More information on PFF is available in Gaff, Pruitt-Logan, and Weibl 2000, Pruitt-Logan, Gaff, and Jentoft 2002, Gaff, Pruitt-Logan, Sims, and Denecke 2003 and at http://www.preparing-faculty.org.)

Rule #4: Developing Cultural Sensitivity among Faculty

A concern pertinent to preparing graduate students who later become faculty members is the cultural sensitivity of an institution's current faculty. To address this issue, in 1992 the former Center for Teaching Excellence at The Ohio State University created a faculty development initiative, called "Teaching for Black Student Retention." A voluntary program, it involved a video presentation that set the stage for discussion and suggested techniques for becoming more culturally sensitive. What a faculty development program can do is help faculty to understand approaches that are welcoming to students of all social groups and to identify stereotypic thinking. Faculty members, for example, have been known to attribute negative or positive characteristics to African American students because of embedded views of their culture. American faculty members are products primarily of a European tradition that leads to a focus on European literature, for example, and eschews African authors. Therefore, faculty development activities can assist faculty in creating curricula that include varied points of view, especially where racial and ethnic scholarship is concerned. Academic departments can create incentives to encourage their colleagues to spend some quality time delving into curricula and pedagogic matters that would help them to be successful with a diverse student body. These sessions must be followed up with consultation with fellow faculty and staff whenever needed (Chism and Pruitt 1995; http://www.diversityweb.org).

Rule #5: Administrative Leadership

If an institution is to embrace cultural sensitivity it must take a robust approach. Despite the fact that the United States has made considerable progress in racial and ethnic equality, the topic of diversity is still an emotionally charged issue. Higher education is still debating affirmative action in recruitment of students, faculty, and administrators; hate crimes still occur on college campuses; and ethnic studies and Black studies curricula are still questioned in some quarters.

The Multicultural Teaching Program (MTP) at The Ohio State University offers an example of a robust approach. Although begun in 1991, it evolved out of the Teaching for Black Student Retention (TBSR) program that was mandated in 1987 by the Provost's Action Plan for the Recruitment and Retention of Black Students.

> The plan identified faculty as central players and it charged the Center for Teaching Excellence and The Office of Affirmative Action with developing and carrying out workshops that would sensitize faculty and Teaching Associates (TAs) to the powerful role that they play in the creation of effective environments for learning and, thus, retention of African American students." (Bonilla and Lumpkins 1992)

Successful procedures require administrators to listen to those forces that try to hamper attention to diversity, but also to capture the strength of those forces that support these kinds of initiatives. Administrators need to respect the preeminence of faculty. Faculty have certain prerogatives regarding whom, where, how, and what they teach; by and large, they owe their allegiance to their disciplines. Because various academic disciplines already address the question of teaching in diverse institutions, many faculty members could already be knowledgeable and, therefore, supportive. Associations such as the American Chemical Society, the American Association of Physics Teachers, and the Mathematical Association of America are examples of societies that are creating ways for their members to respond to the increasing diversity in their classrooms.

The same is true of a college or university's interinstitutional system. These include associations—such as the Association of American Colleges and Universities, American Association for Higher Education, and American Council on Education—where peer institutions make policy regarding teaching and learning in diverse student groups.

Leadership for change should include a staff that represents an institution's diverse student body. Where diversity exists, there are also likely to be informal arrangements that represent diverse ethnic and national backgrounds, such as an African American advocacy group composed of faculty, staff, and students. An assemblage like this would have a stake in the institution's efforts to improve the teaching and learning environment.

Ultimately, the governing arrangement—such as university senate or council—will be central in debating and accepting strong measures to improve teaching. Finally, there is nothing more powerful than external experts. They can come to the campus to present lectures and seminars and be effective where local talent is not; that is to say, one is never a prophet in one's own backyard!

Finally, a shift in the faculty reward system can be used in the service of cultural sensitivity. In addition to research and service, faculty members are accustomed to being rewarded for their teaching. Thus, if members of the faculty realize that items about teaching for diversity will be on standard student evaluation forms, the institution will have provided a significant incentive. Alternatively, the college might ask for evidence of curricular inclusiveness in teaching dossiers or portfolios and weigh this evidence when considering rewards.

A number of factors that traditionally have characterized faculty life—the prevalence of part-time faculty and the increasing use of distance education—are rapidly changing, and they will control the way institutions must approach faculty issues. Considering such factors will influence strategies faculty developers adopt to reach their goals.

The challenge to understand and serve all citizens is not a new one for American higher education; it has been a maxim—although a frustrating one to achieve—since the founding of this nation. I have not discussed how to fix the student, nor have I discussed all of the other considerations that make for student success. Rather, I have focused on the institutions and suggested how they can adopt my rules of engagement. They can, for example, hire more African American faculty members; they can remove the constraints surrounding recruiting and admitting African American graduate students; they can teach those who do aspire to the professoriate how to create welcoming classrooms for all students; and they can design faculty development programs that teach members of the faculty how to improve their sensitivity to African American students. These tasks require leaders who have the will to educate all of the people.

Population projections indicate that minorities—including African Americans—will comprise one-third of the U.S. population by 2015. Moreover, by 2050, Whites—who constituted an 87 percent majority in 1950—are projected to account for only 53 percent of the U.S. population by 2050 (Population Resource Center 2005). This makes the foregoing discussion addressing teaching diverse students critical for both faculty and administrators.

References

Bonilla, James F., and Terrance D. Lumpkins. 1992. *The multicultural teaching resource guide.* Columbus, OH: Ohio State University, Center for Teaching Excellence.

Chism, Nancy V. N., and Anne S. Pruitt. 1995. "Promoting inclusiveness in college teaching." In *Teaching improvement practices: Successful strategies for higher education,* ed. W. Alan Wright, 325–345. Bolton, MA: Anker.

Faculty in academe. 1998. *Update,* 4 (4):3.

Gaff, Jerry G., Anne S. Pruitt-Logan, Leslie B. Sims, and Daniel D. Denecke. 2003. *Preparing future faculty in the humanities and social sciences: A guide for change.* Washington, DC: Council of Graduate Schools.

Gaff, Jerry G., Anne S. Pruitt-Logan, and Richard A. Weibl. 2000. *Building the faculty we need: Colleges and universities working together.* Washington, DC: Association of American Colleges and Universities.

Hurtado, Sylvia. 1996. How diversity affects teaching and learning: Climate of learning has a positive effect on learning outcomes. Diversity Web, http://www

.diversityweb.org/researchand_trends/research_evaluation_impact/benefits_of
_diversity/sylvia_hurtado.cfm.

Ohio State University, Center for Teaching Excellence. 1990. *Making a difference: Teaching for Black student retention*, videotape. Columbus, OH: Author.

Population Resource Center. 2005. Executive summary: A population perspective of the United States. http://www.prcdc.org/summaries/uspopperspec/uspopper spec.html

Preparing-Faculty.org.

Pruitt-Logan, Anne S. 2003. "Making sure you have the 'right stuff' to be successful in graduate and professional school." In *The Black student's guide to graduate and professional school success*, ed. Vernon L. Farmer, 325–345. Westport, CT: Greenwood.

Pruitt-Logan, Anne S., and Jerry G. Gaff. 1999. Preparing future faculty to focus on diversity. *Diversity Web*. http://www.diversity web.org/Digest/F99/faculty.html.

Pruitt-Logan, Anne S., Jerry G. Gaff, and Joyce E. Jentoft. 2002. *Preparing future faculty in the sciences and mathematics: A guide for change*. Washington, DC: Council of Graduate Schools.

Mervyn A. Warren

A native of Dallas, Texas, Dr. Warren began his education in that public school system. He is a graduate of Oakwood College (B. A., Ministerial Theology), Andrews University Seminary (M.A., Homiletics and Preaching; M. Div., Pastoral Ministry), Michigan State University (Ph.D., Rhetoric and Public Address), and Vanderbilt Divinity School (D.Min.). He has taught at all of these institutions in areas of theology, public discourse, homiletics, and methodologies of Martin Luther King on whom his doctoral research focused.

Warren's book, *King Came Preaching* (InterVarsity Press, 2001), catalogs not only his interview with King but also the life, labors, and legacy of the real King. His book has been featured by various media including *The Washington Post* (December 1, 2001), *The Atlanta Journal Constitution* (January 19, 2002), and *Ebony* magazine (April 2002). His other books include *Black Preaching: Truth and Soul; God Made Known*; and *Oakwood College: A Vision Splendid (1869–1996)*. He serves on the boards of the Geoscience Research Institute and the Biblical Research Institute, and he participates in the scholarly activities of the American Academy of Religion, the Society of Biblical Literature, and the American Academy of Homiletics.

Warren is Provost and Senior Vice President at Oakwood College in Huntsville, Alabama, where he has also served as Professor and Chairman of Religion, Vice President for Academic Affairs, Vice President for Student Services, and Assistant to the President.

He is married to Barbara Moseley Warren.

17

OLD WINE IN NEW BOTTLES

Visioning Values in Higher Education

Like a silent shadow, a certain yet often unspoken mission of the academy slips by almost unnoticed. That mission is as real as any visible mortarboard, tassel, or framed degree, but unless you happen to catch it in the typical commencement address that predictably points graduates to moral high ground, you just might miss it. Turned up loud and clear, however, are voices of educators steering students to become badges of academic validation while the companion need for becoming brands of values seems taken for granted and, therefore, left to sort of take care of itself. You could easily get the impression that any attempt toward intentionally welding values and formal education together might interfere with the learning process and more serious content matters of "reading, writing, and arithmetic." Among approximately 4,009 colleges and universities in America, including some eighty-four historically Black institutions of higher learning, are a number of schools that transcend the silent treatment by placing values on the front burner along with academics per se, thereby providing context and purpose for a moral philosophy of higher education. To make it clear that the pursuit of objective truth in the classroom subsumes also subjectivizing truth in the practical lives of scholars so they will both practice truth as well as know truth in daily concourse with other human beings, these institutions give prominence to values in their mission statements and faculty-staff handbooks, thus making it extremely difficult if not impossible for one who might not subscribe to this type of mission to hide behind the veil of academic freedom.

At one of those colleges, a private liberal arts institution where I have had tenure for several decades now, I have witnessed over and over again an uncommon phenomenon; in some sense it is a rather strange act that is a best-kept secret of those schools determined to keep values in focus. In another sense, I am referring to something that is not so much "strange" as it is as an anomaly or maybe even a "subculture" of formal pedagogy. I say this in light of the notion that teaching personal goodness in the classroom, along with excellence in mastering subject matter, runs the risk of being labeled an unnecessary distraction. Implementers of educational programs wedding life values and learning understand full well that the mixture is not automatically love at first sight and might even be considered strange bedfellows. Nevertheless, recruiters at value-sensitive institutions perennially meet students all across this country who willingly and anxiously volunteer to forgo their well-endowed scholarships to more prestigious schools whenever they face the challenge of having to make "either-or" choices between "education without values" and "education with values."

On one hand, to many educators, making such choices might come across as visionary nonsense and venturing into minefields loaded with intangibles and unrealities. On the other hand, to an enormous number of patrons of higher education, principles such as truth, goodness, honesty, beauty, love, and justice are highly esteemed values, even in our world of scientific genius and technological know-how. The obvious need for such values in the world community will not go away but remains the backbone and foundation of society. I am proposing, therefore, that higher education release itself from the general motif of silence or semblance of silence and join the clarion call for intentional integration of learning and love, erudition and ethics, degrees and decency, success and standards. I am proposing that such a union of scholarship and moral values would translate academic capital not only into the gold of professional success and economic security but also into respect for human equity and relationships, appropriate respect and appreciation for trustworthy leadership and authority, respect and appreciation for others, and respect and appreciation for oneself as a contributor to the happiness and well-being of life. For a workable definition of values, I am referring to standards, directions, and parameters of conduct for the best common good of the human race motivated by love and service.

The appeal for an education of values is nothing new when viewed in the historical light of those efforts by missionary societies of the mid- and late 1800s, some of which paternalistically if not racially stressed "proper behavior," including usefulness, virtue, obedience, and even Christianity for the colleges and schools established to educate slaves and their offspring (*The Baptist Home Mission Monthly* 1895). The call today for values, I trust we understand, transcends any suspicion of docility schemed or motivated to perpetuate some "slave-slavemaster" relationship. To the contrary, the call stresses a need for influencing human beings to submit their formal education to positive behavioral patterns on all levels of personal and professional endeavors whether political, corporate, legal, economic, or social (Gates 2004).

Echoes from the Past

As constant companions, the values-education connection, like some integrated couples, might attract curious stares from the suspicious and sneers from detractors; nevertheless, the collaboration does enjoy historical continuity. Notions of fair play and respectful sensitivity to life, liberty, and the pursuit of happiness reach back to early BCE, with the Hebrews and their Torah, which bequeathed to society basic standards of life and relationships upon which we seem not able to improve (Hutchins 1952, 962–990). Early CE brings to mind the likes of Quintilian, the rhetorical philosopher who was not satisfied to define effective public address in strict communication terms alone, but rather explained it as a "good man speaking well" (Thonssen and Baird 1948, 92).

One of the reasons we continue revisiting the famed Booker T. Washington–W.E.B. DuBois "debate" is, in my opinion, that we somehow realize that irrespective of whose side you align yourself with, the overheard subliminal message to Black higher education from both proponents sounds a clear note speaking to the power of preparation and service whether you elect the industrial-technological curriculum or the more liberal philosophical-scientific curriculum. Each thinker speaks from a perspective of his sincere conviction on the best route for an oppressed people to progress from poverty of spirit, poverty of selfhood, poverty of economy, poverty of security to a plain of preparedness and a parity of participation in America's total life (Colon 1991, 69–76; Moore 2003, 117–121). Moreover, I hear DuBois campaigning not merely for the "talented tenth" but likewise for the "trustworthy tenth," and Washington appealing not solely to "let down your buckets where you are" but certainly "filling your buckets with competence, moral worth, dependability, and responsibility."

From 1888 to 1915, when Washington established and operated Tuskegee Institute University, his national visibility and popularity resulted from his persuasive theme of gradual but sure progress epitomized by the successful program there. A research project led me to the Tuskegee campus a few years ago where I discovered that amid his whirlwind of myriad presidential duties at Tuskegee, Washington especially cherished his "Sunday Evening Chapel Talks," when he addressed the student body about such values as independence, respect, honesty, thoroughness, dependability, spirituality, courtesy, and, to wit, personal grooming. Let us laud him for realizing that these and like standards cannot be assumed as automatic or as already having been taught by someone else, even by parents, but must be formally addressed, emphasized, and reemphasized at some time, somewhere, somehow. And what better milieu is there than the educational setting while scholars are in a conscious process of equipping themselves for the real world? Would that more educators in this, our twenty-first century, caught Washington's and DuBois's vision of values!

Of course, a lecture about values in the undergraduate or graduate classroom might appear so rudimentary and come across so elementary, like sandbox child talk, as to be seen as wasting valuable time in fantasy land. The resultant risk of ignoring values, however, can be ultimately devastating in terms of certification without character, honors without honesty, money without manners, promotion without probity, and the list could go on and on ad infinitum.

Here are examples from Washington's "Sunday Evening Chapel Talks" of a few basic values to which he called attention during his heart-to-heart chat with Tuskegee students:

The Sunday evening talk of February 8, 1903, points students to the idea that the greatest possibility of success results from early planning for specific areas of life work rather than drifting into the future depending on happenstance. Washington highlights the advantages of living in more rustic areas rather than in crowded urban conditions, one of these being that the environs of rural dwellers are more conducive toward being "stronger in their morals." That his conclusion inevitably leaves itself open to challenge is not so significant, in my opinion, as his endeavor to assert the pertinence of addressing values in the context of education (1903a). About a month later, in another chapel talk, Washington encourages students to avoid any tendency to be "unreliable," "untruthful," "dishonest," or engaging in "stealing." He asks the question, "What are you going to do, young men and young women, when you go out as leaders?" Then he summons them to the task of "setting for our people a high and proper example" in matters of "money," "food," "clothing," "privilege of voting," eschewing "impurity in our homes" inviting youth to set an example to live "purely" and "virtuously" regarding their sexuality, and, in financial economy, "bank accounts" and the need to "invest money in land." A very poignant statement, as relevant today as it was then, forms a part of his conclusion when he declares: "Only through the work, through the clean, high, pure, sensible lives of such young men and women as go out from this institution, and others [sic]. And I speak to you plainly, frankly, concerning all these subjects. I want to let you know that you are going to be watched and weighed, and unless, in all these matters, you set a high example, one in which no one can find a flaw, the progress of the race will be slow" (1903b). In the last chapel talk before his death, delivered on October 17, 1915, Washington stressed a number of principles, namely, "teamwork" as a people; being "on time" to keep appointments; keeping down "waste"; fostering "cleanliness" and "beauty"; "honesty" in work, studies, examinations, use of other people's property; and development and maintenance of clean morals and character. His theme of teamwork specified one's "spiritual life," "religious life," "prayer meetings," "preaching services," "devotional exercise," and public organizations, such as "YMCA, YWCA, Bible School, everywhere"! I believe it becomes quite apparent that the galaxy of values Washington highlighted are as up to date as tomorrow morning's newspaper, and that although societal, political, and economic paradigms do change, human nature remains essentially the same. Furthermore, positive values continue their unvarying course, leading us to high moral ground in academic success and professional service. There are other examples, I am certain, of echoes from the past that speak to the education-values alliance but probably none so explicitly promoted and documented in the arena of Black higher education as Booker T. Washington's. I hasten to add, moreover, that although the direction of his overall educational philosophy bristles with disputed points, his blending savory ingredients of values into the casserole of higher education does provide a fundamental recipe for modern education to put together a nutritious academic cuisine.

Sounds of the Present

Voices aplenty today are swelling to a crescendo for standards and values to be reflected across the broad spectrum of African American life. Vernon Jordan avers that one's "life pursuit" should be "honorable" (2001, 316.) Henry Louis Gates, in his insightful volume, *America Behind the Color Line*, edited a phalanx of dialogues with African Americans who, among their varied perspectives, expressed their take on the status and hopes of African Americans. Several voiced their conviction that values constitute valid requisites for meaningful success, and I would like to summarize accordingly: Gates himself dares the "black middle class to use their clout and wealth to fight structural and institutional racism . . . and to become more effective role models for dispirited millions of black youth thus left behind and that they no longer have to aspire to be white to obtain our share of the American dream" (2004, 16).

Colin Powell knows what positive thing "our youngsters are capable of doing" but fears that "there are too many of them adopting hedonistic lifestyles" and that "too many of our television stations are exploiting this kind of lifestyle and peddling it all over the airways, and other youngsters see it and hear this kind of language and see this kind of dress and this kind of behavior. Our humor has gone from Bill Cosby down to the worst kind, deep in the gutter" (Gates 2004, 23). According to Vernon Jordan, we need to be "committed to excellence and hard work and sacrifice" as well as "have some moral and ethical boundaries and standards for . . . behavior" and "march in the ranks of honor" (Gates 2004, 34). We are challenged by Maurice Ashley to "hold on to a set of strong values," "deferring gratification" and the pitfall of some "professional athletes who make millions of dollars and then five or ten years later are flat broke" even after being "full of opportunity and hope." Sometimes "we seem to defeat ourselves . . . [and] go after the appearance of success instead of investing in our abilities for the future" (2004, 72–73). Willie W. Hernton worries that we are "disconnected," have "lost a resilient faith and the belief in God that helped us endure the harsher treatments we received," and "lost the work ethic we once had" instead of holding on to the traditional tenet that "if we got a good education and we worked, we were going to achieve" (2004, 175–176). That "God put me here; put this passion in my heart to do good work" epitomizes the passion of Nia Long, who appeals that we "continue to lift each other up and be there for each other and support one another and really try. Even if we don't agree with the choices that we make, we are black people. We have to give each other love and not be so critical and not tear each other down and not be envious, even though this [movie] industry is set up for people to act that way" (2004, 287). Bernie Mac insists, "Our mentality, not just blacks, but a lot of minorities, has fallen. It has fallen from where we were. The spiritual guidance has gone and left us, for number one, and that's a very dangerous thing. And the mentality in terms of microwaves has risen. We want things overnight. It's a fast-food, instant-gratification, efficiency-not-quality society. We hate ourselves. Oh yes, we hate ourselves. We hate anything that has uplift in it. It's just constructed that way and I see it in everyday life as I talk to the schools. I see it in our young people. I see it more and more in our society, whereas our desire to be more and to be better has just disappeared" (2004, 323–324).

Much of the negative counterculture that opposes the positive values espoused by the voices mentioned above streams from the hip-hop generation (Kitwana 2000, 77). While much that is congratulatory may be said about the overall hip-hop originators who carved out for themselves a media genre through which to express and progress themselves and who literally created for themselves a new economic industry, the flip side reveals a lifestyle rife with self-centeredness and prison culture reflected in "the use of language and styles of dress to extensive commentary on crime and prison life. With so many Blacks entering and exiting prison this influence is inescapable" (Kitwana 2000, 77). That hip-hop culture is alive and well and here to stay is an understatement that has prompted efforts to influence hip-hop performers to broadcast more positive, value-based messages. Results of these efforts are yet to be determined. What a powerful impact if hip-hop artists would place their influence behind rapping such values alliterated by Frank Hale, namely: "Purpose, Pride, Planning, Persistence, Punctuality, Personality, Persuasiveness, Purity, Productivity, Perspective, and [divine] Providence"! (2000, vi).

Interestingly enough, the widely touted reality TV show, *The Apprentice*, during its December 19, 2004, finale inadvertently complimented the notion of values when Donald Trump decreed the imminent "you're hired" to the winner, Kelly Perdew, whose strictly business and intellectual attributes were not appreciably better than those of his co-finalist, Jennifer Massey. So what tipped the scale in behalf of Kelly? Comments from the live audience generally spoke of the plus factor evident in the "humaneness" of Kelly versus the more "hard-core leadership" qualities that both finalists possessed. Beyond leadership attributes and rich experience in software executive management, a B.S. in national security in public affairs from the U.S. Military Academy at West Point, an M.B.A. from Anderson School of Business at UCLA, and a J.D. from UCLA School of Law, much of which was matched by Jennifer, who is a Princeton and Harvard graduate, comments made about Kelly pointed to such qualities as a "good guy" or "fine human being" and one who comes across as a person you can trust versus the stark contrast of the sardonic tongue and arrogance of his distaff competitor. The significance of the value dynamics of this particular *Apprentice* episode might very well serve notice to higher education as a microcosm of what the macroworld at large is expecting more and more.

Right on the heels of that *Apprentice* program, the National Football

League kicked off its playoff games to decide which team would eventually make it to the 2005 Superbowl. One of the games between the Denver Broncos and the Minnesota Vikings saw a brilliant Vikings wide receiver catch a pass and dash for the end zone in victorious fashion but then proceed to celebrate through an obvious display of lewd gestures unfit for public consumption but in full view of thousands in the stadium and millions on national TV. Needless to say, the commentators' outcry was consistently one of outrage and disappointment. When asked after the game why he would do such a thing, the talented player responded, "It was something I just felt like doing" to which he later added, "I don't give a d—what nobody thinks. Just so you give us the 'w'"—meaning the win. One sports commentator remarked, "There's not enough popularity or money to excuse that type of end zone obscenity." The response by another commentator really caught my attention: "This just goes to show that *talent* and *class* don't always come in the same package." Transposing this assertion into the higher education world, you might say also that "academia and values don't always come in the same package."

Irrespective of any apparent reticence to teach values intentionally and explicitly in the higher education classroom, we can take courage that value-education seems to enjoy regular exposure in elementary and secondary schools. One of the best accounts I have come across lately is the work by Janice E. Hale, whose treatment of "Character Education" and "Cultural Education" delineates such values as "truthfulness, honesty, integrity, individual responsibility, humility, wisdom, justice, steadfastness, and dependability"—excellent seeds to fertilize and plant in all gardens where learning takes place (2001, 153–170).

In October 2004, I delivered an address for the Twenty-third Annual Dr. Martin Luther King, Jr., Memorial Scholarship Trust Fund in the New Haven, Connecticut, area. Five young high school scholars were celebrated and awarded an average of $20,000 each to attend the college or university of their choice. Honoring the person for whom the scholarship fund was named, I planned my speech around the thirst for learning and motivation for excellence that the teenage Martin Luther King himself embodied. I remembered a very poignant statement by young Martin, which I had quoted in my recent book, *King Came Preaching*, a statement he wrote in a 1948 article, entitled "The Purpose of Education," for the Morehouse College campus paper, *Maroon Tiger*. The nineteen-year-old honor student argued quite persuasively that education should equip persons with "noble ends rather than means to an end." King continued:

At this point, I often wonder whether or not education is fulfilling its purpose. A great majority of the so-called educated people do not think logically and scientifically. Even the press, the classroom, the platform, and the pulpit in many instances do not give us objective and unbiased truths. To save man from the morass of propaganda, in my opinion, is one of the chief aims of education. Education must enable one to sift and weigh evidence, to discern the true from the false, the real from the unreal, and the facts from fiction.

The function of education, therefore, is to teach one to think intensively and to think critically. But education which stops with efficiency may prove the greatest menace to society. The most dangerous criminal may be the man gifted with reason, but with no morals.

The late Eugene Talmadge, in my opinion, possessed one of the better minds of Georgia, or even America. Moreover, he wore the Phi Beta Kappa key. By all measuring rods, Mr. Talmadge could think critically and intensively; yet he contends that I am an inferior being . . .

We must remember that intelligence is not enough. Intelligence plus character—that is the goal of true education. The complete education gives one not only power of concentration, but worthy objectives upon which to concentrate. The broad education will, therefore, transmit to one not only the accumulated knowledge of the race but also the accumulated experience of social living. (Warren 2001, 27)

What more shall we say? If my premise is valid—that values are as old as civilization itself and could stand a resurgence in formal higher education settings today—which for some educators may mean a new thing, then I move that we delay no longer to pour this fine wine of values into new bottles of academia for a better future of learning and love for the good of all humankind.

References

Ashley, Maurice. 2004, Chess masters. In *America behind the color line*, ed. Henry Louis Gates, Jr. New York: Warner Books.

Brown, Titus. 2002. *Faithful, firm, and true: African American education in the South.* Macon, GA: Mercer University Press.

Clark, Reginald M. 1983. *Family life and school achievement: Why poor Black children succeed or fail.* Chicago: University of Chicago Press.

Colon, Alan. 1991. Race relations on campus: An administrative perspective. In *The racial crisis in American higher education*, ed. Philip Altbach and Kofi. Lomotey. Albany: State University of New York Press.

Freeman, Kassie. 1998. *African American culture and heritage in higher research and practice*. Westport, CT: Praeger Publishers.

Gates, Henry Louis, Jr., ed. 2004. *America behind the color line*. New York: Warner Books.

Hale, Frank W., Jr. 2000. *A letter to African American males*. Bloomington, IN: 1st Books Library.

———. *What makes diversity work in higher education: Academic leaders present successful policies and strategies*. Sterling, VA: Stylus Publishing.

Hale, Janice E. 2001. *Learning while Black: Creating educational excellence for African American children*. Baltimore: The John Hopkins University Press.

Hall, Peter M., ed. 1997. *Race, ethnicity, and multiculturalism: Policity and practice*. New York: Garland Publishing, Inc.

Hernton, Willie W. 2004. Keys to the city. In *America behind the color line*, ed. Henry Louis Gates, Jr. New York: Warner Books.

Hutchins, Robert Maynard, ed. 1952. *Law*. Vol. I of *The great ideas: A syntopicon of great books of the Western world*. Chicago: Encyclopedia Britannica, Inc.

Jones, Lee, ed. *Making it on broken promises: African American male scholars confront the culture of higher education*. Sterling, VA: Stylus Publishing.

Jordan, Vernon E., Jr., with Annette Gordon-Reed. 2001. *Vernon can read!* New York: Basic Civatas Books.

Justiz, Manuel J., Reginald Wilson, and Lars G. Bjork, eds. 1994. *Minorities in higher education*. Phoenix, AZ: American Council on Education Series on Higher Education.

Kitwana, Bakari. 2002. *The hip hop generation: Young Blacks and the crisis in African American culture*. New York: Basic Civatas Books.

Long, Nia. 2004. Life purpose. In *America behind the color line*, ed. Henry Louis Gates, Jr. New York: Warner Books.

Mac, Bernie. 2004. The chameleon. In *America behind the color line*, ed. Henry Louis Gates, Jr. New York: Warner Books.

Mannoia, V. James, Jr. 2000. *Christian liberal arts*. New York: Rowman & Littlefield Publishers.

Moore, Jacqueline M. 2003. *Booker T. Washington, W. E. B. DuBois, and the struggle for racial uplift*. Wilmington, DE: Scholarly Resources, Inc.

Smiley, Tavis, ed. 2001. *How to make Black America better*. New York: Anchor Books.

The Baptist Home Mission Monthly (October 17, 1895): 36.

The principal's Sunday evening talk in the chapel. 1903a. *The Tuskegee Student*, XV (7) (Feb. 8).

The principal's Sunday evening talk in the chapel. 1903b. *The Tuskegee Student* (March 1).

Thonssen, Lester, and A. Craig Baird. 1948. *Speech criticism: The development of standards for rhetorical appraisal*. New York: The Ronald Press Co.

Turner, Caroline, M. Garcia, A. Nora, and L. Rendon, eds. 1996. *Racial and ethnic diversity in higher education*. Needham Heights: Simon & Schuster.

Warren, Mervyn A. 2001. *King Came Preaching*. Downers Grove, IL: InterVarsity Press.

White, Ellen G. 1952. *Education*. Mountain View: Pacific Press Publishing Association.

Willmer, Wesley K., ed. 1996. *Advancing Christian higher education*. Washington, DC: Coalition for Christian Colleges & Universities.

As an educator I am deeply offended by those critics who by careless, cavalier, or calloused thinking dare to dismiss the importance and role of Black institutions of higher education in our society. Their value has been their accessibility to all, regardless of race, status, or wealth. In this regard, they have underscored the principle of equal justice when other institutions of higher education restricted the access of African Americans into the Halls of Ivy. These institutions took the first steps in making our nation's proclamations of high democratic principles far more easily implemented and sustainable than those who articulated platitudes totally inconsistent with their practices.

We can measure the genuine success of historically Black colleges and universities by their ultimate contributions to humanity. We are not just discovering their countless achievements. There would be no Black middle class in America if these institutions had not been available to provide the education and undergirding for those with far fewer opportunities than most Americans. They enabled Black Americans, in part, to weather a dismal history of national neglect in education. For whatever failings these institutions may have had, they became a wholesome alternative to what was an almost impenetrable system of dehumanizing racism. They prepared a bank of professionals who, over time, helped to reduce the incidence of ignorance, poverty, and disease among our people. These institutions have nobly and in a self-sacrificing manner clothed Black youth with dignity and value. They have lifted them into a meaningful universe of self-confidence where they will no longer allow themselves to be regarded as a zero or a cipher.

Throughout our national history, historically Black colleges and universities (HBCUs) have produced leaders whose greatness met the nation's needs. Witness Booker T. Washington, Samuel Dewitt Proctor, Mary McLeod Bethune, Andrew Young, Ronald McNair, Howard Thurman, Leontyne Price, Jesse Jackson, Maynard Jackson, and Oprah Winfrey, whose greatness and influence stemmed not so much from their personalities as from the principles and causes they enunciated and implemented.

There are thousands and thousands of Black youth who will take advantage of Black higher education in years to come, and I view that prospect with excitement. My excitement comes from the knowledge that the growth in demand for higher education among our youth is one of the most striking phenomena in our history. It has been a constant factor since the assassination of Dr. Martin Luther King, Jr. Black youth are aware that education is the highway to the dignity of human life and to shared political power. Educational advancement carries them beyond the status of being passive participants and second-class citizens to becoming voices of empowerment, agents of change, and champions of transformation.

We already know that young people lacking in educational preparation face a vicious cycle when it comes to employment and the possibility of increasing their standard of living. Those of us who have served in Black institutions of higher education know that our young people possess great potential for personal fulfillment, meaning, challenge, and satisfaction when we are able to provide the conditions that enable them to achieve in those areas. Black institutions of higher education do not take the position that Black students underperform because they come from the inner city for the most part.

The fact is that students fail because the school system so often fails them. The reality is that the most serious chaos in education are most strikingly apparent in the manner in which educators are unable to see that students are not only creatures of their cultural deprivation, but they are also products of the stoic resignation and neglect of those who have written them off as social problems without any possibility of redemption.

On the other hand, Black institutions of higher education have accepted the challenge of unlocking the secrets of Black students' potential. They have made a conscious effort to improve, enhance, and refine the creative essence of their students. They begin with the proposition that they expect these students to succeed. They seek to preserve and restore the intellectual capacity of students; the aspirations of students are inextricably bound with the expectations of teachers. Black colleges and universities have been very aggressive in helping their students to achieve self-definition and identity, and the role of these institutions has been crystallized into a self-perpetuating philosophy since their beginning.

F.W.H.